THEM AND US

STRUGGLES OF A
RANK-AND-FILE UNION

THEM AND US

STRUGGLES OF A RANK-AND-FILE UNION

by JAMES J. MATLES
and JAMES HIGGINS

PRENTICE-HALL, Inc.
Englewood Cliffs, New Jersey

Them and Us: Struggles of a Rank-and-File Union
by James J. Matles and James Higgins
Copyright © 1974 by James J. Matles

Printed in the United States of America

Prentice-Hall International, Inc., London
Prentice-Hall of Australia, Pty. Ltd., North Sydney
Prentice-Hall of Canada, Ltd., Toronto
Prentice-Hall of India Private Ltd., New Delhi
Prentice-Hall of Japan, Inc., Tokyo

10   9   8   7   6   5   4   3   2   1

Library of Congress Cataloging in Publication Data
Matles, James J.
    Them and us: struggles of a rank-and-file
union.
    1. United Electrical, Radio and Machine
Workers of America. I. Higgins, James,
joint author. II. Title.
HD6515.E3M33   331.88'12'1306273   73-19656
ISBN 0-13-913079-9
ISBN 0-13-913053-5 (pbk.)

TO
Esther Matles

FOREWORD

Much public attention was being paid in the early seventies to American workers and the American labor movement. This had its origins not only in developments of the period but in the history which had gone before, dating especially from the rise of CIO industrial unionism in the thirties, an event which placed an indelible mark on the modern labor movement.

Scholars and journalists, as well as some people with direct labor movement experience, have made contributions to study of the subject. Little, however, has yet been forthcoming from national leaders actively engaged in labor movement struggles in basic mass production industries, from early CIO days into the seventies: the first major battles for industrial union organization and recognition; the great strikes; negotiation of contracts with large industrial corporations; the day-by-day work of trade unionism through the Second World War and the years of cold and hot wars that followed for a quarter of a century, bringing their inevitable pressures upon workers, unions and the labor movement.

James J. Matles, coauthor of this book, left his machine shop job in the mid-thirties to serve as a young industrial union organizer. From 1937, when he was elected first director of organization of a union that became the third largest in the CIO—the United Electrical, Radio and Machine Workers of America, known as the UE—Matles continued in active labor movement leadership as a top UE officer. At the time this book was being written he held the post of UE general secretary, to which he had been elected in 1962 after the death of one of the union's founders, its first general secretary, Julius Emspak.

The friendship between Matles and coauthor James Higgins began in the mid-forties when Higgins, having been graduated from Harvard University, spent several years as a shipyard sheet metal worker and later joined the international staff of the CIO Industrial Union of Marine and Shipbuilding Workers of America. The two friends remained in close touch while Higgins served from 1950 to 1970 as editor of a nationally known newspaper, The Gazette and Daily of York, Pennsylvania. Since 1970 he has been a teacher of journalism at Boston University, a lecturer in the Institute of Politics at Harvard, and an independent writer.

The book is based primarily on the experience of the UE rank-and-file, its shop stewards, local union and district leaders, the international union staff and officers. The UE archives and library at the union's New York headquarters, as well as personal papers of Matles, provided documentary source material. All responsibility for the content of the book, however, is naturally assumed by the authors.

JAMES J. MATLES
JAMES HIGGINS

New York, N.Y.

CONTENTS

THEM AND US

STRUGGLES OF A
RANK-AND-FILE UNION

PART ONE

ORGANIZING

1
Roots of Rank-and-File Unionism

I   In the winter of 1969–70, mass production workers belonging to industrial union organizations shut down plants of the General Electric Company—largest and richest manufacturer of electrical equipment in the world—for one hundred one days. When the strike ended in negotiated settlement between GE and the unions, a major newspaper and a national news magazine reached back thirty-five years into labor history for standards by which to measure the long struggle.

Said *The New York Times:* "In symbolic terms, settlement of the strike of almost 150,000 General Electric workers represents the greatest union 'victory' since labor overcame Tom Girdler, Harry Bennett and other champions of the open shop in the New Deal era."

Time magazine: "Many of the 150,000 workers were as united in bitterness against their employer as any band of workers who fought the U.S. industrial class wars of the 1930's."

Strange words to find in the press of those days. It was almost as if the writers were astonished to be confronted by the fact that there really was a working class in the United States of America—and a militant one at that—ready to engage in class struggle in organized ranks. Such things were supposed to be buried safely in the past. Thus it was to the past the reporters looked to get their bearings.

The parallel they drew was with the organization of the CIO, the Congress of Industrial Organizations, in the years between the Great Depression and the Second World War. For many Americans that period may indeed have seemed far

3

away and long ago. The expectations aroused by the tidal wave of organization that swept through mass production industry in the 1930s, carrying industrial unionism into the plants of the most heavily guarded anti-labor corporate concentrations of all time, had been tremendous.

Never before the CIO had there been so vast and spontaneous a surge of American working people into "unions of their own choosing," to quote the New Deal Wagner Act, which gave sanction of federal law to the freedom of workers to organize. Never before had there been so rapid a transformation of mass spirit into great organizations made up of the rank-and-file of workers in the shops—skilled, semiskilled, and unskilled, white and black, young and old, men and women, united in common purpose and supported by progressive people from a variety of professions and occupations.

The essential breakthrough of democratic industrial unionism—an objective of militant workers in basic industry for many years—seemed to have been achieved at last. The class consciousness of American workers, which had never reached the level of workers in European labor movements, appeared to have come into its own.

Soon after the Second World War, however, corporations enriched with wartime profits amounting to $117 billion mounted a powerful offensive to stop the CIO right where it was. The cold war provided favorable anti-CIO atmosphere. In almost as short a time as it had taken to develop what had the complexion of an irresistible movement of industrial organization, the CIO was divided and effectively immobilized.

By 1947 the proud CIO industrial union banner of the thirties, emblazoned with the slogan *Organize the Unorganized!*, trailed in the dust. The CIO sweep in mass production industry before the war had been a significant labor movement achievement, with several million workers organized in new industrial unions. But total union membership in the United States never exceeded one-third of all nonagricultural workers. Further, as the country's work force increased, the ratio of union membership shrank from 33 percent in 1949 to 27 percent in 1970. The corporate offensive had done what it had set out to do.

4

II   It was ironic that a labor movement of such modest size—the smallest percentage of organized workers in any industrialized nation—came to be known, of all things, as "Big Labor." Such popular myths, however, do not develop by accident. They are prompted. No ruling class in history has wielded the image-making power of the economic royalists who reign over the media of the United States: newspapers, magazines, books, radio, films, television above all—and school classrooms as well. Two of the major myths about the working class impressed upon the American public as the employers' postwar offensive against the labor movement proceeded were those of (1) Big Labor and, (2) Affluent Workers. What message did these myths carry?

The first was that Big Labor with its membership of one quarter of the working class enjoyed power equal to that exercised by Big Business, dominated by two hundred corporations controlling worldwide empires and billions of dollars in assets; and the second, that workers were raking in so much money that they had resigned from the working class and become members of what some social scientists described as the affluent middle class. The facts were different. In 1972 the average annual pay for all workers in private industry, organized and unorganized, was $7,254, about $4,000 less than the moderate annual budget for a family of four called for in U.S. government calculations. Net corporate profits in 1972, however, had reached $52.6 billion as compared to $18.5 billion in 1949—a 185 percent increase.

These facts of economic life were bound to have their eventual effect upon the mood of working people in the shops, who became increasingly restless and rebellious as the pressures upon them increased. In November of 1968, manifestations of this mood came up for discussion at a meeting of members of an industrial union. The setting was a shop steward leadership training class of the independent United Electrical, Radio and Machine Workers of America, known as the UE, which has regularly conducted such sessions for shop stewards and local union officers ever since its founding in 1936.

Speaking to the group assembled in a union hall in Latrobe,

Pennsylvania, the UE's general secretary, James J. Matles, coauthor of this book, remarked:

> The labor movement is faced with the most serious challenge since the 1930s. I would like to discuss tonight only one phase of the challenge. It involves the young people in the organized shops, who are involved in a revolt which is growing day by day. It is not based on ideology. It is not political in character. It expresses itself today solely in economic terms, but as it develops it is bound to have far-reaching political consequences. Young workers are in revolt against the company establishment in the shop, they spark the protests against grievances, they are among the most militant fighters on the picket lines.

The UE leader, however, did not place young workers in a special isolated category. Toward the close of his discussion he said:

> If we combine the experience of the old-timers with the natural militancy of the young, we will have an unbeatable trade union combination. We will learn that it takes the unity of all, the skilled and unskilled, the young and the older, the men and women, the white, the black, and the other minority groups, to win a better life for all.

The UE leader's references in 1968 to "an unbeatable trade union combination" projected the kind of unity that prevailed just one year later among strikers on the picket lines at GE plants across the nation. Further features of this struggle were wide-ranging support measures from the entire labor movement, from students and college faculty members, from public officials and people in the communities where GE plants were located. True enough, as *Time* magazine noted, it was all reminiscent of the "U.S. industrial class wars of the 1930's."

What gave the 1969–1970 strike its special character, however, was its connection with events that had occurred not only in the 1930s but also in 1946. In that first year after the Second World War the CIO took on powerful corporations who were resolved on keeping for themselves almost every nickel of the billions they had received from the wartime production effort

6

of the workers. Massive strikes spearheaded by CIO industrial unions, chief among them the Auto Workers, Steel Workers, and UE, involved five million working people before the year 1946 came to a close. The solidarity of the workers and the popular support they received all over the country accomplished results that staggered corporations confident of having their own way.

One of the corporations was General Electric. Immediately after the strike settlement with UE in 1946, General Electric gave priority to a cold war offensive against the unity of the workers in their strong industrial union. This offensive, coordinated with the general corporate attack on CIO unity, succeeded. General Electric was then able year after year to impose its contract terms upon the workers, who remained organized but divided into several different unions.

It took twenty years before conditions developed which enabled workers once again to conduct a unified struggle against GE. That was the basic significance of the 1969–1970 strike. It brought about the first negotiated settlement with GE since that corporation had destroyed the unity of the workers in 1949. Their 1969–1970 militancy demonstrated that they had learned many a lesson from the bitter experience of twenty lean years.

III Such lessons from experience have always played a part in new battles fought by workers. Matles, in his 1968 remarks at the UE leadership training class in Latrobe, Pennsylvania, observed:

"The lessons of the past, from our own union and from the rest of the trade union movement, become a priceless guide in the battles to meet the challenge of today." He was speaking, fundamentally, of lessons in the kind of unionism defined by the preamble to the UE's constitution, adopted at the founding convention in 1936 and never altered since:

We, the Electrical, Radio and Machine Workers [UE], realize that the struggle to better our living and working conditions is in vain unless we are united to protect ourselves collectively against the organized forces of the employers.

Realizing that the old craft form of trade union organization is unable to defend effectively the interests and improve the conditions of the wage earners, We [UE] form an organization which unites all workers in our industry on an industrial basis, and rank-and-file control, regardless of craft, age, sex, nationality, race, creed or political belief, and pursue at all times a policy of aggressive struggle to improve our conditions.

We pledge ourselves to labor unitedly for the principles herein set forth, to perpetuate our union and work concertedly with other labor organizations to bring about a higher standard of living of the workers.

UE members compose a cross-section of American working people: young and older; radical, moderate, and conservative; men and women; black and white, Puerto Rican and Chicano; Catholic, Protestant, Jewish, and other believers and non-believers; Democrats, Republicans, admirers of George Wallace, socialists, communists and other partisans. Like all other unions it bargains with employers, conducts strikes, handles grievances, engages in political action, collects dues, keeps financial books, publishes an official newspaper, maintains a headquarters—in the one-time Manhattan townhouse, no less, of "robber baron" Cornelius J. Vanderbilt—from which its three top officers administer a staff of organizers, a legal staff, a research department, and a publicity department. There are also full-time district officers, and some full-time local officers, in areas throughout the United States and Canada. As with other labor organizations embracing memberships in Canada, the UE is thereby known as an "international union."

The geographical framework of the UE, consisting of about two hundred fifty local unions—representing in 1972 a total of approximately one hundred sixty-five thousand workers—is based upon the continental range of the electrical manufacturing and machine industries. The "radio" part of the union's original name could just as well be deleted, because radio and most television manufacturers began to go "multinational" after the Second World War and moved their plants to such U.S. economic colonies as Taiwan, South Korea, certain countries of Latin America, and other overseas locales—a process by no means confined to just radio and television production as the years went along.

Companies organized by the UE extend from Massachusetts and Vermont in the East to California on the Pacific, and northward into Canada. Workers who are covered by UE contracts in electrical manufacturing make everything from giant turbines and generators to toasters and clocks; in the machine industry, everything from locomotives and machine tools to delicate instruments and small hand tools. The UE holds collective bargaining contracts with, among other companies, General Electric (sales of $10 billion in 1972), Westinghouse (1972 sales, $5 billion), Sylvania, Ex-Cell-O, United Shoe Machinery, American Standard, Allen-Bradley, Textron, and Honeywell.

IV The survival of militant rank-and-file industrial unionism in the structure and functioning of the UE, throughout a period when this kind of unionism was nearly crushed to death, has puzzled a number of observers of the labor movement. "It would be useful to discover," wrote Professor F. S. O'Brien of Williams College in 1968, "just how the UE has been able to hold on." In his article in the professional journal *Labor History*, he said he would attempt no general answer to the question but would simply offer some comments:

> The UE is a democratic union, as unions go, and its leaders seem dedicated and hard-working. It employs only a relatively small number of organizers, relying primarily on the rank-and-file to spread organization in their immediate vicinity. It appeals to new members entirely in terms of local economic issues rather than ideologies. For a further explanation of UE tenacity, historians will have to look elsewhere; perhaps sociologists and psychologists can help.

Perhaps. But it is not easy for outsiders, however expert they may be in a particular area of social science, to understand the internal workings of an organization based upon the

9

principles of militant rank-and-file industrial unionism. For example: Professor O'Brien, when he writes that the UE "appeals to new members entirely in terms of local economic issues rather than ideologies," misses a fundamental point. Ideology is very much involved. It is the ideology of members running their own union, of members themselves, through union organization, learning to handle "local economic issues" that affect their lives as workers. The power of the ideology of democracy accounts primarily for the survival of the UE, just as it accounts for the appearance, reappearance, and survival of rank-and-file unionism in other sectors of the labor movement through the years.

The ideology of rank-and-file unionism is spelled out in the UE constitution, just as the ideology of American democracy is spelled out in the Declaration of Independence, and the U.S. Constitution and its first ten amendments, known as the Bill of Rights. The fight to secure such rights, however, is never-ending. Once down on paper they have to be constantly practiced and preserved in action. They have to be fought for again and again. Endless struggles to preserve democratic principles explain what militant rank-and-file industrial unionism is all about—and why, when it is practiced by affording all members an equal chance to have a piece of the action, such unionism is difficult to destroy.

V   The UE constitution is marked on almost every page by the enumeration of one principle or another of rank-and-file unionism. For example: Union officers from shop steward to local, district, and international officers are elected annually by the memberships they represent; all negotiating committees are elected—and negotiations themselves are conducted with the participation of rank-and-file elected representatives of the members; proposed contracts are voted upon by the workers they cover; strikes are called and concluded only by membership vote.

The constitution provides that the pay of the three top officers shall be in line with the pay of the most skilled workers in the shops and defines this principle with salary ceilings that cannot be exceeded. The 1972 constitution provided that the salary of the three top officers "shall not exceed $284.14 per week"; that the salary of international representatives "shall not exceed $215.14 per week"; and the salary of field organizers "shall not exceed $197.60 per week." When union officers and organizers are away from their home city on union work, they are paid the cost of their hotel room and are given a modest daily allowance for meals. There is a strict accounting of union funds with a monthly report submitted by the international union to all locals. The constitution prohibits the investment of union funds in corporate stocks, bonds, or any other similar ventures.

From time to time the subject of officer and staff salaries has come up at UE annual conventions. The officers have discussed this subject with the local shop leaders and members on many occasions. Said Matles to the delegates at one convention in the late sixties:

> Yes, some people think we're just a bunch of nuts. Why do we have an international union where our officers are living the same lives as the rank-and-file? The fact of the matter is we have always been convinced that if you want to maintain the rank-and-file nature of our union, if you want to maintain democracy in our organization, if you want officers and representatives to whom no shop grievance is too small to handle, no matter whether it affects one worker or one penny, you must have an organization where your officers and your organizers feel *like* the members and not feel *for* the members. There is a big difference.

On another occasion he remarked:

> One argument for higher officer salaries cited is the need to maintain the prestige of our officers. Let me tell you, we have met with presidents of companies who get a half million dollars a year in salaries and again as much in stock options, incentive compensation, and deferred salaries. We had them on the other side of the table and the fact that we were getting only what a skilled worker gets in the shop didn't do a damn thing to hurt us as negotiators.

11

And on still another occasion, Matles said to the rank-and-file convention delegates:

> We officers, organizers, business agents, district presidents, have it all over you as far as the job is concerned. When you walk through that plant gate every morning, most of you hate to do it. If you did not have to earn a week's pay, few of you would ever go near that gate. During the years you have kept me on my job I've been able to stay away from that gate 9,000 times. Instead of going to work every morning for a boss, and hating it, I've been getting up every morning and going in to work at a job I like to do. That's where we officers have it all over you.

VI　　In the UE setup a consistent effort has been made to build a shop steward system where there is one steward to every company foreman. Shop stewards are encouraged and trained to solve problems by themselves on the shop floor where the problems arise—and to solve these in close contact with the rank-and-file members involved in the problem. The method by which union members have been accustomed to arrive at decisions is the method of open discussion and debate, whether the question be one of a small shop with a few workers or one embracing, as did the General Electric strike, thousands upon thousands.

Some UE people in leadership positions have occasionally found this process frustrating, especially when the rank-and-file may reject contract terms which a negotiating committee sincerely believes it has done its level best to drag out of the company. At such times there may be complaints about "just too damn much democracy in this union." Old-timers have not been backward about speaking up when complaints of this sort are expressed. They are quick to remind their union brothers and sisters that there can never be such a thing as "too much democracy."

The democratic relationship between members and leaders is one of the most important features of rank-and-file unionism—and one of the most difficult to describe. That is because it depends not upon formal rules of procedure but rather upon a constant flow of informally conducted exchanges between members and leaders on equal footing in the union. A well-known labor reporter, whose career of writing about workers and unions stretched back to the thirties, commented in a book review in the spring of 1970 that he was fascinated and, at the same time, beyond his depth as he confronted this rank-and-file unionism phenomenon in print.

Among the publications submitted to him for review had been the *UE Guide to Automation and the New Technology*, which contained verbatim excerpts of a conversation between Matles and a rank-and-file Westinghouse machinist about the operation of a tape-controlled horizontal boring mill. "The intense curiosity about the process of work which runs through Matles' questions," the book reviewer said, enchanted and perplexed him.

Curiosity, yes. But it was also Matles's trade union position that motivated the conversation. He was engaged in the practice of leadership in a rank-and-file unionism setting. Matles was assisting a union negotiating committee at the Westinghouse plant. They were plowing through new ground, negotiating wage rates, job descriptions and classifications for new tape-controlled machines which embodied the latest advances in automation and of the new technology. Whatever was done here would serve as a precedent for many years.

Thus, for seven weeks during the negotiations, Matles, himself a machinist, spent his lunch hours in the shop with skilled machinists who were among the first to experiment with these new machines. Questions and answers were the natural way for a rank-and-file leader to educate himself when confronted with a difficult shop problem, new to him and the rest of the union committee.

VII

"Doing what comes naturally" in rank-and-file unionism, however, is not something the UE invented. Far from it. Such unionism—along with the more familiar business unionism—has a long history, dating back to the beginnings of the modern industrial era at the time of the Civil War. Shortly before that conflict ended, President Abraham Lincoln made a comment which is extremely helpful in understanding the nature of the forces that produced the American labor movement and the ongoing struggle between business unionism and rank-and-file unionism. Writing to a friend in 1864, Lincoln said:

"As a result of the War, corporations have been entrenched and an era of corruption in high places will follow, and the money power of the country will endeavor to prolong its reign by working upon the prejudices of the people until all wealth is aggregated in a few hands."

Lincoln, as it turned out, was forecasting the economic and political future of America. "I feel at this moment," he penned in a final sentence, "more anxiety for the safety of my country than ever before, even in the midst of war." Events have proved beyond question that in fearing the prolongation of the reign of "the money power," he was prophetic. The entrenched corporations of which he spoke were mere children in 1864 compared with what they would be a century and more later; the Civil War aggregates of wealth were just small stuff when set beside the billions upon billions of late twentieth-century monopoly.

Nevertheless, "the money power" of his day, and its corruptive potential, deeply worried Lincoln from the perspective of his office as President of the people. From another perspective, that of a young iron molder turned labor leader, it also worried and enraged William Sylvis, founder of the first national organization of workers to challenge what he too, shortly after the war, called "the money power." In 1868 he elaborated:

"Capital blights and withers all it touches. It is a new aristocracy, proud, imperious, dishonest, seeking only profit and the exploitation of workers." The only alternatives such a system left to the workers, Sylvis said again and again—until, burned out by his organizing efforts, he died at age forty-one—were organization and struggle. He insisted, moreover, to fellow trade unionists, who with him were establishing the National Labor Union, that affiliates of the organization must accept all

14

workers without regard to color or sex. Black workers and women workers, he said, had to be "our companions in advancement."

He went further still. Too exhausted to attend the founding convention of the National Labor Union in Baltimore, he sent word that not only should it unite workers industrially but should also organize an independent political party composed of labor, the black people, and the farmers. Like Lincoln, Sylvis can be described as prophetic. The principles he urged upon workers until his death in 1869 were those which have animated rank-and-file unionism from that time forward.

VIII   Organizing the unorganized, an industrial form of organization, aggressive struggle, no discrimination, independent political action, these are the working class principles to which "the money power" derived from the Civil War gave rise, as it applied the screws to workers in the factory system that was just beginning to develop. The National Labor Union failed in the face of aggregate wealth. An employer had told Sylvis he was going too far, especially when the young organizer declared "the whole united power of labor is necessary to the successful resistance of the power of capital."

Said the employer, "the day will come when men now active in the labor movement will be forced upon their bended knee [by] the widespread and universal organization of capitalists for the avowed purpose of destroying your unions." Six years— 1866 to 1872—was the life span of the National Labor Union. It collapsed after the majority of its membership came to be composed of professional and small business people, whose concentration upon currency reform replaced the essential rank-and-file union objective of organizing workers industrially for aggressive struggle.

Efforts to create democratic industrial unions, however, continued. By 1886 the Knights of Labor, organized on an industrial basis, had a mass membership of 700,000, among which were skilled, semiskilled and unskilled workers. But neither then, nor for some years, would industrial conditions be favor-

15

able for such a form of organization. The American Federation of Labor, founded on craft union lines in the very same year—1886—when the Knights of Labor membership was at its peak, soon attracted most of the skilled workers from that industrial organization, which little by little fell apart.

The skilled craft union leaders who formed the AFL were mostly socialists—including first president, Samuel Gompers—whose political outlook derived from the European socialist movement. The original founders referred to "a struggle going on in the nations of the world between the oppressors and the oppressed of all countries, a struggle between capital and labor which must grow in intensity from year to year." The AFL also based itself upon such declarations of purpose as "working people must unite and organize irrespective of creed, color, sex, nationality or politics." But it was not long before AFL leaders and their craft unions abandoned in practice many principles which still remained on the federation's books.

Discriminatory membership policies were adopted. Early commitments to independent political action were replaced by the Gompers' formula of "rewarding one's friends and punishing one's enemies" among the two major political parties. Class collaboration with the bosses was substituted for class struggle. In 1901 Sam Gompers—who remained at the head of the AFL until his death in 1924—became a vice president of the National Civic Federation. This numbered among its members some of the most powerful industrialists, bankers, and politicians of the era. The National Civic Federation dedicated itself "to the fostering of harmony between organized capital and organized labor," a far cry from the objectives to which the AFL had dedicated itself at its birth.

The leaders of the American Federation of Labor, in short, were falling victim to the corrupting influence of "the money power." By the turn of the century, as Lincoln had feared, this had made itself felt upon just about every institution in the country. Federal, state, and local governments were under its sway. So were universities, churches, the newspapers, the professions, organizations of every sort. Within the labor movement this corrupting influence produced a brand of unionism which came to be known as business unionism.

IX   It is well-named. Business unionism simply means unions run like a business. Customarily, in the practice of business unionism, rank-and-file workers have no active role in negotiating contracts. Not infrequently, moreover, they are not allowed to help formulate contract demands or to decide on calling a strike or ending it. All these things are left to the discretion of the business union "experts," who, after settling with the boss, announce the terms to the members. When business unionism is carried to such lengths, members have no opportunity to reject the terms. At best they have a paper right to approve them. And even when the boss violates provisions of a contract to which he has agreed, workers cannot fight their own grievances. Everything is handled by others.

The rank-and-file under this system plays little or no part in shaping the conditions under which they labor or the conditions under which their families are obliged to live. This is the fatal flaw of business unionism. It fails to recognize that the manner in which workers achieve results is equally as important as the results themselves.

Constant association with corporation executives, and with prominent professional and government personalities, often has a decisive impact upon business unionists. They aspire to the standards and styles of life of the big shots. Their outlooks and perspectives become very different from those of the rank-and-file. In their dealings with the boss, who has become their model of what it means to be successful, they fail to fight for an important human principle which Abraham Lincoln once defined with characteristic simplicity.

Whenever there was a conflict between "the man and the dollar," wrote Lincoln, it could only be resolved by putting "the man before the dollar." But business unionists do not follow the Lincoln philosophy. They permit the boss to do what a boss does automatically. They permit the boss to place the dollar before the man.

Since neither unions nor working people live and function in a social vacuum, no union in the country is immune to, or entirely free from, the corruptive influence of business unionism. As long as "corruption in high places" persists, the strong

17

temptation of business unionism will continue to pose a constant threat to the labor movement and its members. Faced with these conditions, the best any union can do is to practice preventive medicine—aggressive economic and political struggle to protect and improve the lot of working people and their families, hand in hand with education in the principles of rank-and-file trade unionism.

X This is what such dedicated militants as Eugene Debs, Big Bill Haywood, William Z. Foster and others were getting at when they founded the IWW, the Industrial Workers of the World, in 1905. "Industrial unionism," said Debs, "is the principle upon which the IWW is organized." He continued:

> In the Industrial Workers we have a union recognizing the equal rights of all and extending its benefits equally to all. Industrial unionism means actual unity of purpose and action. It means the economic solidarity of our class. It means that the grievance of one is the concern of all and that from this time forward the craft division is to be eliminated.

The founders of the IWW saw unmistakable signs that mass production industry, mingling thousands of skilled, semiskilled, and unskilled workers in great plants, was in the process of making the industrial union form of labor organization imperative. New large corporations backed by aggregates of wealth, such as General Electric (founded in 1892 by Morgan interests) and Westinghouse (founded by Mellon interests in 1891), were getting themselves into mass production gear.

The corporations immediately recognized that they would not be able to work out any "harmony of interest" deal with the IWW, as they had done with the craft union leaders of the AFL. They feared, in fact, that AFL rank-and-file workers, many of whom were conducting their own struggles for militant democratic unionism, would find in the IWW a national organization which met their needs. For that reason the corporations unleashed an all-out war against the new industrial union movement.

18

The IWW fought a heroic battle for survival. But the weight of the forces arrayed against it, combined with certain internal weaknesses, eventually led to the decline of the IWW as an effective labor organization. Among the weaknesses were IWW attitudes toward political action and toward the negotiation of contracts with employers. Debs himself warned that when the IWW renounced a policy of independent political action and adopted "direct action" strategy—including adventuresome clandestine moves carried out by individuals and small groups of militants—it was separating itself from traditions accepted by American workers. Said Debs:

"Direct action can never appeal to any considerable number of workers while they have the ballot and the right of industrial and political organization."

He practiced what he preached. On four occasions he campaigned as a presidential candidate on a program of socialism. In his last effort in 1920, while still in a federal prison to which he had been sentenced because of his opposition to U.S. participation in the First World War, he received almost a million votes. He opposed involvement in the war—as did the IWW—on principle, regarding it as a squabble among aggregates of wealth in various nations for domination of world resources and markets, something which had nothing to do with the interests of working people.

The IWW position on the war was one of the factors which made it vulnerable to attack in that period. It was vulnerable, also, because it had no strong base in the shops. While IWW leaders were incomparable in rallying workers in strikes and in protest mobilizations, the organization viewed the signing of contracts with employers as a form of collaboration with the boss. This feeling stemmed from IWW contempt for the "sweetheart contracts" negotiated between AFL business unionists and employers. But in practice it prevented the IWW from building solid shop organizations capable of carrying on consistent trade union action.

Although the Industrial Workers of the World was practically destroyed in the "Red Scare" hysteria generated by the corporate-government establishment after the First World War, its place in labor movement history was assured. The IWW principles of militant democratic industrial unionism never died.

19

They remained alive not only in memory but in the persons of many active trade unionists who helped to sow the seeds for the industrial unionism of the CIO in the 1930s.

XI The ground for such unionism was already being prepared in the shops during and immediately after the First World War. Many strikes and stoppages, conducted by AFL craft unions, erupted in basic industries such as electrical manufacturing. One strike after another occurred at key plants of this industry—at General Electric in Schenectady, N.Y.; Lynn and Pittsfield, Mass.; Fort Wayne, Indiana; Erie, Pennsylvania; and at Westinghouse in East Pittsburgh, Pennsylvania. The major basic industry battle of that period, however, was fought in 1919 in the steel industry.

For almost four months, three hundred sixty-five thousand steel workers struggled to extract a measure of what they had coming to them from the profits the industry had piled up in the war. The AFL had assigned organizer William Z. Foster to lead the strike. He did so brilliantly. But his insistence on conducting a militant strike on an industrial union basis, with no distinctions drawn between skilled, semiskilled, and unskilled or between white and black workers, ran contrary to the craft union bias of AFL president Sam Gompers and other top AFL leaders. Their sabotage of the strike, achieved by refusing Foster adequate staff and finances, permitted the steel industry to bust it.

While AFL leadership may have calculated that its antagonism to industrial unionism and its policy of class collaboration had won it an acceptable place in the corporate profit system, the leadership had another thing coming. The great steel strike, and the continuing unrest in other basic industry shops, indicated to employers that AFL unions were not being "properly conducted"—to quote the words of the famous American humorist, Finley Peter Dunne.

"And how would employers have unions properly conducted?" Dunne had his fictional bartender philosopher, Mr. Dooley, say to a friend. "I'll tell you. No strikes, no shop rules, no rates, hardly any wages and damn few members."

Such was the prescription for "properly conducted" unions which employers in the early 1920s proceeded to apply to the AFL, whose leaders felt content and secure after the war with an AFL membership of about 3½ million. Very soon, however, its craft organizations fitted Mr. Dooley's definition: "damn few members." In General Electric and Westinghouse, for example, as in all other basic industries, craft unions were swept out by the corporations and replaced either by company unions or no unions at all. AFL craft unionism had come to a dead end in the shops of mass production. And the AFL leadership wrote them off. It gave up.

Militants, however, didn't. Among them was Foster, who with other socialists founded the American Communist party in 1920. Later he helped to set up the Trade Union Education League and the Trade Union Unity League, which he headed, to fight for the cause of industrial unionism in mass production industry. In the shops themselves were individual rank-and-file workers of militant cast—communists, socialists, IWWs, other radicals and a number of workers of no particular political persuasion but deeply dedicated to the realization of honest, democratic, progressive trade unionism.

Throughout the country the seeds of a rank-and-file movement for industrial unionism were in the ground when the storm of the Great Depression broke in 1929. At that time one of the authors of this book, Jim Matles, having completed his four-year apprenticeship, was working as a young machinist in a shop in Brooklyn, New York. Here is the way it was then and there, as Matles remembers it . . .

21

2
Depression Days in the Shops

I   There was quite a buzz in the machine shop in Brooklyn when we got our first pay cut. The top rate had been 60 cents an hour. It was late in the year 1929. We had no union. During lunch hour, while we were talking about the cut, the fellows agreed to get a committee together to see the superintendent.

We tried to pick out skilled people who would be least likely to be fired. That evening, after work, five of us went into the superintendent's office and very meekly asked him not to cut our pay. We said:

"It's hard for us to stand this cut. Do you have any complaints about us or our work that make you cut our pay?"

He said he had no particular complaints but that business was bad. He claimed: "If we don't cut your pay, a lot of you will have no jobs."

Nobody said much more. When we got out of the door we felt as if we had escaped from a lion's den. We told the fellows who were hanging around outside, waiting for us, what the boss had said. It was Friday night.

On Sunday we held a meeting. About fifty showed up. We talked and we decided that on Monday morning the committee would go back in to see the boss—and the rest of the people would hang around the shop but not start work until the committee came out to report.

We tried it. The boss went right past us out of the office and said, "All you guys better go back to work or the whole shebang will be fired."

Without another word we picked up our tools and got busy on the job. A while later, we were discussing the thing and we agreed that the reason we didn't get anywhere was because we didn't have a union and that we had to have one.

One of the fellows suggested that there was an organization in the American Federation of Labor that sounded as if it would be up our alley: the International Association of Machinists, the IAM.

We went to an IAM office in a dreary building in Brooklyn, an AFL labor temple, as they are called. There was an old, old man in the office. He was an IAM business agent. We told him about our pay cut, said we wanted a union, and asked if he would take us in—all of us, the whole shop, about two hundred workers.

He looked at us as if we were crazy. He said that only a few maintenance and repair machinists in printing shops and breweries were left in his IAM local, now that the union had been busted out of the bigger machine shops. We didn't fit into either category, he said, so there was nothing he could do for us.

We didn't argue. To us, at that time, getting a union was like buying a pair of pants. If you went into a store and they said they had no pants, or no pants the right size, you didn't argue, you just went away. So that's what we did.

II   But we kept scouting around and one day we heard of a nearby group of old-timer union men. It turned out they had no shop organized in their small, independent Metal Workers Industrial Union—just individual members in various shops, this place and that. The old-timers were all skilled mechanics.

They had been members of the Micrometer Lodge of the IAM in Brooklyn during the First World War. After the war, the bosses had broken up their organization, regarding the members as too militant. For a long while they had no union at all.

Then some of the old-timers got together in this little group to talk over what they had been through and to "spread the gospel of unionism," as they said to us. They welcomed us with

23

open arms. We signed application blanks. The initiation fee was 50 cents, the dues 25 cents a month.

Our committee in the machine shop decided to call a meeting of the men in our shop and we got the same meeting room the old-timers used. When our committee went to the room it was freezing cold. The caretaker told us he had a kerosene heater at home we could borrow. About forty men came to the meeting. All but three or four signed the union cards. We collected 50 cents apiece.

The next Monday, in the shop, we began very quietly to sign up certain fellows, while staying away from others we were none too sure of as far as carrying word to the boss was concerned. One at a time, slowly, we signed people up. We kept it going all that winter of 1930 and by spring we had about eighty in the union.

We had no leaks, no firings, and no meetings. Nobody in the shop but the five fellows on the committee knew who all the members were. That was important in those days. There was no such thing as making a complaint to the government about an "unfair labor practice." If you joined a union, and the boss found out about it, he would just fire you. That would be the end of that.

We felt good about the progress we were making. We'd say to each other, "The big day is coming!" We didn't know exactly what the big day would be but it made us feel good to say it. Then, as spring came, we didn't feel so good. The layoffs started. People everywhere were saying, "It's a depression."

Every week, one or two or more would be laid off. The 10 percent pay cut became a minor issue. We forgot about it. Our jobs were on the line. Of course no such animal as seniority existed. If two men were on the same kind of job, the company would keep the youngest and strongest, the one the boss thought he could get the most work out of.

As those layoffs kept mowing us down, it took the heart out of organizing in the shop. We didn't dare think of trying to get recognized as a shop organization—or even trying to settle a grievance as a committee. From day to day we were all wondering who would be the next ones let go. We had no alternative but to lay low and keep picking up individual mem-

24

bers as we could. If we had come out in the open we would have invited the boss to crush us entirely.

III Stymied in the shop, we were impatient. We didn't want to stand still. Our union, the independent Metal Workers Industrial Union, decided it might be possible to make headway in other shops. Our old-timer machinist friends would go with us in the early mornings, before starting time, to plant gates, and we would stand around. Or, if we had been laid off, we would turn ourselves into volunteer organizers and maybe hit the plants at lunchtime, and after work too.

Some of the plants we hit were Mergenthaler Linotype, American Machine and Foundry, Intertype, E. W. Bliss, Eiseman Magneto, Johnson Machine, Arma Engineering, F. S. Smithe Machine Co., and a lot of smaller companies. The old-timers would catch sight of someone they had once worked with. They would get him aside, introduce him to us younger fellows—we were in our very early twenties—and we would say we had an organization going. We'd ask if he knew a few people in the shop who might be interested in meeting with us.

We met with small groups. Sometimes it would be with a shop committee, sometimes with individual members. We would exchange information with them on how the union was getting along, and on job conditions, wage cuts, and the layoffs that were going on all around. We would try to keep each other up to date on all developments. Sometimes these meetings were at a fellow's home, sometimes in a saloon, sometimes at our own office which we had by now rented at eight or nine dollars a month out of our initiation and dues money.

If we could get a group moving in a shop, we aimed at spreading out from department to department or at least finding out the situation in different departments. Then our procedure was to put out a little shop paper with news from several departments. In that way we would not put a finger on our men in one department and pinpoint them for firing.

The fellows from the shop furnished the news for the papers but never so they could be identified with the material. They never distributed the papers at their own shops, either. They would have been let go on the spot. Workers from other shops, or unemployed people, did the distributing.

IV   These little shop papers created a sensation whenever they appeared. The first one we put out at Mergenthaler Linotype took the company completely by surprise. We gave out all the copies we had produced. Nobody interfered. We congratulated ourselves at having a clear field at Mergenthaler. When we had a second issue of the paper ready, six of us from our shop went back there to distribute it.

The minute we got near the plant a bunch of goons, who had been hiding in the entrance, jumped us. They threw our papers in the street and started working us over. They shoved us into the street and beat and kicked us as we rolled around. Traffic came to a standstill. A policeman on the corner who could see what was going on just stood there blowing his whistle once in a while.

We escaped as well as we could. We didn't want to get arrested and lose our jobs. Later on, the fellows from Mergenthaler told us the goons came from "the agency." I don't remember if we ever found out what agency—or if we even tried. In those days there was nothing we could do about it. If a boss heard of a union coming around the shop, he would hire an agency to send out the goons to beat up anyone at the plant gates. Also, he would have the agency give him some spies he could put to work in the shop to inform on who belonged to the union. Agencies doing such business were the Pinkertons, the National Metal Trades Association, the Railway Audit and Inspection, and plenty of others.

V   At Mergenthaler we had a taste of both kinds of agency operations, the beating and the infiltration, though not at the same time. It was quite a while after we got beaten up by the goons, and after we had made some progress in organizing the Mergenthaler plant, that a young fellow turned up at the office of our Metal Workers Industrial Union. He said that he had been a member of a small independent union of radio workers in New York. He told us he was interested in union organization and would like to help us out.

He was a good-looking, fast-talking young man. He bragged a lot, but was always very generous and obliging—always ready to run an errand or do someone a favor. He seemed to have a little money and used to offer people small loans or hand out pawn tickets for clothing and such things. We took him pretty much at face value. We were more or less innocent then. All of us had a lot to learn.

When he landed a job at Mergenthaler, we were surprised. Jobs were awfully hard to get then. Some people in the plant were suspicious of him from the start. He was given a job in the tool room, a big department of about one hundred seventy-five tool and die makers, which at that time was our stronghold of organization in the shop. Much later on, after certain things happened, Ray Keefer, a toolmaker and our committeeman in the department, recollected and wrote it out in an affidavit:

I saw a fellow in the tool room. A new fellow. Although he didn't do much if any work, he was running around in the tool room. He was in the plant only two weeks. During that period he would be one day on the job and off the next. He was supposed to have hired in as a machinist's helper. During my entire experience in the Mergenthaler Co. they never hired such a worker before. They hired kids who would have gone through the apprenticeship school of this company, and in this way they'd go on to become full-fledged mechanics.

The first stewards' meeting was arranged for the purpose of discussing ways and means for the union to come out in the open and prepare to call an open meeting. Much to my amazement, when I came to the meeting of the stewards I noticed this fellow at the front of the hall. He continued to stay at the front of the hall watching all the stewards coming into the meeting.

After this meeting, he never returned to the shop. When I asked at the union about him, I was told that he had said he had quit his job and had a week's pay coming to him. Several days later, I, as committeeman in the tool room, and fifteen other active union men in the tool room, were fired. It was a very severe blow to us.

VI   Of course the general layoffs kept going on. This made it natural for small new organizations like the Metal Workers Industrial Union to take an interest in the local councils of unemployed people that were springing up. The councils were active in neighborhoods, fighting evictions and demanding food and other necessities for families of workers without jobs. We observed that the old-line AFL unions had neither a real program for helping unemployed people nor any program for combating unemployment. At first, in fact, they opposed altogether the idea of unemployment insurance.

A tremendous demonstration of the unemployed took place in New York City. It developed out of the local councils getting together. Their members had become extremely militant. In defiance of sheriffs, they moved the furniture of evicted people right back from the sidewalks—where the sheriffs had dumped it—into the homes. They also staged mobilizations at welfare offices, city and borough halls, and storefronts where food for the jobless was being handed out. A big head of steam was building up.

It was at the big meeting in New York that the demand for unemployment insurance was raised for one of the first times as a matter of program. The newspapers were screaming "Red Revolution." Even unemployment insurance, later to become a universally accepted feature of American life, was denounced as coming straight from Moscow.

Some of us from the Metal Workers Union attended the unemployed demonstration where more than one hundred thousand people had gathered. The police charged on horseback from side streets into the huge crowd, clubbing people and sending them sprawling. Many were hurt and many were arrested. Such things were happening all over the country.

VII   Out of the city demonstrations came marches on Washington. There were "bonus" marches by veterans, "hunger" and other marches of unemployed people, all with the objective of petitioning the federal government for assistance. One caravan, in which some of our union members participated, set out with the intention of asking Congress to pass an unemployment insurance law. That was some time in 1931.

We never got into Washington. A swarm of police met us about twelve miles out. While we were camped there by the roadside arguing for three days—they finally let a small committee go through to see some congressmen—the farmers in the area fed us. We shared among us what we received from the farmers—eggs, chickens, meat, fruit, vegetables, and milk.

In 1931 and 1932 the Metal Workers Industrial Union concentrated on trying to organize old, established, important shops such as Mergenthaler and American Machine and Foundry. These firms were practiced in blocking unionism. People, with good reason, were deathly afraid of the boss. It took much time and effort in those big shops to get one contact and, in the end, perhaps sign up just one worker. But the organizing work never stopped and was gradually spreading from one shop to another.

(The preceding personal recollections by Matles of early organizing days were first recorded for UE members in 1955, a period of severest trial for the union.)

VIII   For quite a while in the machine industry the Metal Workers Industrial Union had the organizing field all to itself. It did not have to worry about competition from the AFL craft unions. They were in bad shape. The anti-labor offensive of employers through the twenties, and then the Great Depression, had combined to take the steam out of all labor organizations, not only industrial unionism. Most of the AFL membership of less than 2 million was restricted to the building trades and miscellaneous industries, nothing basic.

These were conditions prevailing when a few workers decided in 1930 to found the Metal Workers Industrial Union affiliated with the Trade Union Unity League. Realistically, they had no great expectations. None of them felt that overnight they were going to rebuild the labor movement and enlist masses of working people in the cause of industrial unionism. They were not complete romantics—just romantic enough to believe that somehow, at some future time, they didn't dare to think when, industrial unionism would succeed.

The Mergenthaler experience of disaster was repeated time and again. All too often, the young activists of the Metal Workers could not escape the vengeance of company-hired spies and goons. For that reason the Metal Workers adopted for the most part the strategy of organizing cautiously and secretly. It seemed to be the only intelligent way of trying to stay alive in the enemy territory of the machine, metal, and electrical shops of the period. The objective was to build union-conscious groups, however small, in these shops and to do it with as few job losses as possible. Some progress in this direction was made in the years 1930 to 1933.

Groups formed in Brooklyn, Manhattan, and Queens. Also in Newark, Harrison, Paterson, and other New Jersey towns. A Metal Workers local was organized in Philadelphia, consisting of several tool and die shops. More groups formed at the Yale and Towne Co., Stamford, Connecticut; at Pratt and Whitney Aircraft, and Pratt and Whitney Tool, in Hartford; at a metal fabricating shop in Jamestown, New York. Another local established a base in Cleveland; another in Minneapolis; still another in Chicago. Slowly but surely, the union was putting together a string of component parts here and there.

IX　Most significantly, however, in terms of the future of industrial unionism in the electrical manufacturing industry, members of the Metal Workers—mainly skilled mechanics—organized groups in the key plants of the giant corporations of that industry: General Electric in Schenectady, New York, and Westinghouse in East Pittsburgh, Pennsylvania. By the time of the inauguration of Franklin Roosevelt as president in March 1933, when the hopes of working people for recovery from depressed economic conditions could be more and more openly expressed, the young organizers of the Metal Workers Industrial Union had established skeleton crews in dozens of shops in the machine, metal working, and electrical industry.

These active, volunteer organizers were full of zeal and determination but, at the start, very inexperienced. They had to learn the hard way to keep a constant eye out for agents planted by the companies. Soon it came to be taken for granted that in any large shop where union-building was under way, at least one company spy was in the works somewhere.

Nobody, however, knew the extent of this spy operation. It was not until 1936, when the LaFollette Committee of the U.S. Senate initiated a two-year investigation of industrial espionage against labor unions, that it became clear what the industrial unionists had really been up against. A nationwide network of professional spies and strikebreakers, employed by private agencies who sold their services to the most powerful corporations in the land at an annual cost of $80 million, had been operating night and day against union-minded men and women.

There was expectation in the air in those early New Deal months. Workers everywhere were stirred up by the feeling that real political change was about to occur. Nevertheless, it took a while for organizational movement of any size to get underway in larger industry, where fear of the boss had been well implanted in the minds of the workers. Not until the first practical measures of New Deal reform were instituted did these workers, in any great numbers, begin to feel free to let loose their instinctive desire for industrial unionism.

The legislative act of the New Deal Congress that started the ball rolling was the National Industrial Recovery Act of April 1933. Ordinarily referred to by its initials—NIRA—the act aimed to treat "a national emergency productive of widespread unemployment and disorganization of industry . . . which effects the public welfare and undermines the standards of living of the American people."

X   The agency set up in Washington to administer the NIRA was known by the initials NRA: National Recovery Administration. Its task, in general, was to formulate "codes of conduct" for every industry. The law contained only one important provision for labor—section 7A—which related the rights of working people to the prospective codes by declaring: "That employees shall have the right to organize and bargain collectively through representatives of their own choosing, and shall be free from the interference, restraint or coercion of employers of labor or their agents."

While the NIRA was indeed law, it did not provide the NRA with enforcement powers. For the moment, then—pending the enactment in 1935 of the Wagner Act—the rebuilding of weakened unions, and the initial work on the organization of new industrial unions, rested in the hands of the unionists themselves, using to what advantage they could the explicit statement of section 7A. The United Mine Workers, for example, dispatched to the coal fields organizers with leaflets by the thousands carrying the slogan: "The President wants you to join a union."

Corporations, individually and through such combinations as the National Association of Manufacturers, declared war on section 7A. Quoting their law firms as authorities for the claim that the law was unconstitutional, they refused to obey it. As future events revealed, however, section 7A did help to promote the exercise of the legal rights and liberties of working people. It ignited the spark that started the organizational engine humming in mass production.

Now the possibilities of the quiet work done over a period of four years by the pioneer industrial unionists, who had pulled together a leadership corps in hundreds of shops, became apparent. They were on the inside. They occupied posts in the automobile plants, electrical plants, machine shops, large foundries, rubber plants, and others. There were tens of thousands of workers employed in these shops. As activists among them launched open organizing campaigns, new young local unions knocked on the doors of the AFL, requesting support and industrial union charters.

It is an understatement to describe the AFL craft union high command as being totally unprepared for so extraordinary a development. The AFL old guard was about as ready to receive industrial unionists as had been the old IAM business agent in the Brooklyn labor temple in 1930, when the machine shop committee representing two hundred unorganized workers knocked on his door and he didn't know what to do with them.

The craft union fathers of the AFL confronted a crisis of unwanted children: the industrial unionists. Officials of seventy craft unions got together in special conference to decide if there was any way out of the dilemma. The gathering was dominated by two elements in the AFL structure, the Building Trades Department and the Metal Trades Department. Every construction craft was represented in the Building Trades Department; every craft union in the metal trades belonged to the Metal Trades Department. The leaders of the unions in the two departments traditionally wielded just about supreme power in the AFL.

An almost forgotten clause of the AFL constitution was resurrected. It authorized the AFL high command to issue charters to so-called federal labor unions—individual locals unaffiliated with any craft organization and directly under the jurisdiction of the AFL headquarters. In 1933 there were very few federal locals in existence. It seemed, however, opportune to issue a flock of such charters without delay to the local unions in mass production clamoring for industrial union charters. The scheme amounted to a holding operation. A local federal charter was intended to rope the workers in a given plant into a general AFL group. But only temporarily.

Once the workers were roped in by the federal local charter, the various craft organizations would then select their moment for picking off those particular workers which each craft decided belonged in its organization. These would be the skilled mechanics of the different trades. As for the rest, mainly the unskilled, they would be left in the federal local to shift for themselves, and industrial unionism as a form of organization would go down the drain.

The chief crafts of the Metal Trades Department of the AFL which sought to take advantage of the strategy of federal labor union charters were the International Association of Machinists (IAM), the International Brotherhood of Electrical Workers (IBEW), the Moulders, the Pattern Makers, the Sheet Metal Workers, the Plumbers and Steamfitters, the Metal Polishers, and several others. They hoped to reap a harvest of members by cultivation of AFL federal locals. But, out in the field, a pattern of organization was developing, which, in the three years from 1933 to 1936, was to make a shambles out of the craft union scheme.

XI   Two distinct categories of local unions formed this pattern of organization in 1933. In certain plants the workers accepted the offer of AFL organizers, who were scouring mass production territory under orders from AFL Washington headquarters to distribute federal labor union charters. In other plants the workers chose to maintain an independent status. All these industrial union groups were carrying on a fight for recognition by the plant management.

Where the fight was successful, victory came about by one of two methods: through strikes or through plant representation elections conducted by the NRA under section 7A. The work of organization, and the campaigns for recognition, were led in many cases, no matter what type of local industrial union was involved, by skilled craftsmen. Plainly, such a phenomenon had deep implications. The old-timer skilled mechanics were versed in the ways of craft unionism. They had experienced its restrictions of membership and its failures—in great part because of selective membership rules—to adequately represent the general welfare of the workers. It was this instructive lesson of history which prompted skilled craftsmen to join hands with unskilled union activists, in the early thirties, in organizing local industrial unions in the plants.

Among the plants organized was that of General Electric in Lynn, Massachusetts. There, in West Lynn and at the River Works, the second largest complex in the GE chain, skilled pattern maker Al Coulthard helped to lead the struggle for industrial organization. He had long been a member of the AFL Pattern Makers League. Similarly, in the first-ranking GE plant in Schenectady, New York, skilled turbine inspector Bill Turnbull took leadership in 1933 in organizing an independent local union, which immediately received the full support of the group of Metal Workers members established there in 1932.

Like Coulthard in Lynn, Turnbull in Schenectady had an AFL background. He had belonged for many years to the IAM, one of the craft unions which had been driven out of GE in the twenties. Coulthard, who was forty years old, and Turnbull, past fifty, fell into the classification of old-timers in the movement. Both British-born, they had arrived in the United States as experienced trade unionists, former members of the British Labour party.

Another independent local union had been organized at the RCA plant in Camden, New Jersey, just across the Delaware River from Philadelphia, where a group of RCA toolmakers were members of the Metal Workers Industrial Union. They took the organizing lead in the giant RCA plant, largest radio manufacturing installation in the nation. At the home plant of Westinghouse in East Pittsburgh, Pennsylvania, much of the leadership work of organizing an independent union was done by Logan Burkhart, a skilled generator inspector whose experience in the AFL had convinced him of the practical need for industrial unionism.

Metal Workers members such as K. M. Kirkendahl helped to organize an independent union at the mammoth refrigerator manufacturing plant in Dayton, Ohio, of the General Motors Electrical Division, where ten thousand workers produced Frigidaires. This GM division operated several other shops: in Dayton and Warren, Ohio, and in Rochester, New York.

The AFL issued federal charters to a number of local industrial unions. One was at the Westinghouse Turbine Works in South Philadelphia, where a group of Wobblies and other militants led by skilled pipefitter John Schaefer spearheaded organization at this second-ranking plant of the Westinghouse chain.

Other AFL federal charters were issued to locals at Philco Radio in Philadelphia, where two young leaders, James Carey and Harry Block, had sparked organizing efforts; at the Westinghouse refrigerator plant in Springfield, Massachusetts; the GE electric motor shop in Fort Wayne, Indiana; and King Colonial Radio in Buffalo, New York, which made radios under its own name but was also the chief supplier of radios to Sears Roebuck.

35

No longer, as between 1930 and 1933, did the Metal Workers Industrial Union need to feel alone. Although its leaders and members continued to be in the forefront of organization, the Metal Workers as such was being absorbed in the broad mass movement of workers proceeding with self-organization, their spirits refreshed by the New Deal political atmosphere. Tremendous energies had been released, as thousands of workers got themselves together in local industrial organizations. Now the next problem: How to organize the organizations, how to bring them into touch with one another and create a common understanding as to objectives and direction. Contacts among the groups obviously had to be greatly expanded.

3
Pounding on AFL Doors

I   One reason for the unusual rank-and-file character of the UE, with its strong tradition of local autonomy, lies in the manner in which the union was assembled over a seven-year period—1930 to 1937. In the early stages of its development there was no "big plan" for organization of all the workers in the industry into one industrial union. The UE grew together out of a number of locally organized industrial unions which, at the beginning, were hardly aware of one another's existence. All of them, however, had a general sense of somehow starting on the road toward formation of an industrial organization in the industry, which they hoped to further by securing a national charter from the AFL.

It could be said that it was this common objective—the idea of an industrial union within the AFL—which little by little drew them together and, at length, led to the founding of the UE. But it could be said, too, that the problems they encountered from the dominant craft unions of the AFL were responsible for the remarkably complicated route they were obliged to travel, as they struggled for seven years to reach their industrial unionism objective. The major problem which they all confronted—whether they were units of the Metal Workers union in machine shops, whether they were independent locals or AFL federal locals in electrical and radio manufacture—was the insistence of AFL craft unions on their own jurisdictional claims.

Only in the machine industry, however, was there an AFL organization—the International Association of Machinists—in a position to make a claim that had to be realistically faced. Even though the corporations had wiped the IAM out of mass production plants and large machine shops in the twenties, the union held on to a membership in Navy yards, U.S. arsenals, and railroad shops. It also had members who were maintenance machinists in such places as printing shops and breweries. There was no reasonable expectation that the AFL would consider granting a new industrial union charter to any group in the machine industry.

In electrical and radio manufacturing, however, the situation was different. There, no AFL craft union could possibly argue jurisdictional claims on the basis of membership in the industry or in comparable shops. For this reason the federal and independent local industrial unions of that industry anticipated that by assembling sufficient strength of numbers, and by concerted effort, they would be able, in time, to secure an industrial union charter from the AFL.

The federal locals began to pull themselves together into a radio workers council. The independent local unions based in electrical manufacturing combined forces with the independents in the machine industry, setting up an organization they called the Federation of Metal and Allied Unions, in which each group maintained a distinct identity. This would permit them to deal flexibly, on behalf of industrial unionism, with AFL jurisdictional questions.

All the groupings and consolidations of the local industrial unions had a common purpose—the achievement of industrial union standing within the AFL. As the newly organized Federation of Metal and Allied Unions put it: "To labor for the amalgamation of our two affiliated groups with the American Federation of Labor, on conditions that will best serve the interests of the membership." In this sense the federation was understood to be a temporary means of organizing forces to advance the common purpose. But in another sense the federation had permanent significance. Principles set down in its constitution—among them, organization of the unorganized in the industry on an industrial basis, no discrimination against any workers because of race, creed, sex, skill, religion, or political beliefs—served as a model for the constitutional preamble which the UE would later adopt as the foundation stone of the union.

The federation decided that its two groups, aiming at the same destination, would take different paths toward the AFL.

The workers in the machine industry felt the only way they could hope to get there was by amalgamating on an industrially organized basis with the IAM, while their colleagues, the independent industrial unionists in electrical manufacturing, planned a joint campaign with the federal locals for a new AFL industrial union charter in that industry.

As these plans were being developed, important rank-and-file struggles took place in early 1934. In Minneapolis, on May 15, five thousand AFL teamsters led by the militant Dunne brothers—Vincent, Miles and Grant—defied Teamster union president Dan Tobin and launched a strike against the city's trucking companies. Their struggle for recognition of their union was eventually joined by tens of thousands of Minneapolis workers and persisted for more than three months before it was settled with a written contract.

The historic General Strike in San Francisco, which began on July 15, 1934, developed out of a rebellion of rank-and-file longshoremen in May against the collaboration of the shipowners and King Joe Ryan, lifetime president of the International Longshoremen's Association. This was the strike that brought Harry Bridges forward as the outstanding rank-and-file leader of the AFL. Thousands upon thousands of San Francisco workers, in solidarity with the longshoremen under Bridges' leadership, shut down the city in July, an event that set off a chain reaction of militancy in the unorganized mass production industries and had a profound impact upon developments within the AFL.

These 1934 rank-and-file rebellions helped set the stage for the battle at the November 1934 AFL convention between the old guard craft unionists and the industrial union forces headed by John L. Lewis, president of the United Mine Workers. At this convention Lewis took the floor to make a powerful speech for the cause of industrial unionism.

II   The Lewis speech burst like a bombshell in the faces of the AFL craft union leaders, who regarded as heresy his demand for all-out AFL backing in support of a drive to organize industrial unions in mass production industry. But the young rank-and-file organizers out in the shops of the industries were heartened by the appearance of a champion of their cause inside the AFL. They also took note of a clever and obstinate antagonist, John P. Frey, head of the AFL's Metal Trades Department, who, at the 1934 convention, assumed the role of strategist and advocate of the craft union point of view.

Frey represented the position that in any organizing that was done, or in any charters for new unions in mass production issued by the AFL, the claims of the craft unions must be given first consideration. Unlike Lewis, Frey had few gifts as an orator. But he made up for that by calculated maneuvering behind the scenes of the AFL, with such people as Matthew Woll, an AFL vice-president, who was more an insurance executive than a union leader, Dan Tracy of the International Brotherhood of Electrical Workers, Arthur Wharton of the International Association of Machinists and Bill Hutcheson of the Carpenters Union. They all opposed industrial unionism one hundred percent.

Industrial unionism, however, had its own lineup of AFL support: not only the United Mine Workers but also the Amalgamated Clothing Workers, International Ladies Garment Workers, Oil Workers, Textile Workers, and the Mine, Mill and Smelter Workers—this last union a lineal descendant of the pioneer industrial union which Big Bill Haywood headed, the Western Federation of Miners. Another devoted champion of industrial organization in mass production industry was Charles P. Howard, president of the AFL craft union of typographical workers. After the 1934 convention, Lewis and other leaders joined to map plans for continuing the fight for mass production industrial unionism which Lewis had launched on the convention floor.

III   The rank-and-file organizers of industrial unionism in electrical manufacturing and the machine industry continued to develop their joint strategy for approaching the AFL. On July 19, 1935, the fledgling Federation of Metal and

Allied Unions wrote to AFL president William Green, citing its membership in "some of the largest machine shops and electrical and radio plants in the country," and asking Green for a conference. He replied three weeks later by referring the new federation to Frey in his position as head of the AFL Metal Trades Department. Frey agreed to meet with a federation committee.

Of the four committee members who traveled to Washington AFL headquarters on September 5, 1935, three were old-timers, still on the job in the shop although holding top offices in the new federation: Charles Kenneck, toolmaker in a Philadelphia tool and die shop; skilled turbine inspector Bill Turnbull from GE Schenectady; Tom Molloy, Hartford, Connecticut, machinist from Pratt and Whitney Tool Company. The fourth committee member was James J. Matles, then serving full-time as the federation's secretary-treasurer at a salary of twenty-five dollars per week.

They discovered, on being ushered into Frey's presence, that they would also be meeting with two other AFL craft union leaders: Arthur Wharton, president of the International Association of Machinists, and Dan Tracy, president of the International Brotherhood of Electrical Workers. So it was that "riff-raff" industrial unionists came face to face for the first time with the power elite of the AFL: the tall, austere Frey, known to his colleagues as "Colonel," that title having been conferred by a governor of Kentucky; Wharton, descendant in part of a North American Indian tribe, short in stature with a broad forehead and piercing eyes; and Tracy, the image of a self-assured business unionist. Their greeting was polite and to the point: "Gentlemen, what do you have to say for yourselves?"

It might have been assumed that these men, who had been union officers for a long time, would be aware of what was happening organizationally among workers in mass production. But it turned out that much of what the committee members had to tell them about the state of affairs in the industry of electrical and radio manufacturing, and in the machine industry, was news. The committee pointed out that the experience to date of organizing local unions in the mass production industry of electrical and radio manufacture showed, beyond question,

41

that the approach of industrial unionism suited the conditions prevailing in the industry, dominated as it was by several great corporations operating chains of plants.

Frey and his associates, however, didn't see it that way. They were quick to say—in a sort of "father knows best" fashion—that AFL craft organizations were the appropriate forms of unionism for workers in electrical manufacturing mass production plants. Frey advised the four rank-and-file committee members that, in any event, he and the Metal Trades Department were not authorized to issue charters to new unions. The power to decide such questions, he said, belonged only to the highest tribunal of the AFL, the Executive Council, headed by President Green. The industrial unionists, in short, having been bounced by Green to Frey, were now being bounced back again.

That much out of the way, the committee proceeded to put the cards on the table for Wharton of the AFL Machinists. The federation's locals in the machine industry, representing shops with about eight thousand workers, were prepared to amalgamate with Wharton's IAM on certain conditions, some of these being: that the form of industrial unionism be maintained, with memberships of skilled, semiskilled, and unskilled —from the sweeper to the skilled tool and die maker, men and women, black and white; that no existing locals of the IAM claim any members of the industrial locals; that industrial unionists inside the IAM be free to pursue industrial organization of new plants in the industry, which would enter the IAM as industrial locals and remain as such, without interference. Wharton said the proposition could be discussed further by an IAM committee meeting with a committee from the new unions.

So, that was how the two-hour conversation at AFL headquarters wound up. The question of an industrial union charter in electrical and radio manufacturing, it seemed, would be taken up by the AFL Executive Council. The question of amalgamating the machinists' industrial locals with the IAM was to be discussed later by representatives of the concerned organizations.

IV   At the time of the meeting with Frey, Wharton and Tracy, the 1935 AFL convention was only about two months away. Hopes of the industrial unionists were high. John L. Lewis and his allies in the AFL, preparing to wage a battle for AFL commitment to industrial organization of the unorganized, sponsored a convention resolution which began: "In the great mass production industries, industrial organization is the only solution." Lewis himself led the fight on the floor. When the resolution was defeated by a margin of about two to one, leaders of the craft unions gloated. One such was Bill Hutcheson, president of the Carpenters Union, weighing all of three hundred pounds.

As Hutcheson tried to shut up a young industrial unionist from the Rubber Workers by shouting, "Point of order!" Lewis walked across the convention floor and said something to him. Hutcheson's reply was hardly out of his mouth when Lewis let him have one. It became famous as a blow struck for industrial unionism against a symbol of the stubborn craft union attitude that would not change, regardless of real conditions in industry and regardless of the almost incredible militancy of workers in the shops of mass production.

Three weeks after the 1935 convention, the presidents of eight AFL unions, led by Lewis of the United Mine Workers, formed the first CIO, the Committee for Industrial Organization. It had a twofold purpose: to continue the battle for industrial unionism inside the AFL; and to give encouragement, aid, and assistance to any group of rank-and-file workers struggling to build an industrial union of their own.

One of these, the Federation of Metal and Allied Unions, was still hot on the heels of the AFL for an industrial union charter in electrical and radio manufacturing. Delegates from AFL federal locals in the industry had raised the issue at the AFL convention but had gotten nowhere. Their request was referred —just as Frey had referred the independents' request—to the Executive Council, scheduled to meet in January 1936. On January 27, 1936, in the form of a telegraphed order from Green to all federal locals in electrical and radio plants, the Council announced its decision:

43

Executive Council decided best interests of radio workers including those you represent would be served through their affiliation with the International Brotherhood of Electrical Workers [IBEW]. . . . I urge you to confer with President Tracy and his associates for the purpose of arranging for all members to be transferred to the IBEW. . . . Executive Council is of the firm opinion that this course should be pursued rather than create a new national union of radio workers.

As soon as the telegrams were received, both independents and federals in the electrical industry agreed to combine forces without delay. In a matter of days—on February 22, 1936—their representatives got together. They quickly rejected the order from Green to join the IBEW. They made plans for a March convention of independents and federals to form a new union, the United Electrical and Radio Workers of America, their own organization, the UE. Just as soon as the convention was held, and the new union founded, the nine former federal locals which participated in the UE convention got word from Bill Green that their AFL federal charters had been revoked.

It didn't bother them. Now they were looking forward, as affiliates of a new industrial union, to entering the AFL on that basis. In that same month of March 1936, in accordance with agreed-upon plans, their old friends the industrial machinists completed their amalgamation as an industrially organized group, eight thousand strong, with the IAM. They did so on the terms originally presented to IAM president Wharton at the Washington meeting in Frey's office in September 1935.

The stage was set for a two-pronged organizing drive, one by the UE in electrical manufacturing, the other by the industrial machinists of the IAM in major machine shops in several northeastern states. The campaign of the young UE and the IAM industrial machinists, proceeding in complete cooperation, began to gain momentum. They were gathering ammunition, in the form of many new members, to be used at the coming AFL convention to support the cause of industrial unionism.

V Plans launched back in the month of March were working like a charm. So much so that in July the IAM industrial machinists, who were organizing shop after shop in the machine industry in New York, New Jersey, Connecticut, and Pennsylvania, wrote Wharton saying: "The interests of the IAM, in our opinion, coincide with those of the CIO unions, in as much as the main object of the IAM must be to organize the large numbers of workers in industrial plants."

The letter reached Wharton at a time when the whole AFL craft union leadership was viewing the march of industrial unionism with extreme alarm. Inspired by the CIO, thousands of workers, particularly in the automobile, electrical, and rubber industries, were defying the craft unions, whose chiefs figured they had stopped Lewis and industrial unionism at the 1935 AFL convention. Quite the opposite. All signs pointed to a November 1936 AFL convention showdown, where Green, Frey, Tracy, Hutcheson, Wharton, and other craft chieftains would have a real fight on their hands. That was the last thing they wanted.

The AFL Executive Council, at a meeting in August, decided to serve an immediate ultimatum on each CIO union. The Council ordered these unions to disband their Committee for Industrial Organization and to cease and desist from the promotion of industrial unionism in mass production. The order fixed a deadline: September 5, 1936. Either the unions were to obey the dispersal order by that date or face automatic suspension from the AFL.

No one in his right mind would have believed that the old guard of the AFL, furious as it might be, intended to throw a million members out of an AFL which then had a total of no more than 3 million members. A third of the membership to be summarily ejected? Rational men wouldn't do such a thing. But the old guard did, thereby creating a whole new set of labor movement conditions which had an almost immediate effect on the CIO, the UE, and the industrial machinists.

The CIO simply ignored the AFL deadline of September 5, at which time the UE, holding its second convention in Fort Wayne, Indiana, resolved to apply for a charter from the CIO

—which was issued. This cast the die for CIO industrial unionism distinct from the AFL. In effect, a second house of labor was established by the CIO decision to admit into its ranks for the first time a new mass production industrial union, the UE, and also another new organization, the Industrial Union of Marine and Shipbuilding Workers.

Two weeks after the CIO unions had ignored the AFL suspension deadline and issued a charter to the UE, the industrial machinists, attending their first IAM convention held in Milwaukee, prepared to fight for two resolutions. For all practical purposes, one was defeated before it got off the ground. It proposed to put the IAM on record in support of the CIO organization drive and in favor of organizing the machine industry on an industrial basis within the IAM. With the CIO unions suspended, the resolution on CIO industrial unionism didn't even reach the convention floor.

Worse happened when the industrial machinists brought up a resolution which Wharton himself, less than a year previous, had promised to support. The industrial unionists had entered the IAM with the understanding that they would all go in—skilled and unskilled, men and women, black and white—according to basic constitutional principles of the Federation of Metal and Allied Unions.

One of these principles, in direct conflict with IAM rules, was that of no discrimination by color or race. An IAM secret ritual restricting membership only to "Caucasians"—workers with white skins—was something the industrial unionists didn't intend to live with in an organization with which they were associated. They had entered the IAM with membership intact as agreed by Wharton, who simply "waived" the ritual for the industrial group which included black workers. The IAM president had also agreed to support, at the September convention, a move to get rid of the ritual altogether. However, this solemn promise, given before the time that the AFL Executive Council suspended the CIO unions, was repudiated by Wharton.

When a demand by the industrial machinists for the abolition of the ritual reached the floor, the convention became bedlam. Wharton ordered an executive session. He cleared out representatives of the press along with visitors and observers.

46

As the industrial unionists then rose to speak, chairs started to fly. The young delegates could hardly be heard amidst the hooting and hollering. At the height of the uproar, Wharton banged his gavel, declared the ritual inviolate and adjourned that session of the convention.

That was not all. After the industrial unionists returned from convention to the organizing field, suddenly other AFL metal trades craft unions came crawling out of the woodwork. The electricians, molders, patternmakers, plumbers and steamfitters, sheetmetal workers, and others demanded that members of their crafts organized by the industrial machinists be turned over, like so many heads of cattle, to the respective craft unions. The young organizers confronted Wharton: What about the agreement on industrial integrity of our locals? Wharton answered by admonishing them to adopt cautious and reasonable attitudes, in view of the changed circumstances in the labor movement.

VI   Wharton and "Colonel" Frey next proceeded with a scheme to use the industrial machinists against the CIO. As part of the amalgamation agreement, the new industrial locals of the IAM had been given the right to choose their own grand lodge representative, who in other unions is called international representative. They selected Matles for this position.

On March 25, 1937, Matles received a wire from Wharton which read: "Owing to my inability to cancel previously made engagements, I am designating you as my representative to call upon Mr. George Huston and Mr. Harris Hoblecelle, Eddyston, Pa. in connection with matters discussed with a mutual friend." Mysterious. Who were these gentlemen? What was the errand? And the mutual friend? His name?

It turned out to be none other than "Colonel" Frey himself. As for Misters Huston and Hoblecelle who had discussed matters with Frey, they were disclosed, respectively, as president of the Baldwin Locomotive Company and president of General Steel Casting Company. At that time, too, the Baldwin man was president of the National Association of Manufacturers.

In Philadelphia, the young grand lodge representative met with them separately, by their preference, but the subject matter was the same.

They said that in their conversations with Frey they had expressed their distaste for the organizing drive presently being aimed at their shops by the CIO Steel Workers Organizing Committee. They'd be better off, they felt, in Frey's AFL Metal Trades Department, where presumably the union that would handle the situation was to be the IAM. At least so Frey had indicated.

When the grand lodge representative reported back his shock and dismay, Wharton replied with a soothing message telling him to take a practical view of things and try to grow up to the realization that the CIO, as a danger to bona fide unionism, must be fought by all means.

Following this incident, Wharton sent out a "directive" from supreme IAM headquarters to vice-presidents, grand lodge representatives, business agents, and general chairmen of the union. Dated April 30, 1937, it began:

> Since the Supreme Court decision upholding the Wagner Labor Act many employers now realize that it is the Law of our Country and they are prepared to deal with labor organizations. These employers have expressed a preference to deal with AFL Organizations rather than Lewis, Hillman, Dubinsky, Howard and their gang of sluggers, communists, radicals and soap box artists, professional bums, expelled members of labor unions, outright scabs and the Jewish organizations with all their red affiliates.
>
> We have conferred with several such employers and arranged for conferences later when we get the plants organized. The purpose of this is to direct all officers and all representatives to contact employers in your locality as a preliminary to organizing the shops and factories.
>
> We have not hesitated to tell the employers we have met, that the best manner in which to deal with us is on the closed shop basis, because we are then in a position where we can require the members to observe the provisions of any agreement entered into, this with our well-known policy of living up to agreements gives the em-

48

ployer the benefits he is entitled to receive from contracts with our organization and it also places us in a position to prevent sitdowns, sporadic disturbances, slowdowns and other communistic CIO tactics of disruption and disorganization.

That finished it up for the IAM industrial unionists. The time had come for a clean break with Wharton and his IAM in cahoots with Frey and the corporations. Matles, the grand lodge representative, submitted his resignation to the IAM president in a letter which said in part:

During the past year hundreds of thousands of workers joined the ranks of organized labor only because of the program and leadership of the CIO and thereby increased wages and improved their working conditions.... Events of the past few months have proven beyond a shadow of doubt, that the Executive Council of the IAM by its unprincipled efforts to undermine the CIO and its leadership ... has lost the opportunity for becoming *the* Union in the Machine Industry.

If I am to retain the confidence and serve the best interests of the thousands of members who have elected me as their representative, I am compelled to resign as a Grand Lodge Representative of the International Association of Machinists, effective this date.

The "thousands of members" were almost double the number which the industrial machinists had brought into the IAM in March 1936. Then there had been eight thousand members. Now there were fifteen thousand—testimony, on the face of it, that some organizing had been going on. Every local voted to leave the IAM forthwith. There was no question about where they were heading. They returned home in June 1937, to be reunited in the UE with their industrial union companions and fellow workers of the Federation of Metal and Allied Unions, and with all others of the federal labor unions who had helped to found the new industrial organization.

Three months later, three long-established IAM lodges in Minneapolis, with six thousand members, also left the IAM for the UE. The Minneapolis lodges, progressive and militant, had jointly fought on the side of the other industrial machinists at the IAM convention the year before in Milwaukee against the "Caucasian-only" secret ritual. At the September 1937 convention of the UE in Philadelphia, with AFL jurisdictional problems no longer an issue, the union, embracing now both the electrical and machine industries, became the United Electrical, Radio and Machine Workers of America.

VII   More than thirty years of history furnish an intriguing comment on the unsuccessful attempt in the 1930s to persuade the IAM to accept the principle of industrial organization. By 1972 the IAM's large membership in the aerospace and other mass production shops had been recruited by organizing the workers on an industrial basis.

4
The UE's Baptism of Fire

I   The UE founding convention in Buffalo, on March 21–22, 1936, took place in the midst of a fierce spring snowstorm—so heavy a fall that it prevented delegates of the East Pittsburgh Westinghouse independent local, and the GE federal local of New Kensington, Pennsylvania, from getting through. But snow or no snow, the union was born that weekend, a time chosen because of the rank-and-file composition of the delegates, all of them shop workers planning to leave for Buffalo after work on Friday and be back on the job Monday morning. In a mood of enthusiasm and confidence, the fifty delegates from seventeen local unions got a lot done in those two days.

They adopted a UE constitution, drew up a budget, elected officers, and staked out general organizing objectives for the immediate and long-range future. Their principal concern, from beginning to end of the convention, was to insure constitutionally the democratic rank-and-file control of the union they were establishing—and to prepare themselves to embark upon the basic task of organizing the unorganized in a corporate empire employing three hundred fifty thousand workers.

Objectives and principles of the union, spelled out in the preamble to the constitution, were the same as those which had been embodied in the constitution of the temporary Federation of Metal and Allied Unions. In Buffalo, Al Coulthard, from the Lynn GE independent local, served as chairman of the constitution committee, just as he had done several years before when the federation had set forth the principles of industrial organization, membership rights, aggressive struggle, and labor unity vital to the workings of effective rank-and-file unionism. Here, too, at the UE founding convention, the delegates approved other important constitutional policies, such as those of annual conventions; annual election by the membership of all local and international union officers; salaries for officers not to exceed the highest weekly wage paid to workers in the industry. In 1936 this was determined to be fifty dollars a week.

Union income from sixteen thousand dues-paying members—although the "book membership" stood at thirty thousand—made necessary an extremely modest budget for an organization planning to tackle corporations whose wealth and power derived from annual production of $2.3 billion worth of electrical equipment. Delegates apportioned the amount of $2,400.00 a month for "general organizing and operating fund"; $800 a month to support a weekly union periodical to be mailed to each member; $800 a month to go into a strike fund. The monies allocated to the general fund were specifically assigned for payment of the salaries of the UE president and secretary-treasurer and for one office secretary; for office administrative expenses such as rent, light, heat, telephone service, stationery, printing, and so forth; and for salaries and expenses of four organizers.

It's worth taking a close look at the manner in which the two top officers were chosen, to observe the principles which governed these decisions. The call to the convention had been issued by a Committee of Eight, four each elected from the independent locals and the federal locals respectively. The committee agreed that top leadership would be shared between independents and federals, with the federals nominating a candidate for president and the independents a candidate for secretary-treasurer. The claim of the federals to the office of president was based upon proportionate dues-paying membership figures. In 1933, Philco had conceded a union shop to the AFL federal locals in the plant in return for a commitment by AFL president Green not to seek additional wage increases unless these had first been established in competitive companies and incorporated in NRA codes for the radio industry. At the time of the UE founding convention, the dues-paying membership at Philco was about sixty-five hundred.

Two separate convention caucuses, one made up of delegates from the federals, the other from the independents,

52

agreed to support the other's choice of a candidate for union office, according to the plan worked out by the Committee of Eight. The federals selected Philco local leader, twenty-five-year-old James Carey, as candidate for UE president. Julius Emspak, thirty-year-old tool and die maker from the GE home plant in Schenectady, was nominated by the independents for union secretary-treasurer. Both were unanimously elected by the convention delegates, at which point the distinction between federals and independents disappeared. In the following year, when the industrial machinists left the IAM and re-united with their old UE allies, the union's constitution was amended to establish a third top office, Director of Organization. James J. Matles was chosen to fill the new post.

II   Overall, the delegates at the March 1936 convention represented local unions in plants employing a total of about fifty-five thousand workers. Although some thirty thousand had signed up as local union members, only the sixteen thousand on whom the budget had been based were then regularly paying dues. These statistics were a measure of the organizing job that had been done—and of the job that remained to be done in plants where cores of local unions had been established.

The major representation of the federal locals at the convention came from locals at Philco in Philadelphia; Westinghouse in Springfield, Massachusetts; General Electric, Fort Wayne; and King Colonial in Buffalo. These shops were in the "light side" of the industry. Philco and King Colonial made radios; Westinghouse at Springfield, refrigerators and appliances; GE Fort Wayne, small fractional horsepower motors. Philco and King Colonial held written contracts, the others did not. All these federal locals had been in existence since 1933.

Most of the independent local delegates participating in the founding of the UE represented unions in the central fortresses of the industry—heavy equipment plants of General Electric and Westinghouse, producing turbines, generators, and such, and large complexes operated by RCA and by the electri-

53

cal division of General Motors. The GE plant at Schenectady, for example, was the company's headquarters for production and research, paralleled by the plant Westinghouse maintained in East Pittsburgh. Schenectady dominated the GE chain, East Pittsburgh the Westinghouse.

Each plant employed about eleven thousand workers in 1936. Each contained a company union council, wielded by the companies as instruments to fend off organizing efforts by the independent unions and to deny them recognition. The part the company unions played in GE and Westinghouse anti-labor policy could be estimated by the percentage of workers represented by independent union delegates at the UE founding convention: approximately 20 percent in GE Schenectady, not much more than 10 percent at East Pittsburgh Westinghouse.

The same held true for delegates from the independent locals at RCA, Camden, New Jersey, and the Frigidaire plant of the General Motors electrical division in Dayton, Ohio—each employing more than ten thousand workers. At RCA the independent local union membership did not exceed three thousand. Less than one thousand workers belonged to the independent local organized in the Frigidaire plant. The only relative bright spot was to be found at the second-ranking plant of the GE chain in Lynn, Massachusetts, where the 1933 election victory of the independent industrial union had paved the way for company recognition of a union committee to represent workers with grievances. No independent union, however, had won a written contract.

Another comparatively strong local industrial union, holding an AFL federal charter, existed at the number two plant in the Westinghouse chain in South Philadelphia. There, under the leadership of a group of rank-and-file-minded members of the Industrial Workers of the World, and other militant trade unionists, the organization in a plant of thirty-five hundred workers had won company recognition but not, as yet, a written contract. This local, however, wasn't represented by delegates at the UE founding convention. But everyone assumed correctly that before long its members would affiliate their organization with the UE. The local at South Philadelphia was a UE natural.

54

The logical direction in which the new UE had to turn for effective organization of the unorganized and for securing union recognition was toward the "heavy side" of the industry: GE Schenectady and Westinghouse East Pittsburgh. Also, to the largest radio plant in the country, RCA; and largest in refrigeration, GM's Frigidaire. These were the union objectives as its two young officers set up shop at 1133 Broadway, New York City. UE headquarters consisted of a couple of rooms, at $27.50 a month, outfitted with second-hand office furniture, telephone service, and printed stationery.

III   The union, confronting an industry with three hundred fifty thousand workers in plants throughout the United States and Canada, immediately issued charters to every local whose delegates had attended the founding convention. Among them were Local 301 at Schenectady GE; Local 601, Westinghouse, East Pittsburgh; Local 801, Dayton Frigidaire; and Local 103, RCA Camden, which had almost one-third of the ten thousand workers in the plant signed up in the union. On May 20, 1936, UE representatives approached RCA with demands for exclusive baragaining rights, a union shop, abolition of the company union, and a wage increase. That really started something.

A little background helps to explain the level of development which this local union had reached. In the spring of 1933, RCA announced a new wage-payment system which, like most such gimmicks, was a formula for speedup. A group of toolmakers, members of the Philadelphia local of the Metal Workers Industrial Union, organized a protest that shut down the tool room. Next, they formed a local independent union at RCA, giving it the name of Radio and Metal Workers Industrial Union. RCA promptly responded by creating an employees' representation plan, a company union, which the Radio and Metal Workers local attempted, without success, to win over.

At the same time, RCA was trying to put the Radio and Metal Workers out of business. Fearful that under the NRA the employee representation plan might be considered illegal, RCA disguised it. An Employees' Committee Union appeared on the scene, to which RCA gave every support and help possible in the hope of liquidating the local of the Radio and Metal Workers.

As time passed, two other unions entered RCA. One was an AFL federal local consisting of a group of skilled trouble-shooters and testers. The other was the AFL electrician's craft organization, the IBEW, which issued an RCA charter in 1935 for the purpose of blocking the fast-growing independent Radio and Metal Workers, transformed in early 1936 into UE Local 103. All of these elements were in the picture as UE representatives began, on June 8, discussions with plant management. After several unproductive sessions, the president of RCA, David Sarnoff, took a direct hand.

IV   Sarnoff had no intention of allowing the new union to represent workers in the Camden plant. In contrast, however, to many other industrialists who were openly fighting the New Deal, the Wagner Act, and Franklin Roosevelt, Sarnoff had developed a liberal image which he wanted to keep—that of a self-made success in America, having risen from a poor young immigrant boy to his position as head of a large corporation and thus presumed to be in sympathy with the aspirations of ordinary working people.

Across the Delaware River in Philadelphia, Philco, the chief competitor of RCA in radio manufacture, had been operating under contract with the two federal local unions for three years and doing very well. With the founding of UE, these former AFL federal locals had become UE Locals 101 and 102. But Sarnoff of RCA wanted no part of UE Local 103's demands for the wages and conditions, as well as the union shop, prevailing at Philco. He attempted to deal with the dilemma in which he found himself by hiring as RCA "labor advisor" a former New Deal big shot, General Hugh Johnson, one-time director of the NRA. Johnson stepped into the negotiations.

Things went from bad to worse. On June 23 the talks collapsed. Local 103 called a mass membership meeting at which workers—once they learned of Johnson's wholesale rejection of their demands—approved a strike. Unprecedented picket lines went up at RCA. Hardly three months after the founding of the UE, the members and leaders of the new union found themselves engaged in battle at one of the four key plants on which they had set their organizing sights. Among those who received a baptism of fire in the strike was Julius Emspak, the new secretary-treasurer of UE, who moved into the situation and stayed until the finish.

Now that the chips were down, Sarnoff's concern for his liberal image disappeared. RCA hired a thousand outside strike-breakers, whose passage in and out of the plant was to be insured by a large number of private armed guards, also hired by the company from the Sherwood Detective Agency to which, according to research by the Twentieth Century Fund, RCA paid $244,930. Both the Employee Committee Union and the IBEW joined the RCA opposition to Local 103. Some of their constituents entered the ranks of the strike-breakers. Others helped the armed guards. And the two groups called publicly for "law and order"—by which they meant an open shop for strikebreakers—and for more and more Camden police to bully the picket lines.

Every day strikers were hauled off to jail. The many women among them proved to be among the most undaunted members of Local 103. More than $2 million had to be put up in bail bonds—furnished by members of the sister UE locals at Philco —to free strikers jailed during the course of the strike. It was a situation made to order for the IBEW of the AFL. They seized the opportunity to try and engineer a backdoor agreement with Sarnoff. This called for support action for UE Local 103 from the industrial machinists, now grouped in the AFL's IAM, who joined the picket line and spoke out against IBEW activities.

Meanwhile, General Johnson, doing his utmost to earn his pay from Sarnoff, spent a lot of time in Washington, endeavoring to use the influence he had acquired as NRA director to have the strike broken or sabotaged from on high. Johnson even went to John Lewis of the CIO, but got nowhere. At the RCA plant, in spite of the fact that bloody clashes and arrests on the picket line were increasing, the strikers' solidarity actually grew stronger day by day. Also, day by day, RCA was taking an economic beating from its competitor Philco, whose radios kept flowing off the assembly lines while RCA was in trouble.

These two factors led to an agreement which settled the strike on July 28, 1936, although RCA's and Sarnoff's reputations were also involved in the company's decision to conclude an agreement. The strikebreakers, goons, picket line riots, arrests, suppression of civil liberties, and a National Labor Relations Board finding that RCA was indulging in company unionism all contributed to community and national disapproval of the tactics of the country's largest radio manufacturer. But, General Johnson had still another scheme up his sleeve.

V The RCA settlement provided that the issue of union recognition would be resolved by means of an NLRB election on August 16. RCA, taking Johnson's advice, confidently expected to defeat the UE in this election. The Johnson strategy called for a boycott of the election by company unionists and IBEW people, thereby making it impossible for the UE to secure a majority of the eligible voters in the plant.

The strategy worked as far as the boycott went, but otherwise it backfired. The vote count in favor of UE was 3,116 to 51. True enough, this did not constitute a majority of eligible voters. However, the overwhelming UE plurality and the fact that the NLRB ruled that the Wagner Act required that a representation election was to be decided by a majority of those voting and not of those eligible to vote, furnished ample evidence of the blunder General Johnson had made. The NLRB certified UE Local 103 as the exclusive bargaining agent at RCA Camden.

Johnson, still advising, told RCA to ignore and defy the NLRB—by not recognizing the certified UE local and by refusing to rehire about five hundred discharged strikers—whereupon unrest and stoppages became the order of the day at RCA. The contest moved from picket line to plant, which endured industrial guerrilla warfare for months and months.

These were the exact months that the challenge of anti-labor industrialists to the constitutionality of the Wagner Act was moving up through the judicial process to the Supreme Court for final decision. The strategic advice Sarnoff continued to accept from General Johnson was based on hopes that the NAM and Liberty League campaign against the Wagner Act would be successful. But, in April 1937, the Supreme Court upheld the act's constitutionality.

Sarnoff reacted by firing General Johnson and taking on as RCA vice president of labor relations Ed McGrady, a man who had served as assistant secretary of labor in the Roosevelt administration. McGrady, an AFL official before entering public life, was known to some of the UE leaders. Almost as soon as he came on the job for RCA he asked for an informal meeting with the local and international union officers, which was then followed by several months of formal negotiations with Local 103's rank-and-file committee, assisted by Matles.

Sarnoff now relied on McGrady to undo the damage done by Johnson's advice and get RCA labor relations on an even keel. McGrady's experience had shaped him into a shrewd, hard bargainer, who made nothing easy for the UE. Unlike Johnson, however, he negotiated. When agreement was reached in October of 1937 after several months of bargaining, the union committee headed for the ratification meeting at the Camden Armory, jampacked with several thousand workers.

Quite a scene. And quite a meeting. The president of Local 103, chairman of the negotiating committee, reported on the agreement article by article, each one punctuated by prolonged cheers. He had to ask constantly for quiet in order to proceed. One minute, thunderous cheers in the air. The next minute, absolute quiet, so everyone could hear what came next. Finally he announced reinstatement of the five hundred fired strikers, news which just about tore the roof off. Then the president added: All strikers would be going back to their jobs with full back pay for the months they were out. Pandemonium, nothing but, broke out at that point.

The long but success-crowned UE struggle at RCA, one of four key organizing objectives of the union, served notice on the industry in general that it would have to reckon with this young union. Other corporations could hardly misread signs of what the strike and settlement meant to workers in their plants. Furthermore, the results had national implications throughout all of mass production industry. The UE struggle was among the first waged by the new industrial union forces since the CIO had been created under John L. Lewis's leadership in November of 1935. It therefore represented a pioneer breakthrough in the mass production field.

5
"Miracles" of Organization

I UE conventions, from the very beginning, have been working sessions, with emphasis on the basic question of organizing. The founding convention, in March 1936, laid out plans for concentration on organizing drives at GE Schenectady, Westinghouse East Pittsburgh, RCA Camden, and Frigidaire of the General Motors electrical division in Dayton, a major competitor of GE and Westinghouse in the electrical appliance industry. In September of 1936, when the second convention of the union was held in Fort Wayne, with Local 901 of that city's GE plant acting as host, reports came in from the field on how things were going. Between March and September all UE eyes had been focused on RCA and most everybody knew of events there. But what about the other places? What was happening?

British-born old-timer Bill Turnbull, the skilled GE turbine inspector, reported on Schenectady, where in the five months since the founding convention five hundred eighty three new members had joined UE Local 301. Four factors, Turnbull said, had helped organizing move along: the creation of the UE as the union in the industry; the example set by the members of Local 103 in the RCA strike; the assistance rendered to the Schenectady local by the well-established UE Local 201 at the GE works in Lynn; and a spontaneous sitdown by Schenectady workers in the wire and cable department of the plant, a protest that had brought in quite a few new members.

From Westinghouse East Pittsburgh, skilled generator inspector Logan Burkhart made the report. A test was shaping up. Local 601 would soon be approaching the company to demand recognition of the local as bargaining agent in the plant. In short, progress was being made at Schenectady and East Pittsburgh. But in Dayton the going was rough and

61

slow. K. M. Kirkendahl, a skilled worker at Frigidaire, explained why. "The local is meeting great opposition in its organizing drive. No other union in Dayton can be counted on as a friend. In fact, the AFL crafts in town have been and are indulging in vicious attacks against UE."

This reflected the real situation in Dayton. It was a company-controlled community. Nevertheless, Kirkendahl said in conclusion, Local 801 was holding itself together, carrying on organization work member by member, and would succeed in due time.

There were seventy delegates at this September convention, a modest increase of twenty over March, representing the establishment of seven more UE local unions. Part of the delegates' job consisted of examining the state of their new international organization, its financial position, its needs and prospects.

Up to that time, everything of an administrative nature had been on a very small scale, as indicated by the inventory submitted to the convention of property owned by the international union: twenty-two chairs, one typewriter desk, one roll-top desk, one steel cabinet, one wooden filing cabinet, one small table, two standing ash trays, five wastepaper baskets, one coat rack, one postal scale, one Underwood typewriter (noiseless), one desk lamp, one national office seal. That was it in terms of real property. The union's treasury balance didn't add much more: $3,226. Such were the material assets of a group of organized workers setting forth to challenge the entrenched power of multimillion dollar corporations.

If the force of rank-and-file unionism depended upon financial wealth and real property, in the manner of corporations and business unionism, no organization like the UE would ever get off the ground. But although the administrative responsibilities of a rank-and-file union have to be carefully handled, the secret of success lies in spirit. At the convention the delegates heard welcome news of the spreading strength of industrial unionism from CIO representatives—officers of the Mine Workers, the Amalgamated Clothing Workers, and the Flat Glass Workers. And they, in turn, by meeting with rank-and-file people of a new industrial union, already proving itself in the field of organization and on the picket lines at RCA, got their batteries recharged, as older union leaders can only do by making contact with youth.

II   Bill Turnbull's convention report on Schenectady touched upon an important adjustment Local 301 had made in its strategy of organization. Of all companies, General Electric was most masterful in its control of workers by the practice of paternalism, sourced in the temperament and philosophy of its president, Gerard Swope. After the AFL craft organizations had been shattered by GE in the twenties, Swope set up Works Councils, which were company unions. But the NRA of 1933, affirming the right of workers to form their own unions, compelled some changes in the GE policy of company unionism.

The Works Councils had consisted of representatives from wage-earners and from the management side. This was in accord with the Swope idea of General Electric as one big family, with him at the head of it. However, the advent of NRA led Swope to reorganize and rename the company union councils. Now they were to be made up only of representatives of the workers, not management, although managers and foremen closely supervised the elections in which the representatives were chosen. The new name was Workers' Council. Their function, of course, remained the same: to maintain a roadblock against genuine trade unionism, specifically, in 1936, UE Local 301.

The independent industrial union which Turnbull and others organized at GE Schenectady in 1933 had a first conducted direct combat against the company union. In 1935, when the Federation of Metal and Allied Unions was formed, the GE electrical workers' local at Schenectady, sizing up the changes made by Swope, took a different tack. Its members decided to operate inside the Workers' Council, a tactic continued by UE Local 301 in 1936. It was not a matter of giving up, of adopting the motto "If you can't lick 'em, join 'em," but rather, "You got to join 'em in order to lick 'em." Turnbull put it this way at the convention:

Because of the nature of paternalistic plans that tie all workers to the company, it is difficult to get men with long service to join the union. However, inroads are being made in the company union by Local 301. Members, including the president of our local, have been elected to the Workers' Council. Much effective work is being done in this way. It is hoped that by such tactics, it will be possible eventually to do away with that company union.

Turnbull's cautious "eventually" came sooner than he, or anyone else, may have expected. Three months after he spoke of "much effective work being done" in his report to the September 1936 convention, an NLRB election was held at Schenectady GE. The results: 5,111 votes for UE Local 301, a total of 4,033 for the company union.

Thus by the end of 1936, RCA, locked in struggle with Local 103 even after the union had won an NLRB election, was nonetheless on the way to liberation by the UE. Schenectady GE had fallen into the UE fold. Two of the union's four key objectives were just about secured, with the UE only nine months old. At the next convention of the union, in September of 1937, the question of organizing the unorganized brought Bill Turnbull again to the floor.

One of his purposes, Turnbull said, in presenting a review and analysis of the process which had led to the victory at Schenectady GE, was to make a Local 301 contribution to the UE's general organizing aims. Perhaps the Schenectady experience would prove of interest, to young delegates particularly, of whom he noted quite a few at the 1937 convention, he said in his opening remarks.

III Turnbull's report, delivered extemporaneously, held the delegates' attention for close to an hour. UE people, from rank-and-file to top officers, almost always talk off-the-cuff at union gatherings, to the extent that this practice can be described as rank-and-file unionism's manner of speaking. It is informal, candid, and often laced with humor, even in the darkest of hours—or perhaps especially so then. The sense of humor of the American working class has on many an occasion been the saving grace of militancy, baffling opponents who figured they had pinned the workers to the mat, only to have them laugh and come up fighting.

On the other hand, when the situation itself is full of cheer, as in the case of Local 301's success at Schenectady, the rank-and-file unionism custom is to treat the facts thoughtfully and seriously, so that no lessons will be lost in the emotional enthusiasm of the moment. This was Turnbull's form of address to his fellow-workers. His remarks at the 1937 UE convention constitute a good sample of rank-and-file talk by a shop worker about important union matters. They were unusual only in length.

He began with the impressive statistics of UE Local 301: In 1936, six hundred fifty members; at 1937 convention time, eight thousand. But then, immediately, a significant word about the original six hundred fifty: "Such membership as we had," said Turnbull, "was fixed in determination to establish the union as the major factor in the plant." Determination among workers can often produce what seem to be miracles. Really, however, they are almost invariably the result of determination and optimism, combined with the sort of keen analysis of conditions to which Turnbull next addressed himself:

> What we confronted in our organizing was the long-established Workers' Council, the highly perfected company union of GE, with which many of our delegates are familiar. Recognition of a kind had been extended to UE as a minority group, which permitted us to bring grievances before the management. In substance, our official standing in the plant did not go much beyond this grievance work. And because of our limited membership, of which management was only too well aware, we were able to win grievances only in those departments where we were strong. There were not very many of those. We realized, however, that the grievances were the keystone on which an organization was to be built.

Turnbull did not claim that the band of industrial unionists at Schenectady GE had hit upon bedrock organizational truth. He was, after all, speaking of one particular event at one particular time in labor movement experience. But his words, nonetheless, can be weighed against the fate of innumerable progressive enterprises whose leaders, while irreproachable as to ideals, failed to understand that solid organizations are built on the ideal of people doing something themselves about the immediate injustices that afflict them. And that the first duty of organizers is to bring these grievances out into the open, for recognition and action. Turnbull went on:

> Twelve years of company unionism had accumulated literally thousands of serious complaints among the workers which required settling. While developing our union as an independent organization, fighting hard for the workers' demands with the management in the office, we at the same time employed the method of raising questions inside the company union.

This, he explained, had two results: It demonstrated the quality of the UE leaders who were active in the Workers' Council; and it exposed "to shop workers generally, the hollowness of the company union and its ineffectiveness as an instrument for improving their conditions." The Schenectady workers had known that their complaints made through the company union weren't getting to first base. Persistent agitation by UE members in the shop, however, continued to strip away the covering of the Workers' Council, revealing that its failures were not due to personnel deficiencies or lack of know-how but to the fact that it was part of the company system.

Hand in hand with this work of unmasking the company union went diligent work to show what Local 301 was all about. Turnbull said:

> We made it a practice to acquaint all men and women in the shop with every detail of our activity ... our successes in the departments where we had a strong membership in our own union. We issued leaflets at the rate of at least one a week. And we made extensive use of the official organ of our international union, filling the workers in on general news of UE accomplishments and providing local details as well. We distributed thousands of copies of the paper weekly, reaching into every department in the plant.

66

It is worth noting here that the decision of the UE's founders to allocate budget monies for an international union publication was serving its purpose where it counted—in organizing. The workers at Schenectady, reading the UE paper, could relate themselves and their grievances to workers in Lynn, Erie, Fort Wayne, Pittsfield, and other GE locations, as well as to workers elsewhere in the electrical manufacturing industry. Geographical separation, one means by which American corporate interests have promoted their classic strategy of divide-and-rule against working people, was being broken down. A sense of working class interest in one large industrial organization was developing.

IV   Still another divide-and-rule technique in vogue at Schenectady GE under Swope's paternalistic policies involved wage increases. Favoritism governed the system by which any wage increases were granted, as the company handed out raises individually and in varying amounts. Turnbull explained how Local 301 approached this question:

> We recognized that a 10-cents-an-hour increase demand brought before the company union by our delegates for more than a year reflected the real aspirations of the men and women in the Schenectady plant. Local 301 took over this demand. We made it our central issue. Our union members raised it on the company union floor in so sharp a manner that plant executives themselves had to speak on the question, dropping their pose of impartiality in order to defeat it.

The Schenectady plant manager vetoed the increase demand, at which stage the UE proposed taking the demand directly to Swope. Such a stroke was made possible by Swope's principles of paternalism, whereby he held himself available as a high court of appeal, his door always open to "his people." Indeed, the so-called contract of the company union provided for such appeal. Local 301, in suggesting this route, was experimenting with a strategy which the UE, in its later dealings with General Electric, would develop and employ on a large scale. But as Turnbull told the delegates, the UE local union found that the battle for representation rights in the plant had to be fought further within the company union, before the limits of Swope's "democratic paternalism" could be truly tested.

The Swope personnel policy, often conveyed in statements to the GE family, did not involve opposition to unions as such. GE was not "anti-labor" in the fashion of those employers, such as the Liberty Leaguers, who had formed an army to oppose industrial unionism, the Wagner Act, Franklin Roosevelt, and the whole New Deal social reform program. Gerard Swope took the position that in a company under his direction, the workers' interests didn't require any unionism except that reflected by the Workers' Council. His attitude was that the will of GE employees could be adequately expressed there. So there it was that Local 301 members pressed the demand for the 10-cent-an-hour wage increase, until they forced a roll-call vote the favorable outcome of which was concealed by the company union.

Then, said Turnbull, "Members began to join us in such numbers that we felt the time had come to place before the NLRB a petition for an election in the plant, to determine the exclusive bargaining agent of the workers." Local 301 submitted the petition. Weeks went by. The UE learned that lack of company consent was holding up the works. "This was a national period," Turnbull commented, "when employers were resisting industrial unionism and hoping to have the Wagner Act declared unconstitutional."

Local 301 circulated petitions among all workers calling upon the company to consent to an NLRB election in the interests of democracy. Next, the union's members on the Workers' Council availed themselves of a provision in its constitution to request a special meeting, at which a resolution demanding GE to consent to an immediate election was approved. At length, GE consented. And, UE Local 301 prevailed.

V   When a union wins an election its job is far from over. In fact, the job of union-building has usually just begun. This is true in most cases, but particularly when the vote in the election, as at Schenectady—where the UE had an edge of about one thousand out of slightly more than nine thousand votes cast—indicates that deep divisions of sentiment must be quickly healed. Turnbull described what Local 301 did along those lines:

> Our first step was to extend the hand of friendship to committeemen of the Workers' Council, workers who up to that time had taken no part in our affairs, sincerely hoping that the company union could function effectively for GE workers. They joined our ranks. Today they are among some of our most active people. We set up organizational teams from among active UE members. We scheduled them according to buildings, floors, and departments to visit other workers at lunch time and to carry on the work of mass sign-ups. About fifteen hundred new members entered the union in this way.

Within a few days after the election, which occurred on December 15, 1936, Local 301 began to get its grievance machinery into shape. Departmental meetings were held to elect committeemen and -women. "Today," Turnbull reported to the delegates, "we have two hundred and nineteen committee people in the plant, who in the past six months have handled or settled twenty-six hundred grievances in the shop on the floor with foremen." He continued:

> Following the setup of our sister Local 201 at Lynn, Massachusetts, any grievances not adjusted on the floor go next to the level of the executive board of the local, which deals with management on the case. Two hundred and ninety grievances touching on fundamental policy were handled in this way. In these we were most cautious, understanding that we were setting precedent which would be used in the future. We consider that the adjustment of grievances is the basic activity of the union.

These were the procedures—a friendly hand to sincere Workers' Council people, systematic organizing, and swift effective treatment of a logjam of grievances—that brought the mem-

69

bership of Local 301 from six hundred fifty to eight thousand in a year's time. "About twenty percent are women," Turnbull said, "which fairly represents the proportion of women workers in the plant. Young workers as well are coming into the union in large numbers." During the year, also, the 10-cent-an-hour wage increase was realized "for virtually all the production workers" at Schenectady GE.

Turnbull then proceeded to draw some distinctions between previous business unionism setups at GE Schenectady and the procedures of Local 301. "We find it an interesting commentary on the nature of industrial unionism," he said, "that we are able to conduct the affairs of our local with only one full-time business agent, while, in the old craft union days"—which he knew at first-hand as an old-timer in the shop—"with something like thirty-six different craft union locals in the plant, each supported its own full-time business agent." Turnbull didn't mean that the one Local 301 business agent did all the work there was to be done. He explained in terms of Local 301 at Schenectady the role leadership plays in developing shop leaders of a rank-and-file union:

> We hold on the average about forty-eight departmental meetings a month, which we have found offers one of the best opportunities for education of the membership. The free discussion of conditions in the shop, and the consideration of problems that have to be thrashed out, are features of these meetings. We find a deep need for education of the hundreds of new members coming into our union, also the new leaders and young leaders who are stepping forward. This fall we intend to initiate a labor institute on a big scale, where we will offer membership classes in economics, trade unionism, parliamentary law, and public speaking. We plan too, to develop a program of recreational and cultural activities, to make our union the center of the lives of the GE workers.

VI   The years 1936 and 1937 comprised a period of unprecedented industrial union organizing in the United

States. Hundreds of thousands of workers in mass production—auto, steel, electrical manufacturing, the machine industry, rubber, cement, glass, transport, oil, shipbuilding, and others—were liberating themselves from the open shop and founding their own CIO unions. Sometimes they had to occupy the shop to secure their independence. It was the era of the historic sitdowns, initiated at 2:00 A.M. on January 29, 1936, by workers in the Firestone Tire Plant No. 1 at Akron, Ohio, and raised to dramatic heights by the auto workers' occupation, from December 30, 1936, to February 11, 1937, of the General Motors Chevrolet and Fisher Body plants in Flint, Michigan.

The 1936 stoppage in the wire and cable department of Schenectady GE, to which Bill Turnbull had referred in his report to the UE convention in September of that year, had been a sitdown. (It was not without precedent there in Schenectady. As far back as 1906, IWW industrial unionists had inspired an effective sixty-five-hour "folded arms strike" in the plant.) But there were a number of significant differences between the kind of organizing required in most mass production industry and that in which the UE engaged. The 1937 drive on the open shop steel industry was mainly conducted from outside the plants by the Steel Workers Organizing Committee, with publicity men, statisticians, batteries of lawyers, thirty-five subregional offices, one hundred fifty-eight field directors and full-time organizers, eighty-five part-time organizers, supplied largely by the manpower and financial resources of the United Mine Workers.

This organizing strategy was employed in steel. Not so in electrical manufacturing. The UE grew indigenously in most shops, giving it a character in its origins which remained through the years and had an all-important bearing on its development and survival. In Schenectady, not even a single full-time staff organizer from the UE international union was assigned to the campaign. On the contrary, Local 301 helped the international union. From the founding convention of March 1936 to the convention of September 1937—the span of months in which Local 301 membership went from six hundred fifty to eight thousand—the local paid $12,217 in dues and initiation fees to the international union. It received back in financial aid a total of $482.50. The difference signified the support Local 301 gave UE organizing efforts in tougher territory, such as GM's electrical division plants in Ohio.

Bill Turnbull's 1937 convention report illuminated another aspect of the Schenectady local's contribution to the struggles of working people for militant unionism. It should not be forgotten that the spirit animating workers in mass production also had its effect upon established AFL organizations. Willing or not, they had to respond to the surge of rank-and-file people. Said Turnbull:

> Our influence in the community, and the surrounding area, has been extensive. We gave our full aid to the American Locomotive Company workers when they were organizing their union. We assisted also the store workers, the cleaners and dyers, the transport workers, the petroleum workers, the laundry workers, the meat packers, the textile workers, and many others. We worked hand in hand with AFL unions, helping to negotiate with them when they asked us. We actually organized a local of the Teamsters Union and turned it over to the Teamsters AFL.

VII   During the peak period of the Schenectady campaign in late 1936, Julius Emspak, UE secretary-treasurer, one of the first industrial unionists in the GE plant and a Local 301 member in good standing, hadn't been spending much time in the New York office. He had hardly returned from weeks in Camden in the RCA battle when he set out for Schenectady to join with Turnbull, young leader Leo Jandreau, Julius's brother Frank Emspak, and others to wind up organization of the plant there. It was a natural move for the UE secretary-treasurer, whose choice of lifetime work in industrial unionism had been made after he finished undergraduate studies at Union College in Schenectady and then gone on to graduate school at Brown University in Providence, Rhode Island. He had come out of the shop to enter Union College by virtue of one of Swope's employee benefit programs—scholarship loans

72

for promising young fellows. When Emspak completed his studies he returned to the shop in Schenectady, where, earning the pay of a skilled tool and die maker, he paid off the Swope loan, meanwhile serving as a volunteer organizer for the union that was to become UE Local 301.

It was natural, too, for Tommy Wright to accompany Emspak back to Schenectady for the final weeks of the UE organizing drive. Tommy, first editor of the international union's official publication—a post he held until he retired in 1967— was a Schenectady newspaperman in the early 1930s, fired from the *Schenectady Gazette* for union activity in helping to organize a local of the CIO Newspaper Guild. Before and after the firing he had served as a volunteer pamphleteer for the industrial union at the GE plant, writing leaflets and, once they were printed up, taking a handful to do his share in distributing them at the plant gates. He was one of many people with special skills who enlisted, in those days, in the cause of industrial unionism. The CIO wouldn't have been what it was without them.

VIII Bill Turnbull's report on the subject of organizing to the 1937 convention was comprehensive and detailed. Matt Campbell's was short but just as sweet. Campbell, from the Westinghouse plant in Springfield, Massachusetts, reported as president of the UE's New England district, saying:

> The growth of the UE in New England has been so abnormal in the last year that it is impossible to give a report on each individual local. We have chartered forty different groups in twelve months. The membership in our district has increased from twelve thousand to thirty thousand. A few small strikes have been settled satisfactorily to the workers. Our weak spots remain in Maine and Vermont, predominantly agricultural states, where there are only a few mass production plants but plants nevertheless that must be organized.

Campbell's story of what had happened in New England between the UE convention of September 1936 and that of the same month in 1937 contained in capsule form the story of what had happened just about everywhere in the country. Even beyond. UE locals were establishing the foundations of the union in Canadian plants, many of them owned or controlled by U.S.-based corporations. Seventeen locals had been represented at the foundation convention, twenty-six in September 1936 in Fort Wayne. The delegates meeting on 1937's Labor Day weekend in the Benjamin Franklin Hotel in Philadelphia came from two hundred seventy UE local unions.

Secretary-treasurer Emspak's report revealed in fact and figure how far the union had advanced in twelve months: a dues-paying membership of seventy-one thousand; income for the period, $127,000; a staff of thirty-five full-time and part-time organizers, whose pay ranged from $10 to $30 a week; expenditures on strikes and organizing, $106,000; a balance of about $21,000 in the UE treasury. As far as the temper of the delegates was concerned, it could have been $21 million. They had written a success story to date the equal of anything ever accomplished by workers of the American labor movement. And, they had done it, really, on a shoestring.

In St. Louis, for example, one young organizer, Bill Sentner, working with rank-and-file leaders from the shops, carried on a drive that in relatively short order organized plants employing fifteen thousand workers. Two thousand of these were in Emerson Electric, where the UE conducted one of the longest sitdown strikes on record—fifty-five days—before winning recognition and a written contract. Century Electric, Wagner Electric, and others became UE shops. The swift pace of industrial union organizing in that year was nowhere more in evidence than in Sentner's activities. As soon as the St. Louis shops had been organized he headed for Newton, Iowa, not far from Des Moines.

Maytag Washing Machine Company, the UE objective, was to Newton what the electrical division of General Motors was to Dayton. In each case the company ran not only its plant but the town as well. It turned out, however, that the workers at Maytag were among those generally described in Bill Turnbull's final words to convention delegates at the Benjamin Franklin Hotel in Philadelphia:

74

The tremendous growth of our international union, its high prestige throughout the nation, its progressive, militant and democratic policies, have given the UE a reputation which is a beacon to workers everywhere. They are willing and ready to join with us if we can put our program before them.

Exactly as occurred at Maytag in Newton, Iowa. Before the Maytag company could catch its balance, the union won an NLRB election. Such was the momentum that the company had no recourse but to recognize the union and agree to a contract settlement that satisfied the organized workers. Almost overnight, a company town had been given an industrial union complexion. It summed up, for the most part, the events of that epic year, 1937.

IX Certain general conditions, of course, contributed to making the months of 1937 favorable for industrial union organizing, which in turn led to the greatest economic improvement in the lives of working people and their families since the crash of 1929. The militancy of the workers in mass production found expression in a period when production and employment were on the rise. Furthermore, the Supreme Court decision in April affirming the constitutionality of the Wagner Act—something which stunned corporation leaders, especially the Liberty League brand such as Tom Girdler of Republic Steel—accelerated the response of workers all over the country to the massive CIO campaigns. It was in 1937, too, that Franklin Roosevelt began his second term, meaning that a progressive political climate still prevailed, that the winds blowing from the executive branch of government in Washington favored the interests of working people.

Stage by stage, the long-range organization strategy of the UE was operating according to plan. First had come the struggle and organizational success at RCA. Next, in November 1936, the AFL federal union in the Westinghouse South Philadelphia turbine plant, second most important shop of that company, had fulfilled expectations by leaving the AFL to become UE Local 107. Then, in December of the same year, 1936, the success of Local 301 in Schenectady. And an equally significant victory at the Westinghouse fortress in East Pittsburgh.

There, as in Schenectady, the corporation relied on a company union representation plan. The UE tactic once again was to work from inside the company union, while carrying on concurrently a UE program of organization and pressure demands upon Westinghouse. In November 1936, elections were held for positions on the executive committee of the company union, called the "Joint Conference Committee." Five UE leaders, running as candidates, among them the key UE leader Al Burkhart, were elected. A sixth committeeman, not a UE member, pledged to support the UE demand for a 20 percent increase in wages.

In April 1937, UE Local 601 petitioned the NLRB for certification as the bargaining agent at Westinghouse East Pittsburgh, submitting seventy-two hundred signed membership cards from the eleven thousand five hundred employees in the plant. The NLRB certified the UE local union. At this stage the executive committee of the company union voted not to oppose the NLRB decision. The International Brotherhood of Electrical Workers, IBEW, bowed out even before the hearing was held, having been unable to gain enough interest from the workers to make any claim at all before the NLRB.

Once the central fortresses of the two great corporations in the industry had been organized by the UE, the union took steps aimed at reaching the next objectives—national GE and Westinghouse contracts covering all plants containing UE local unions, and further organization of the unorganized in the other plants of these major corporations. In the spring and summer of 1937, the union conducted negotiations with GE and Westinghouse in an attempt to win national contracts. Both efforts failed at that time. For different reasons.

Analysis of the failures, however, and discussion on the matter by delegates at the September 1937 convention led to a convention decision that was to have far-reaching influence on the future relationship between UE on the one hand and GE and Westinghouse on the other. By request of GE and Westinghouse delegates, the convention authorized the establishment of two conference boards, to be composed of representatives from local unions in each corporate chain of plants. The GE Conference Board and the Westinghouse Conference Board would be responsible, with the assistance of the international union and its top leadership, for preparing demands and negotiating national contracts with the corporations. This turned out to be one of the most important decisions made by the confident, enthusiastic and purposeful delegates at this happy UE convention.

6
Signing up Swope's GE

I   The opposition of Westinghouse to a national contract—or, for that matter, to a written contract of any sort—stemmed from the line taken by those employers who were in the forefront of the corporate war against industrial unionism. Their symbolic leader was Tom Girdler of Republic Steel in Chicago, who has gone down in history as the man most responsible for the Memorial Day, 1937, slaughter by city police of striking workers parading peacefully, with their wives and children, near the gates of the Republic Steel mill in Chicago. Girdler, incensed to fury by the Supreme Court approval of the Wagner Act in April, and determined to resist the organizing campaign of the CIO Steel Workers Organizing Committee, put himself at the head of the so-called "Little Steel" group in the industry to defeat industrial unionism.

According to a report by the La Follette Committee of the U.S. Senate, Little Steel spent $43,901.88 for machine guns rifles, revolvers, and tear gas and bombs to prepare for resistance to the CIO. This group of companies, accounting for about a quarter of the nation's steel production, refused to negotiate, provoked a bloody strike, and gave the CIO forces their first major setback. It took four years of struggle by the workers to win recognition of their union and a written contract. During those years Girdler-and-company took the position that even if the Wagner Act was declared constitutional, this didn't mean that employers had to sign an agreement with a union. Little Steel construed the act as obliging corporations to bargain with a labor organization—meaning talk it to death —but not obligating them to enter into written contracts. This was also the Westinghouse position, which explained the inability of the UE to negotiate a national agreement with Westinghouse in 1937.

The union's failure in that year to secure a contract from GE had other causes. Swope was no Girdler. He wouldn't go near the anti–Roosevelt, anti–New Deal, anti–CIO Liberty League gang of employers. Nor did he associate himself with the campaign of the National Association of Manufacturers against the New Deal's reform program, above all the Wagner Act. He had cultivated an image of GE as a broadminded, fairminded employer. However much his pride may have been hurt by the Schenectady workers' repudiation of his preference for company unionism, it could be expected, on the record of Swope's paternalism, that he would be amenable to working out an agreement with the UE.

Furthermore, 1937 was an opportune year for new industrial unions to be negotiating contracts. Not only were economic conditions good but by the time the UE approached General Electric, the CIO Auto Workers had signed with General Motors; and U.S. Steel, giant of that industry, an open shop since 1919, had suddenly come to terms with the CIO Steel Workers Organizing Committee. John L. Lewis hailed the auto and steel successes which he had played a key role in helping to achieve.

II   A rank-and-file committee from GE plants sat down in mid-1937 to negotiate with the company. From local 301 in Schenectady came Bill Turnbull, Leo Jandreau, and Frank Emspak; from Lynn Local 201, Al Coulthard, and Bill Murphy; also present were representatives from the other four UE local unions in organized General Electric plants. The international union was represented by its president, James Carey.

The rank-and-file committee members carried the ball in negotiations with GE. Some, like Turnbull and Coulthard, had put in years in the shop, accumulating plenty of trade union experience. All committee members were acquainted at first hand with present conditions and problems on the job. None of the international union leaders, at this early point in their careers, were in a position to make the contributions to negotiations which lay within the competence of the rank-and-file committee people. Such a setting as negotiations with General Electric, in fact, furnished an excellent chance for the young international union officers to gain necessary leadership education.

As the series of meetings moved along, the rank-and-file committee members were astonished and angered one day by the news that Carey had made a public announcement on "progress." In a manner that suggested an endeavor to match the Lewis statements on the GM and U.S. Steel settlements, the young UE president had told the press that an agreement with GE was imminent, that the company was about ready to crack. Because this had no basis in the stage which negotiations had reached, and because in the practice of rank-and-file unionism no one sounds off unless it is part of organization strategy—discussed and approved by the group—the negotiating committee members unanimously requested Carey to separate himself from the bargaining sessions. They were hoping that no serious damage had been done to whatever possibilities existed for agreement with GE.

But it seemed that company officers blew their stacks when word reached them of Carey's public statement. One could imagine how Swope himself, not an unproud man, might react to the suggestion by an upstart of a union, with only a fraction of the GE chain organized, that this powerful corporation of his was ready to crack. Negotiations languished and the question of agreement was left hanging in the air for months. When 1938 came around, the UE, unfortunately, was in nowhere near as strong a position for bargaining as it had been in 1937. The union's new General Electric Conference Board faced a very different situation. So did the whole union—and CIO industrial unionism generally.

III   John L. Lewis charged the corporations with responsibility for manufacturing the depression of 1938 to give workers a dose of unemployment and thus halt the march of industrial unionism. Depression times returned in that year for no good economic reason that any CIO labor leader, nor President Roosevelt either, could see. On April 29 Roosevelt warned Americans that depression simply meant suffering for the people and opportunity for the corporations. It appeared plain enough that the "economic royalists," as Roosevelt once called them, having tried unsuccessfully by all means to keep the workers from organizing their new unions, had now decided they needed a depression breathing spell in which to mount a counteroffensive against the CIO—before unions such as UE could consolidate the strength of the tens and tens of thousands who had joined the union.

Hard times began to hit the shops early in the year. There were layoffs and lockouts. In the electrical manufacturing industry, during the months of 1938, more than sixty thousand workers lost their jobs. The UE, all told, had a total of fifty lockouts and strikes on its hands, occasioned by workers' refusals to swallow the wage cuts, which employers announced on a "take it or leave it" basis. Other CIO unions were feeling the same pain.

The workers' organizations had begun to extract in wage increases a greater measure of the profits they created for the corporations. In 1938, the corporations indicated, in no uncertain terms, that they intended to put a stop to that, as well as to any further organizing of the unorganized. If the workers didn't like it, they'd better think twice or they'd be out on the street without a job. The atmosphere was very different from that of 1937, when the UE first tried to negotiate a national contract with GE. How was the union to approach its objective now that conditions had been so drastically altered for working people? What could be done to maintain and strengthen the union—and the CIO—in the midst of depression and the employer counteroffensive? Could organizing go on, contracts be negotiated, under such circumstances?

These were questions discussed by the UE local union representatives making up the General Electric Conference Board and by the rank-and-file negotiating committee. Carey, by his own choice, continued to stay out of the discussions. Although the committee members had requested him to remove himself from negotiating meetings with the company, he would have been welcomed at the committee bull sessions. The members hoped to have him sit in and resume his education in trade union leadership, just as the other two top officers were doing. They encouraged Carey to take part. But he didn't appear.

At one of the discussions the conversation touched on a little printed GE booklet which contained Swope's labor policies—a booklet distributed to GE workers as proof that they didn't need their own union contract since everything was in the booklet, backed by GE's word, which naturally was as good as gold. For some reason the company's published policy documents always bore a cryptic numerical title—in this case GE Q105A. Serving as Swope's labor code, GE Q105A did indeed cover matters usually found spelled out in a union contract, setting forth the prevailing GE policies on wages, hours, overtime, vacations, and employment conditions in the shop.

Procedures on layoffs and promotions, as well as the various benefit plans of the company, were described. Also in GE Q105A was an interesting "no discrimination" statement which surely came from nowhere but the philosophy of paternalistic democracy as conceived by Gerard Swope. It read: "There shall be no discrimination by foremen, superintendents or any executives of the company against any employee because of race or creed or because of an employee's membership in any fraternity, society, labor organization or other lawful organization."

Swope was one of an all-but-vanished species of rare individuals in positions of corporate authority. He never batted an eye when GE's famous electrical engineer in the Schenectady research laboratories, Charles Steinmetz, was elected chairman of the city school board on the Socialist party ticket—and later became president of the Schenectady Common Council. Steinmetz could be a socialist or anything "lawful" he pleased. As long as he was valuable to GE—his genius made millions for the company—he would be kept on the job for that reason. The Swope no-discrimination clause in GE Q105A established the same principle for all employees.

IV   When the UE negotiating committee people discussed Swope and his policies, it was no idle talkfest. Such material had to be explored again and again in those difficult days of early 1938 in order to find a route forward to the objective of a national contract. The committee wasn't concerned with psychoanalyzing a man like Swope to discover what made him tick. There was no point to that. But in driving ahead toward union goals at GE it was rank-and-file wisdom to thoroughly study the lay of the land. In that company almost every feature of the terrain—such as *GE Q105A*—was impressed with something of Gerard Swope's cast of mind.

The committee started to bat around the possibility of an unconventional approach to GE. Perhaps it would serve the union's purpose best to propose to GE—that is, to Swope—that *GE Q105A* be converted into a one-year national contract between the UE and the company—without change, and with only a couple of additions: (1) a preamble stating that the contract covered all GE plants where the union had already been certified as bargaining agent and also any future plants in which the union won certification; and (2) a section outlining systematic and effective grievance procedure.

There was a tremendous restlessness among the workers in the company plants. Countless complaints piling up. Spontaneous stoppages more the rule than the exception. This was poor business for a company which had always operated on the principle that its "contented" work force meant steady production and a steady flow of profits. Swope and GE had to be aware that the old system of paternalism had broken down, and that something was needed to take its place if production and profits were to be maximized—especially in tight depression conditions.

Furthermore, grievance machinery aside, Swope himself had declared it to be company policy to negotiate with labor unions representing GE workers and, if agreement was reached, to sign a contract. How could he reject an agreement identical with the contents of *GE Q105A* word-for-word, except for two additions? The odds seemed to be good that, given the chance, Swope would choose to follow the union-agreement course set by Myron C. Taylor, president of U.S. Steel, rather than that adopted by Tom Girdler and GE's competitor, Westinghouse.

So it might look from the company's point of view. Suppose it did. Was such an agreement in the interest of the workers?

Would it be wise to propose freezing, for a one-year contract term, the prevailing wages and conditions at GE and to abandon for twelve months all efforts to improve the basic wages and job conditions? The members of the UE committee, and the two top international union officers sitting in on the discussions—Emspak and Matles—proceeded to weigh the whole idea in the light of the general 1938 situation in which the UE, with its objectives of organizing the unorganized and negotiating union contracts, found itself. Also very prominent in the picture loomed the challenge confronting CIO industrial unionism under the guns of a corporate offensive.

V

By 1938 the UE had organized local unions in seven GE plants employing about thirty thousand workers, including, of course, the two key company bases in Schenectady and Lynn. The way things were going in 1937, it had been possible to envision a rapid takeoff—from the success of plans to develop strong locals at Lynn and Schenectady—into organization of the remaining unorganized plants of the GE chain, which contained more than forty-five thousand workers. The UE plans were still the same. But the timetable had been rearranged by failure in the 1937 negotiations and by events of depression.

On top of that, with thousands of workers in electrical manufacturing being laid off, and the new local unions not yet firmly consolidated, there was a danger of discouragement and demoralization among already organized workers. What was needed was contract protection, grievance machinery, and a sense of having a union in operation, under local rank-and-file control. The negotiating committee members weren't indulging in guesswork on all this. They themselves were in the shop and knew what was needed.

A national agreement with GE, stipulating that workers in as yet unorganized plants would be protected by the contract once they got a local union recognized, promised to be an invaluable organizing weapon under depression circumstances. It would, in short, support the UE's objectives, given things as they were in 1938.

84

Another advantage in the strategy being discussed by the negotiating committee had to do with the fifty lockouts and strikes in the industry, where workers were dug in against wage cuts. Never in American history had corporations failed to slash wages during a depression. As Roosevelt had said, depressions produce opportunity for big corporations, which make use of the conditions to arrest organizing, weaken or wreck unions, drive wages down, and extend monopolistic control of their industries. The matter of monopoly—or, as the scholars refer to it, economic concentration—is beyond the capacity of any local union, or any individual international union, to tackle effectively. It is a political question for an entire labor movement to deal with by putting a political program of struggle before the workers.

But preventing wage cuts, preserving union strength, and persisting with organization in the climate of depression were precisely the realistic CIO industrial unionism goals in 1938. The effect on these goals of an agreement by a major CIO union, such as the UE, with a great corporation, such as GE, while holding the line on wages and invigorating the organization, was obviously something to think about. The negotiating committee members felt that, everything considered, the idea of proposing a national contract based on Swope's *GE Q105A* was sound—and they so recommended to the union's GE Conference Board, which agreed.

VI   Swope had assigned his vice-president in charge of manufacturing, William Burrows, to the duty of negotiating with the new union. Burrows, like most other GE executives, regarded Swope with genuine admiration. At that time, throughout the company there existed a family of officers and managers whose allegiance to Swope, and whose confidence in him, made GE an extraordinary corporation.

As time passed, such corporate relationships became mostly a thing of the past in industry. But in 1938, when the UE negotiating committee was talking to Burrows, the committee knew full well that it was also talking to Swope. The proposal for a contract on the basis of *GE Q105A*, which took no more than

85

fifteen minutes or so to present, went on the table. The committee was reasonably certain that it would reach Swope without delay.

Burrows and his associates, somewhat taken aback, didn't say anything for a while. Then Burrows began to make carefully formulated inquiries as to the meaning of the proposition, the reasons the UE had come up with it, the projections the union could make of its future significance, and so forth. The committee members explained that the proposal they had just introduced sought to provide a breakthrough, a departure from endless haggling, and an effort to get down quickly to the principal issues of concern to the union.

What the union was asking, the committee said, was evidence of GE willingness to recognize the UE, to sign a contract establishing evidence of recognition, and thus to take a decisive step in closing its books, so to say, on company unionism. Under a written agreement the union could effectively handle the innumerable grievances that were burdening workers and creating difficult conditions in the plants.

Burrows said that he would like to know what the union intended to do at the end of the twelve-month period, when the agreement, as proposed, could be reopened. The committee members replied by first candidly sketching the union's program during the contract year. The UE, they said, hoped to build an operative shop steward system in the seven plants already organized; to develop local union leadership in the plants; to begin the job of working out relationships between the rank-and-file, with their pressing grievances, and the stewards and leadership people, and between the union representatives and the company's supervisors and managers; and to proceed to organize other GE plants with the aim of making the UE universally representative of all the workers in the GE chain. Finally, the committee said that at the end of the twelve-month period the union hoped to be able to negotiate improvements in the contract. At that point Burrows suggested an adjournment pending another meeting.

A week later the parties reconvened. It was at once clear that the matter had been reviewed by Swope. Burrows quoted the GE president as having remarked that the union's proposal represented "a novel idea," which should be explored and pursued. Swope, in other words, had flashed the green light. Work began on putting an agreement together which eventually came into being. It was only six double-spaced typewritten pages long. All union objectives were included, among them: (1) recognition of the UE as bargaining agent for workers in the seven organized plants; (2) the contract to be national in scope, covering the seven plants and any others where UE might later become the certified bargaining agent; and (3) establishment of a shop steward system, whereby workers through the steward could take up complaints directly with the foreman in a department.

VII   In this first GE national contract was laid down the blueprint of the UE grievance machinery and shop steward system, ingredients of rank-and-file industrial unionism which were to remain characteristic of the union's functioning over the years. Both parties agreed on an arrangement of one steward to one foreman; on the desirability of bringing up and settling grievances at that level, on the shop floor; on processing unresolved grievances to the next level of local union leadership and plant management and, if still unsettled there, to top UE and GE officers; on a pledge of no strikes or stoppages while a grievance was in the works, nevertheless reserving the right of the workers to take strike action if the grievance procedure had been exhausted and a grievance had failed to be settled to their satisfaction at the highest level. Arbitration was possible only if union and company agreed. It would not be compulsory.

GE Q105A was incorporated by reference in the contract and attached to it. It would not be changed, both parties agreed, during the contract's twelve-month life. But after that time, if union or company had given notice at least sixty days prior to expiration of the contract, modifications would be discussed in further negotiations. If no notice was served, then the contract was to renew itself automatically for another year. This was the substance of the agreement signed in 1938 by the union and the largest electrical manufacturing company in the industry.

The union committee had proposed, and the company committee agreed, that the contract be negotiated and drafted without the aid of lawyers on either side. There was no need for it since neither party had the slightest intention of going to court to seek interpretation or enforcement of the contract. The grievance procedure, and the right to economic action by the workers, would be the final arbiter.

Among those signing were UE local union officers from Schenectady, Lynn, Bridgeport, Cleveland Lamp Works, Fort Wayne and New Kensington, Pennsylvania—also, the three officers of the international union. On the date the contract went into effect, April 1, 1938, it covered about thirty thousand workers, all of whom had been afforded opportunity, according to customary UE practice, of meeting to consider and vote on the terms of the agreement before it became effective.

When it did, the union embarked upon a program of consolidation and organization. The job of consolidation, of signing up new members, of getting shop steward systems organized and grievance procedure operating, rested in the hands of the rank-and-file elected shop stewards and the local union officers in the seven organized plants. The old-timer leadership, such as Bill Turnbull and Al Coulthard had looked forward to this day for as long as they could remember. And the young leadership they had been helping to bring along—in the international union and throughout the entire chain of General Electric plants—had learned priceless lessons in the skills of union-building. But there was no mood for resting on the laurels of GE national contract victory. The depression was on and the corporate offensive in full swing. They were rough times. There was more work to be done.

7
Company Town in Iowa

I   Among the fifty lockouts and strikes constituting a serious crisis for the UE in 1938 were those at Philco in Philadelphia, Allen-Bradley in Milwaukee, and Maytag in Newton, Iowa. The Maytag situation, in the very months that the national contract was being hammered out with GE, showed signs of developing into a full-blown donnybrook. Maytag had been champing at the bit for a year, just waiting to get back at the union which had swept in out of the blue and organized the Newton plant. Now that the first twelve-month contract was expiring, Maytag lowered the boom, serving a wage-cut ultimatum and other "take it or leave it" downgrading changes in contract terms which added up to nothing less than an intention to throw the union out.

The agreement with GE was in existence only five weeks when, on May 9, 1938, Maytag locked out its workers. Local 1116, representing sixteen hundred working people in the plant, promptly convened a mass membership meeting at which the stand of resistance to a wage cut was reaffirmed and a resolution approved to conduct a strike against the lockout. This is traditional trade union response to lockout action by a company. In essence, the workers strike to compel the company to negotiate. While the most militant struggles of the working class are always exercises of self-defense against the effects upon workers of the profit motive, no struggles more sharply dramatize the contest between the rights and interests of working people and the profit policies of a company than a strike called to resist a lockout.

In a conflict of this sort, the issue can be put plainly and simply, as it was by John L. Lewis in discussions with the young UE international union officers in 1938. They were talking with Lewis about the test presented to the union by the

89

lockouts and strikes in their industry across the nation—a test made even more formidable by the loss in union income because of dues-paying members being laid off. The international union, its budget reduced, had been forced to make a 20 percent cutback in full-time and part-time field staff. Volunteers had come forward from among jobless members. Rank-and-file militancy remained high. These, said Lewis, were all-important factors. In such lockouts and strikes as were underway, he remarked, "Whichever side can hold out one day longer, that is how the outcome is decided."

II Newton, Iowa, was a one-company town in a politically conservative agricultural state, which contained some scattered small industrial shops but nothing of a mass production nature. Unions were few and far between. The organization of UE Local 1116 at Maytag in 1937 had been, and remained, the most substantial CIO penetration in Iowa. In 1936 and 1937 the Maytag Washing Machine Company made a profit of $5.5 million on its capital investment—a dollar profit for every dollar paid out in wages. The argument advanced to support its 1938 wage-cut edict had nothing to do with Maytag's financial position. Company executives said that the railroads had cut wages and so they were going to do the same. Not only did Maytag have comfortable reserves of cash in its coffers at lockout time, but it also had a stockpile of warehoused washing machines—marketable inventories which it had been building up for many months.

The company was well equipped for battle. Furthermore, it would be fighting on the most comfortable terrain any corporation could wish for. In Newton, the political establishment, the courts, the police force, the business community, banks, merchants, real estate companies, and even automobile agencies were all under the influence or control of the Maytag family. Its lines of political communication reached to the state Capitol in Des Moines. These were heavy Maytag assets. The weight the company attached to them could be felt, almost from the first day of the lockout, by members of a one-year-old local union affiliated with an international which itself had been formed only a little more than two years previously.

UE organizer Bill Sentner transferred the seat of union operations in the Missouri-Iowa district from St. Louis to Newton. He was the young man who had already demonstrated his abilities in both cities in 1937, when fifteen thousand St. Louis workers in electrical and radio manufacturing, as well as the workers of Maytag, joined the UE.

Sentner, like many another UE organizer of the period, had been shaped by the Great Depression, a shattering experience for the poor, working class family into which he had been born. He moved from job to job, as he could get hold of one, and at the same time continued his school education. At length he returned to work at a shop job. When the CIO organizing drives started, Sentner decided he wanted to get in on them. Because the rank-and-file character of the UE attracted him, he volunteered his services to the organization.

Once the Maytag local was established, Sentner assumed another duty expected of UE organizers—helping to negotiate a contract. Just as skilled workers in a shop must master a wide range of techniques, UE organizers, in the course of learning their skills, are called upon to handle many different jobs. While most organizers will show particular talent for one phase or another of the work, Sentner had strength in all departments.

He could organize at factory gates and negotiate carefully at the bargaining table; he was an excellent speaker; he could plan publicity, produce pamphlets and leaflets, and handle a labor board hearing; he had both a concern and knack for the training of local leadership, for forging alliances with other sections of the labor movement, for building support in a community, and for directing political action strategy. An all-round UE organizer, that was Bill Sentner, moving into the lockout situation at Maytag.

Almost as soon as the workers were locked out, the company's battle plan started to unfold. First of all, there appeared a "Loyal Workers Committee," set up by the attorney for the Maytag estate. This was the spearhead of a back-to-work movement, bolstered by another company-inspired group, the "Citizens and Taxpayers Committee," which had the assignment of creating community sentiment for the back-to-work campaign. Simultaneously, Maytag foremen and supervisors made the rounds to the homes of the workers, who were solicited to sign up as supporters of the back-to-work movement to break the strike—and to pledge themselves ready, at a given signal, to crash through the picket lines into the plant.

III In a company town such as that ruled for years by the Maytag dynasty, workers often cannot realize, until they attempt to exercise their rights of organization, how securely some of them have been hooked by company-controlled commercial and other institutions. Most home mortgages, for instance, had been written by one of the four lending associations in Newton, all of them connected to Maytag. A company man ran an auto agency from which a number of workers had purchased cars on long-term installment schedules. Both home-owners and car-owners, lacking job income to meet their payments, would be at the mercy of their creditors, controlled by Maytag.

Interwoven throughout the fabric of the entire work force at the washing machine company were persons who had obtained their jobs by way of an employment agency managed by the chauffeur for the Maytag family. Others were sons, brothers, or relatives of company superintendents, managers, foremen, and supervisors. Maytag, to put it mildly, had important built-in resources—in the plant, the town, and the state of Iowa—for its crackdown on the union.

In an early skirmish on the picket line, one would-be scab wound up with a bloody nose. One man. One bloody nose. And the result? Two injunctions were granted by the local courts, against the union and against the picket line as such. The idea was to employ the courts to reduce the picket line—which had been holding firm against the approaches of small groups of scabs—to a size that could be overwhelmed by a larger assault led by the "Loyal Workers Committee." Even as the judge was handing down the injunctions, Maytag supervisors were out organizing people for a big push at the plant gates. This had all the elements of a surprise raid prepared by the high command of a military operation. But as can happen with the best laid schemes, the other side—in this case, the UE—is not always caught napping.

Not long after sunup one morning, scabs under orders secretly assembled in the woods a distance from the plant. Extra town police at the gates were meanwhile moving pickets away from the entrance. When the way was clear, the scabs broke from cover and headed for Maytag. En route, however, and as they bunched up to pass through the gates, several hundred strikers mingled in. Minutes after the strikers were inside the shop they organized a sitdown. Production work was out of the question. The scabs were escorted from the plant and the strikers stayed in, while their union comrades on the outside organized support. At the same time, everyone waited for the next company maneuver. It was not long in coming.

Maytag attorneys dug up an ancient state statute pertaining to sedition and criminal syndicalism, under which the strike leadership, including Sentner, was charged and arrested, for, among other things, an attempt to overthrow the government. The company announced that twelve of the leaders were fired and barred from any further employment. Those arrested were at first held without bail. Finally, the court set a total bail of $150,000 for which the state refused to accept property offered by union members unless the property was secured by a cash surety bond for the whole $150,000. Even then, when the international UE put up the bond, Newton and Iowa authorities haggled for days before agreeing to release the imprisoned strikers.

IV   At this point, with the Maytag public relations operation rolling out releases and statements about "sedition," "revolution," and whatnot—a blaze of hysteria thus enkindled—company officers issued an appeal to Iowa Governor Nelson G. Kraschal, Democrat, to step in and restore law and order. Here the struggle between UE Local 1116 and the Maytag company was escalated to another level, which required the involvement of the labor movement of the state. Its aid was forthcoming. Although nationally the AFL—Bill Green, John P. Frey, and their cohorts on the AFL executive council—was doing its utmost to wreck the CIO, the AFL of Iowa and the independent Railroad Brotherhood unions rallied at the side of the workers of UE-CIO Local 1116 in solidarity against the Maytag scheme to use Governor Kraschal as a strikebreaker.

At length the governor proposed that the union see to it that the sitdown strikers withdraw from the plant. If they did, he said, he would guarantee, by the presence of the Iowa National Guard, that the plant would remain closed. And, he said further, he would direct both union and company—which all this time were meeting occasionally in negotiations—to get down to serious discussions concerning a settlement.

This promise from the chief officer of the state, that no scabs would enter the plant and that he would lend the authority of his office to a renewed effort for agreement, could not help but arouse the hopes of many strikers. Among them, as well as among people in the Newton community, pressure built up to accept the governor's offer. The strike leadership took a long look at the whole situation. There were doubts that the governor would be able to keep his promise if negotiations produced no quick results, if the deadlock dragged on. But the leadership, after considerable deliberation, finally felt that feeling in the community left the union no alternative but to take a chance.

The sitdowners marched out in organized ranks, to be greeted by a mass reception from their fellow workers—who then cheered as the National Guard proceeded to ring the plant. Almost at once it became clear that Governor Kraschal had more in mind than a simple plant occupation. Martial law was declared in Newton. The governor ordered a curfew. Guardsmen, with machine guns, rifles, and bayonets, took up posts outside the gates and on street corners of the city.

In this atmosphere, still another development in the dispute was occurring under the auspices of the National Labor Relations Board, which was conducting hearings on a complaint the board issued against the company. The complaint had resulted from a UE charge, filed with the board, that the lockout represented an effort by Maytag to eliminate the union. At the same time, with martial law in force, with NLRB hearings going on, union and company negotiators continued to get together. But that was about all. No progress whatsoever was made in the talks. A standoff.

V By now the strike at Maytag had attracted national attention and assumed national significance. The CIO, as well as other elements of the labor movement, recognized that this was no isolated adventure by one employer but rather an attack, at a key point, aimed at setting a wage-cut and union-busting pattern to be followed by companies everywhere. Statements by leaders of the Republican Party, smarting under political defeats by the New Deal coalition, which included the CIO, provided evidence for this view of the conflict at Maytag. The strike became big news.

So much so that among the reporters who came to Newton was Ernest Hemingway, just back from covering the war of the Franco fascists upon the elected popular government of Spain. There was a lot of shooting over there in Spain, Hemingway told Sentner and a group of strikers one night while they were having a drink together in the family-owned Maytag Hotel. "Then I got back to the States," the novelist went on, "and I heard about martial law and guns in my own native land, out in Newton, Iowa. So I came to have a look."

As Hemingway and the group of UE people left the hotel and hit the street, they were immediately threatened by a guardsman with rifle and fixed bayonet. He commanded Hemingway and the union leaders to get a move on, to break it up and leave, or he'd clap them in jail.

"Now, son," said Hemingway, turning toward him, "you ought to be more respectful when you address your elders. If you don't behave yourself, let me tell you what I'll do. I'll take that rifle and bayonet away from you and shove it up your ass and blow your brains out."

Fortunately, a National Guard officer nearby, recognizing Hemingway, got the young guardsman out of the tangle before harm was done. That was only one of many tense incidents of that difficult time in Newton.

VI   The day came, as the strike leadership had suspected it might, when the governor broke his word. The heat got to him. The support the labor movement of the state had rendered the cause of the Maytag workers couldn't measure up to the forces the company had been able to mobilize. The "Citizens and Taxpayers Committee," the "Loyal Workers Committee," Maytag itself, prominent Republican politicians, and the press, all put the squeeze on the governor. He announced that the plant would reopen under the protection of the National Guard.

His announcement included a call to the union members to return to their jobs—and a call to the company not to impose the wage cut from which it had never backed off in the almost three months since it had locked out the workers. The governor further directed both parties, following a return to work, to resume negotiations for an agreement. The twelve leaders who had been fired, however, were not to return to work with the others. Their status was to be negotiated with all other disputed issues.

An entirely new set of circumstances had been created by the governor's order. The members of Local 1116 had been locked out because they refused to accept a contract including a wage cut and other curtailed conditions. If they now returned to the plant at the point of a gun, it would be, apparently, without a wage cut but also without any contract at all— and with no assurance of getting one. What was to be the future of their union? Especially since the governor had, for every practical purpose, confirmed the firing of the twelve local union leaders. He had followed the company line on that one, altogether.

This at once became the dominant issue. Nobody talked of anything else. The strikers said: "Order or no order, guns or no guns, we're not going back into that plant without our leaders." You could hear such words all over the town of Newton in those days. Everybody agreed that the deal had been engineered by Maytag, that the governor's office had been captured by the company. When the members assembled for a mass meeting to decide what to do next, they were overwhelmingly of a mood to stay outside as long as their leaders were outside—to go in only if the leaders went in too.

A rank-and-file union leadership never faces a tougher situation. It is very easy, no trick at all, for a leadership at the end of a long strike to return to the members and report the terms of an agreeable settlement. Enthusiasm prevails. The scene on such occasions is one of general rejoicing and approval of leadership for a job well done. It is easy, also, for leaders to go along with the emotional feelings of a multitude of members. No one could doubt that if the leadership of Local 1116, at that mass meeting, had said, "We are going to tell the governor to go straight to hell," cheers would have filled the air. But then what? That's the question a leadership has to ask itself before it takes a position at a time when disaster is blowing in the wind.

The meeting hall was packed to the walls. Bill Sentner and the young local union leaders had talked things over. They stood before the members and outlined the two courses of action which could be followed: (1) to defy the governor, come what may, or (2) to return under the guns to their jobs in the plant and carry on the fight from there. For two hours Sentner and every one of the fired local leaders took the floor to recommend that the second course be adopted, that everything considered, everything analyzed from a realistic point of view, it was necessary to comply with the governor's order. There are never cheers at meetings of this sort. On the contrary. Members who have staunchly withstood weeks on a picket line, and hardship at home, break down and weep without shame. As they did that day in Newton. They had to accept a most painful solution to the problem presented to them. They voted to accept the leadership recommendation and return to work.

When next they gathered in the union hall it was early in the morning on the day of return. They marched slowly from the hall in disciplined formation. On their way into the plant they passed between rows of National Guard troops, whose rifles, bayonets, and machine guns were still on display. In this organized fashion the workers, after ninety-eight days, went back to their jobs at Maytag, resolved—the setback notwithstanding —to continue their struggle for a satisfactory contract.

VII Not many weeks later, Bill Sentner made a report to the fourth convention of the UE on developments at Maytag since the return to work. As fate would have it, the convention had been scheduled a year previous for the city of St. Louis, base of the union district in which Local 1116, Newton, Iowa, was located. When the convention opened on Labor Day, September 5, among the large representation from the Maytag local—some delegates, others observers—were the fired strike leaders and the president of the women's auxiliary, whose members had done picket-line duty, organized food collection and distribution, and helped to rally community support.

Sentner referred the convention delegates to a statement made by the membership of Local 1116 just before the march back to the plant:

> We are returning to work under the forces of military intimidation and coercion. But at the proper time, and in the proper manner, Local 1116 will again present its demands to the Maytag company.

Bravado? Not at all, said Sentner: "Our organization is one hundred percent solid in the plant." He gave an example or two, by way of evidence:

> When the company announced workers could draw wages in advance, over one hundred went to the company and took only a dollar each, telling the paymaster: "That's for August union dues." After receiving their first pay checks, eight hundred and thirty-two members came into the union office on the same day they got their pay, which was very small, and they had been on strike for thirteen weeks, and they paid their August union dues out of that first check, eight hundred and thirty-two of them.

Sentner went on to explain something which Maytag, in its political maneuvering to force the workers back to the plant, had not been able to realize: You can pressure people to the job but you can't make them work. Not if they find the conditions intolerable and if they are a hundred percent solid in their organization. "We have had five or six sitdown strikes,"

Sentner said. "The pet cock of labor production flows as labor in the Maytag plant wants it to flow. It will stay that way until we get a fair and just settlement of the wage questions and all the other issues in the contract."

Already the company had caught the drift. Negotiations were in progress. Maytag had agreed on eight points out of a possible eleven on which the union was insisting. After a short time, predicted Sentner, "we will be able to report...that again Local 1116 of the UE, and the Maytag company, have entered into a contract satisfactory to our membership."

Soon, indeed, a contract was successfully negotiated. No wage cut. No sacrifice of other conditions as first laid down in the Maytag ultimatum to the workers. But there were, just the same, some sacrifices. Twelve of them. Although all fired strike leaders were acquitted at long last of the charges lodged against them under the antique sedition and criminal syndicalism laws—originally put on the books at the behest of employers bent on persecution of militant trade unionists and on maintaining the open shop—none ever got his job back. They had lost them, as things turned out, for the sake and benefit of their fellow workers, who were helped to gain a measure of freedom and economic justice thereby. Not an uncommon story in the annals of the labor movement. What kind of satisfaction did Maytag executives derive from having their pound of flesh in the denial of jobs to the twelve? Well, perhaps only they might have been able to say. That, too, is not uncommon in the annals of corporate behavior, the mean streak that passeth understanding. Two of the victimized local 1116 leaders, Dick Niebur—who had been charged with kidnapping and acquitted—and Bob Kirkwood, one of those freed of sedition and criminal syndicalism charges, went on to serve as UE organizers and elected officers. They devoted their lives to organization of the unorganized and to service in the interests of the union members.

VIII   The remarkable achievement of the UE workers at Maytag—turning a setback into a victory through the exercise of militant solidarity, and doing it in the toughest of depression times—reflected the record of the union as a whole in 1938: all agreements signed without wage cuts, some with increases and improved working conditions; twenty-eight new plants organized, among them shops of GE, Allis Chalmers, Singer Sewing Machine, American Machine and Foundry, and, not least significant, the first small breakthrough in the electrical division of General Motors at Warren, Ohio; and a total of thirty thousand new members.

At the founding convention of the CIO two months later, John L. Lewis made a comment, linking the strategy which the UE had followed by signing its GE agreement early in the year to the general experience of industrial unionism in the previous months:

> Every one of the CIO unions has maintained and even increased its membership in this period of trial and tribulation. They have maintained and renewed their contracts, without wage cuts, in the midst of this depression. New unions have been added to our ranks. A number of unions have made sweeping advances and won national agreements for the first time. Among the examples of new advance made by the CIO in the period of depression is the winning of a national agreement for the first time with the great General Electric Corporation by the United Electrical, Radio and Machine Workers of America.

Militant rank-and-file industrial unionism, united in the CIO, had proven itself a match for the heaviest artillery of the corporate counteroffensive of 1938. Seldom if ever had working class organizations been able to consolidate and move ahead under depression conditions. It was a first. And the job had been done in spite of a thick redbaiting smokescreen under cover of which the employers endeavored to demolish the CIO, to divide and rule the workers, to cry "communism!" and conquer, just as they had done for almost a hundred years. In 1938 it didn't work. But the corporate forces tried hard, as we shall see.

8
Redbaiters, Spies, Union-Busters

I   On August 13, 1938—one day before the workers of UE Local 1116 in Newton had been forced to return to the Maytag plant—the corporate offensive against the CIO opened up a political line of attack in Washington, D.C. In Iowa, the Maytag company, acting in fact if not by assignment as a task force for industry, had conscripted the state government into its service. In the capital city of the nation, industry proceeded to make use of a branch of the federal government. Their aim was not confined, as at Maytag, to one UE local union or one CIO international union. They were out after the whole CIO, industrial unionism altogether.

For that purpose, antagonists of industrial unionism—each with a special interest in view—combined their resources. The corporate masterminds, as is usual when there is slick political work afoot, remained behind the scenes. Up front were reactionary politicians, the chief strategist of the AFL craft unions, and the mass media. Not the least of the services performed by the media at such time is their focus on surface events, the so-called "hard news," and their utter neglect of the decisive role played by corporate elements—public relations personnel and lobbyists included—in developing this "news."

In mid-August 1938, a strange new committee of the U.S. House of Representatives presented as first major witness none other than "Colonel" John P. Frey, president of the AFL Metal Trades Department. So far, things had not gone very well for him and the AFL old guard in their endeavors to insert craft union jurisdiction into mass production industry. Nor for the corporations in such industry. Nor for the reactionary Roosevelt-hating politicians. New Deal policies and militant CIO industrial unions had achieved a series of remarkable economic and political improvements in the lives of working people.

Neither industrialists, AFL craft union leaders, reactionary politicians, propaganda press, depression, Tom Girdler, brutality, or anything else had succeeded in stopping the march of industrial unionism. Employer "Liberty League" efforts to overturn the Wagner Act in the courts had failed. Their schemes to cripple the "freedom to organize" act by pushing legislative amendments through the Congress—an operation to which Frey lent himself and the heavyweights of the AFL craft leadership—had as yet come to nothing. Moreover, New Deal forces in the Congress were preparing legislation aimed at bringing under control those industrialists actively engaged in subverting the Wagner Act. This prospect deeply concerned the lawbreakers in industry.

II   Among the tactics industry was using—in addition to just plain refusal to negotiate or sign agreements with unions representing their workers—were those displayed in the RCA-Sarnoff assault on the UE: contracting, with private union-busting agencies, for use of strikebreakers, spies, strongarm squads, and provocateurs. The Education and Labor Committee of the U.S. Senate, chaired by Senator Hugo Black, who was later appointed by Roosevelt to the Supreme Court where he became an outstanding champion of constitutional rights and liberties, decided to have a look at what was happening. In August 1936, it created a special subcommittee headed by Senator Robert La Follette, Progressive of Wisconsin, assisted by Senator Elbert D. Thomas, Democrat of Utah, to study the situation. The committee came to be well known as the La Follette Committee.

This is only normal congressional procedure, flowing from the constitutional responsibilities of members of the Senate and the House of Representatives. Among their duties, after a law goes on the books, is investigation of its administrative effects, especially in regard to the manner in which the law is meeting the need for which it was passed. The La Follette Committee, although its budget was minimal, had uncovered impressive evidence of employers flouting the Wagner Act's intent—which was, essentially, to guarantee by federal law the liberty of workers to form unions of their own choosing for the purpose of collective bargaining. The documentation assembled by the La Follette Committee comprised a testament to the fact that employers, law or no law, were continuing to interfere with that liberty.

This Senate committee was proceeding with its work when, on May 26, 1938, without much notice or ado, the other branch of Congress, the House of Representatives, approved House Resolution 282, creating something that can be justifiably described as the corporations' answer to the threat they saw in the La Follette Committee revelations.

House Resolution 282 directed the Speaker of the House to appoint a special committee "for the purpose of conducting an investigation of, 1: The extent, character and objects of un-American propaganda activities in the United States; 2: The diffusion within the United States of subversive and un-American propaganda that is instigated from foreign countries or of a domestic origin and attacks the principles of the form of government that is guaranteed by our Constitution, and 3: All other questions in relation thereto that would aid Congress in any necessary remedial legislation."

Point number 3, of course, was inserted to give the novel committee the appearance of having the same kind of "valid legislative purpose" as did the La Follette Committee. But careful examination of the mandate might have disclosed—as committee practices soon established beyond question—that the new House Committee on Un-American Activities didn't have a valid legislative purpose and was itself, indeed, an un-American tool of reaction.

III Frey's performance as a witness in August 1938 laid on the line the real objectives of this unprecedented committee, whose first chairman was Congressman Martin Dies of Texas, unreconstructed southern Democrat, sponsor of House Resolution 282. "Colonel" Frey began by telling committee members, from the witness platform arranged for him, that he and an expert private investigator had worked for many months to prepare the material which he was going to place in the record. The CIO, said the "Colonel," was a giant communist conspiracy to overthrow the government of the United States. He next proceeded to list the names of two hundred forty-eight officers and organizers of CIO unions who, he claimed, were communists. Day by day he added others to his "little list," as the Lord High Executioner in the Gilbert and Sullivan operetta called his roster of those destined to get the ax. By the time Frey finished his four-day starring role on stage, the names of more than three hundred CIO leaders had been entered into the committee records and thus made available to the media, which had a heyday with the material.

IV   That Sunday's *New York Times,* appearing on the day following Frey's initial appearance, headed its report: "Communists Rule the CIO, Frey of the AFL Testifies: He Names 248 Reds." Among the names appearing on Frey's list were those of United Mine Workers veteran John Brophy, director of the CIO; Harry Bridges of the Longshoremen and Warehousemen's Union; Francis Gorman, president of the Textile Workers; Powers Hapgood, CIO representative; James Matles, UE director of organization; Michael Quill, president of the Transport Workers Union; Joseph Salerno, a vice-president of the Amalgamated Clothing Workers; and Walter Reuther, a vice-president of the United Automobile Workers. The names, however, were not all. As testimony unfolded day by day, any number of exchanges occurred between Dies and Frey. On the first day, Saturday, the following took place.

> *Chairman Dies:* Before you secured this information, did you make very careful investigation to determine whether as a matter of fact there was reliable evidence that these individuals were Communists?
>
> *Frey:* I know in some instances they were because I have the police record here.

Over the weekend it apparently occurred to Frey—or someone brought it to his attention—that it just didn't look good for

104

a labor leader to have indulged in collaboration with police departments in putting the finger on other labor leaders. When he took the stand on Monday, he requested the opportunity to clarify his remarks of two days previous.

> *Frey:* I have carefully avoided any discussion with any minor representative of any police department in an effort to secure information. The information I bring before the committee is entirely free from any connection with any police department or any governmental agency. I would like to make that clear and definite. I would not cooperate with police departments with the purpose of getting this information.

Frey went on to elaborate on other matters, such as:

> Last year the [CIO] Steel Workers Organizing Committee held their first convention. And I have a list of fifty-nine delegates to that convention who are members of the Communist Party.

As the "Colonel" concluded his four-day stand before the committee, he delivered one of those statements not unusual in the case of "informers" who anticipate that their motives may be questioned. He elected to don the mantle of patriotism:

> I am fortunate, Mr. Chairman, in being thoroughly nonpartisan. I am not now a member of any political party. And so long as I hold an American Federation of Labor position, I never will be.... I have said nothing critical of the CIO in the past. What I say now is critical, but I believe justified in view of the political problems we are facing as a people.

Greater understanding of the purposes and timing of the hearings at which Frey was featured can be gained by referring back a year or so in history to the hearings of a New Deal committee of the U.S. Congress, the special committee headed by Senator La Follette.

V   *Date:* January 23, 1937. *Place:* Room 247-C, United States Senate Office Building, Washington, D.C. *Occasion:* Hearing of a Committee of the U.S. Senate. *Presiding:*

Committee chairman Senator Robert La Follette of Wisconsin. A witness is on the stand:

Sen. La Follette: Your name?

Witness: James Matles.

Sen. La Follette: What is your occupation?

Matles: Machinist.

Sen. La Follette: Are you a member of any labor organization?

Matles: I am a member of the International Association of Machinists.

Sen. La Follette: Do you hold any office with that association?

Matles: Grand Lodge Representative.

Sen. La Follette: What territory do you cover?

Matles: New York, New Jersey, Philadelphia and Connecticut.

Sen. La Follette: Have you seen the list of names of the members of the National Metal Trades Association who have employed undercover men?

Matles: I have, Senator.

Sen. La Follette: Are any of the firms mentioned in this list located in your territory?

Matles: Yes, there are.

Sen. La Follette: Mention them.

Matles: Armor Engineering Co., Brooklyn; S. W. Farber Co., Brooklyn; Ford Instrument Co., Long Island; Otis Elevator Co., Yonkers; Pratt and Whitney Manufacturing Co., Hartford, Connecticut; Silver and Pewter Manufacturers Association, Brooklyn; F. S. Smithe Machine Co., New York City; Waterbury Tool Co., Waterbury, Connecticut; Worthington Pump and Machinery Co., Harrison, New Jersey; Wright Aeronautical Co., Paterson, New Jersey; Yale and Towne Manufacturing Co., Stamford, Connecticut. . . . These are the principal plants on the list.

VI   La Follette Committee initial procedure involved ordering the well-known big spy agencies to produce their records. Senate subpoenas went out. In this way the committee could secure some of the reports and expense vouchers of the spies in the shops. Each spy, assigned a number by the agency, would identify his weekly reports and vouchers by number, never by his name. If the report was typed, that further concealed identity. But if a specimen of spy handwriting was in the hands of the La Follette Committee, then its staff investigators, who were assisted by a number of volunteer union organizers familiar with the spy racket, could often get a lead.

The organizers were close to the shops. They had learned quickly, in only a few years of field work, that wherever there was an open shop, or a shop with the beginnings of a union, there was also bound to be at least one spy. He was there somewhere. Most likely, too, he would be an active union person, which meant that he had filled out a union application card in his own handwriting.

Between August 1936 and January 1937, when the organizers appeared as witnesses before the committee, they had uncovered some forty spies who had been employed by the agencies in the business. The method of discovery, in most cases, was handwriting comparison: spy reports measured against union cards. When on that basis an organizer was dead sure he had nailed a spy he would say, confronting the spy with the handwritten evidence: "All we want from you is an affidavit for the Senate Committee. You don't have to appear as a witness. The committee isn't interested in you. It simply wants your statement as to who hired you, when, and what your assignment was."

The forty spies nailed down in this fashion were agents of either the Metal Trades Association or the Corporation Auxiliary Company, two outfits operating mainly in the electrical manufacturing and the machine industry. No doubt more than forty could have been pulled out from under rocks. But forty proved the point. Besides, in some instances the organizers felt it was safer not to expose an identified spy. Conditions in the shop were such that the practical thing to do was to keep an eye on him, rather than to take the chance of the agency sending in a new spy, on whom it might take a long while to get the goods.

VII When it came to the work of drawing up a list of spy suspects in a shop, the union had most of them already spotted, because union organizers learned to look for a pattern. Usually a professional spy, employed directly by the agency, followed a set routine. He would hire in as an ordinary worker. Almost at once he would snuggle into the union, if there was one, or move himself next to fellows who were active in organization endeavors. He would make a point of getting close to the union organizer, doing favors for him, running errands, driving him here and there. He would, in some cases, start the organizing in the shop to smoke out workers who were favorable to unions.

In a shop with an established union, he'd make a beeline for union office. His preference would be president, or recording secretary, where he would have access to files of the names of union members, correspondence, and other papers. But otherwise he'd settle for a lesser office, such as sergeant-at-arms, committeeman, or volunteer organizer. Anything to gain the trust and support of the workers. That had a twofold purpose. Even if suspicion fell on him, eventually, it would have the effect of throwing confusion and chaos into the organization, which was the basic objective of the spy, the agency, and the company.

This kind of fellow stayed at a shop only as long as it took to disrupt organizing or ruin a union. Then the agency would send him on to another company to do the same job there. His spy pay, in addition to his plant wage, might be ten or fifteen dollars a week plus small expenses, such as what he spent for union dues, money he put out buying workers a few beers in order to ingratiate himself, or contributions to a shop collection taken up among the workers for someone who had a death in the family or a family member seriously ill. All such expenses went down on the voucher and were reimbursed by the agency.

At the same time, the spy's activities, especially if he got going on them fast, soon after he hired in, could arouse the suspicion of experienced volunteer organizers in the shop. Some spies would be very anxious. The quicker they got into a union post, the more valuable they were to the agency—and then they

108

would qualify for a couple of extra dollars a week. The agencies received big money from the corporations but they paid their professional spies peanuts. Nevertheless, the spies would be so eager for even a small amount of added income that they might move too rapidly, thereby bringing themselves under scrutiny.

There were other clues. The professional was usually an unmarried man. He would live in a boarding house. He would be bumming around. His record of former employment might not hold up. Either he hadn't worked where he said he did—or something had gone wrong with the organizing or the union framework in the shop from which he had come and there had been reason to wonder about him, particularly if he left suddenly under mysterious circumstances. Sometimes, if he hired on as a supposedly skilled man, it was obvious that he didn't know his job. But still the company didn't fire him. That could be a tipoff.

VIII On January 23, 1937, as the evidence on the forty agency spies was being presented in testimony by Matles before the La Follette Committee, the agency chiefs were in the hearing room. They had been subpoenaed. They couldn't get out of appearing. The Metal Trades Association, the Corporation Auxiliary Company, the Pinkerton Agency, the Railway Audit and Inspection Company, all were represented by their top brass. At one point the head of the Metal Trades Association entered an objection: He said that his employees were "operatives," and that he did not relish hearing them described over and over as rats, finks, and stoolpigeons. Senator Thomas, presiding at the time, asked the young organizer witness if he could find some more appropriate language for the undercover operatives. Yes, the organizer replied, he thought he could. Would "cheesehound" do? The spy-agency chiefs did not appear to like it any better.

But what really got them were the affidavits. They squirmed when such material was read into the record. For example:

"John Mohacsi, being duly sworn, deposes and says":
> That I reside in Astoria, Long Island. The following statements are made of my own free will and accord.

109

On or about ... 1935 ... I answered an advertisement in the *New York American*, calling for an experienced machinist. I received a letter on the letterhead of the Atlantic Production Company asking me to come for an interview. I was interviewed by a Mr. G. C. Carter ... who stated that his was a firm of consulting engineers, and that if they placed me on a job I would have to report as to the conditions existing in the plant. I was also given a literacy test.... The job was with the Worthington Pump Company at Harrison, New Jersey. I was to be employed as a tool maker at 78 cents an hour. In addition to this, I was to get $50 per month from Carter for my reports to the Atlantic Production Company....

I was to make reports concerning the type of men I was working with, whether any of the men were constantly complaining about conditions, to get to know what my fellow workers were thinking about, and their attitude toward their pay and working conditions. I was also told that when I incorporated any of the complaints of the men I was to make sure to state the name of the man. I was told to report what I see and what I hear.... I was given a letter to Mr. Bennet, General Manager of the Worthington Pump Company, and was in turn turned over to the Employment Manager....

On or about January 4, 1936, Pat Stewart sent me a letter to come in to see him.... When I came to the office I noticed that the name of Atlantic Production Company was no longer on the door and there appeared the name International Auxiliary Corporation. At this time Pat Stewart told me that he wanted me to join the union, which was organizing at the plant. He handed me the application card of the Tool, Die and Metal Workers Union, which later became affiliated with the International Association of Machinists, Local 1560. He told me that I was to join up with the union and to make detailed reports of what went on at the meetings.

Twice a month I would send in detailed reports on the meetings of the union. On or about October, 1936, I was instructed by the International Auxiliary Corporation

110

not to hand in any more reports on union meetings but to continue only with my reports concerning plant activities. I was instructed not to mention the union meetings in my daily reports. On or about January 4, 1937, I was called into the office by Stewart and I filled out a card resigning my position with the International Auxiliary Corporation. I was then instructed to sign a new contract of employment for handing in of reports to the Worthington Pump Company. I was to receive the same amount of pay but it would come directly from the Worthington Pump Company. All of my reports and activities were to continue in the same way, being supervised by Mr. Stewart of the International Auxiliary Corporation. And there was no change in the manner or place to which I was to send my reports.

After I was contacted by the agent of the La Follette Committee, I called up Mr. Stewart on January 20 and informed him of same. He ordered me to discontinue my work and to resign my position with the Worthington Pump Company on January 23, 1937.

This was the affidavit of a professional spy, whose first job assignment was at Worthington Pump. He knew what he was doing right from the start. Hired professionally, he accepted with his eyes wide open. He wasn't hooked in as an innocent.

IX   Others were, however—such as National Metal Trades Association operative G-321. That's how he appeared in the committee files. The reports of G-321 dealt with the General Electric plant in Bloomfield, New Jersey. A careful study of the reports indicated that G-321 worked in the tool room. But, beyond that, no clues. Reports and vouchers not available. A handwriting check couldn't be run on this spy.

The key union man in the tool room was a little Scotsman, Walter Mugford. Walter, and the union organizer gathering material for the La Follette Committee, went down the list of all the tool room fellows. Every man's history and conduct was reviewed. By a process of elimination, the list narrowed to a single possibility. But it seemed incredible that old-timer George Nelson and operative G-321 were one and the same.

Nelson wore the twenty-five-year membership pin of the International Association of Machinists. He was a skilled tool and die maker, a quiet man, respected in the shop. Nelson held no office in the union and had never aspired to do so. He was a long-time resident of Bloomfield, where he lived with his family in a modest frame house which he owned, free and clear of mortgage. All in all, he fitted none of the specifications for the type of worker who gets sucked into spying. While the organizers had most of the forty spies under suspicion for a long time, this was not so in the case of Nelson. His type of informer was almost never under susupicion.

Could it be possible that the circumstantial evidence developed by Walter Mugford and the organizer was pointing in an entirely wrong direction? It would be a terrible thing even to raise the question of spying in the case of an innocent man. On top of that, to do so would finish the union in the shop. The toolmakers would never forgive such an error. Somehow, an extremely careful move had to be made to establish any definite connection between G-321 and George Nelson.

An examination of the weekly reports of other operatives showed that they were generally made out and mailed to the agency each Friday or Saturday. La Follette Committee investigator Felix Fraser, together with union organizer Matles, decided on a plan. One Friday, after work, Fraser and Matles went into Nelson's neighborhood. The investigator stationed himself close to the frame house. The organizer located the nearest mailbox and took up a position there. From Fraser's vantage point he could see the Nelson family eating dinner. When the meal was over, Nelson sat himself down at a small table where he began typing something.

Before long, the front door opened. Out came Nelson, an envelope in his hand. Fraser followed him along to the mailbox. Just as Nelson approached the box, Matles stepped forward, saying, "Hello, George." Nelson stood stock still. "George," said Matles, "I wonder if you'd mind opening up that envelope for us." Like a man in a trance, Nelson simply handed over the envelope, which contained nothing less than his weekly report to the National Metal Trades Association.

George Nelson, operative G-321, agreed to give an affidavit. What a pitiful story. After he got the whole thing off his chest, that was the end of him in the shop, the community, the United States even. He never showed up at the plant again. He put his home on the market. And when he sold it, Nelson, a citizen of this country, moved himself and his family to Sweden, never to return. He didn't want to face the working people he had been hooked into betraying. For a lousy ten bucks a week.

X The La Follette Committee's investigations were still continuing when its original fifteen thousand dollar funding ran out and it was necessary to return to the full Senate with a request for an additional appropriation. The committee justified the request by presenting a partial report to the Senate on results to date. Much of the partial report dealt with the Pinkertons, who didn't neglect the business of infiltrating spies into the shops but who specialized in supplying the "heavies"—strikebreakers, strong-arm men, goons. Senator La Follette, in addressing the Senate, said:

> Drawn from the underworld, a large number of strikebreakers have criminal records. An interesting example is Sam Cohen, alias Sam Goldberg, alias Chowderhead Cohen, alias Charles Harris, who testified before the committee. His preparatory work in industrial relations included a term in Atlanta for conspiracy, four years in state prison and four years in Sing Sing for burglary, and detention as a material witness in a notorious murder case. Out of thirteen strikebreakers furnished by Railway Audit and Inspection for the General Materials strike in St. Louis in 1932, seven were wanted by the police of other cities on charges including burglary, forgery, larceny, inciting to riot, and assault. . . .
>
> That industry should be permitted to arm unscrupulous men under their own pay, gravely wearing the badge of the law, is startling. That there is allowed to flourish a

113

gigantic commercial enterprise in which employers collaborate with professional spies in assaulting citizens, because they exert their lawful right to organize for collective bargaining, is shocking to any true defender of constitutional government.

From your committee's still fragmentary inquiry in this field of its investigation, it is clear that espionage has become the habit of American industry. Until it is stamped out, the rights of labor to organize, freedom of speech, freedom of assembly, will be meaningless phrases. Men cannot meet freely to discuss their grievances, or organize for economic betterment. They may not even express opinions on politics or religion so long as the machinery of espionage pervades their daily lives.

What legislative means can be adopted by Congress to curb these anti-American practices will not be apparent until the custom is shown in all its ramifications.

The committee received an additional small appropriation, went ahead with its work and by 1939 had prepared a bill. On June 9 of that year, as hearings on the bill—labeled S. 1970—got underway in a Senate room, Senator La Follette addressed a witness:

"Will you proceed in your own way to make your statement concerning this bill?"

He was speaking to Matles—the organizer who had appeared on January 23, 1937, representing the International Association of Machinists. Now in 1939, he represented the UE, in which he held the office of Director of Organization. Matles stated:

On January 23, 1937, my testimony revolved around two points: the use of labor spies and labor espionage, and the use of strikebreakers and finks by a number of corporations who were either members of the National Metal Trades Association or clients of the Corporation Auxiliary Company. Two years have gone by. I now wish to show that the use of labor spies, strikebreakers and finks is still a common practice in our industry.

The UE Director of Organization referred to the experience of the union in that two-year period in conducting an organiz-

114

ing drive in plants of the electrical and machine industries. The drive covered about a quarter of a million workers. Among them were thirty-three thousand workers in forty companies which the La Follette Committee had previously found to employ spies and strikebreakers. Matles reported on the spying:

> One group within the forty companies definitely abandoned such activities. A second group professed to have done so. A third group, a powerful minority, continued to defy the Wagner Act, fired its old spies and hired new ones.

He then went on to provide details of three sample cases from the last group: Yale and Towne Manufacturing Company, Stamford, Connecticut; the Servel Electrolux Corporation, Evansville, Indiana; and S. W. Farber Company, Brooklyn, New York. Efforts by the UE to organize in these plants had run up against spies, provocateurs, and strikebreakers. He continued:

> I could cite many more similar instances to show that the labor spy, strikebreaker and fink still occupy a prominent place in American industry. But that is hardly necessary. We cannot wipe out a labor espionage and strikebreaking institution of long standing through publicity and investigation alone. The enactment of S. 1970, in the UE's opinion, will go a long way in accomplishing the desired result. This is so because employers who continue to employ oppressive practices against their employees: will be deprived by law from receiving Government contracts, loans and subsidies; compelled to pay substantial fines; given the choice of either obeying the law or of serving some time in jail; and discover that crime doesn't pay.
>
> Unless this legislation is enacted without delay . . . the practice of industry in employing spies, strikebreakers and finks will continue to flourish as in the past.

It did. The La Follette Committee bill to prevent such operations never became law. In the year 1939 time had run out for this kind of people's legislation to pass the Congress. The Dies Committee type of politician—southern Democrat or reactionary Republican—was getting back into control. The economic royalists, unable to repress the nationwide popularity of President Roosevelt, concentrated their millions and their election campaign propaganda on support for congressional and senate candidates they could count on. They were on the political warpath. The old story of a tremendously sophisticated political consciousness on the part of the corporate class had started to repeat itself. "Colonel" Frey's appearance before the Dies Committee in the late summer of 1938 showed how the political winds were being shifted by corporate pressure.

9
Winning Westinghouse and GM

I   Neither the corporations nor the AFL crafts were any match for the CIO in mass production industry under free Wagner Act conditions. Thus corporations from their perspective, and AFL craft leaders from theirs, were hell-bent on scuttling that New Deal law. Frey's well-publicized redbaiting of 1938 was only the opening blast in a long-range scheme by corporations and AFL crafts to split the ranks of industrial unionism.

The corporations hoped to save themselves and their treasuries from the militancy of rank-and-file industrial unions. The AFL crafts, on their part, dreamed desperately of recovering their preeminent labor movement status by bagging skilled workers in mass production industry. Both knew it couldn't be done at the plant gates, either by corporate strikebreaking or AFL craft union appeals to workers to sign up with them. Both were aware that the job required a complete change in the political climate of the country, which they had in mind to produce. In 1938, however, Frey's charges of communism failed to frighten the workers in the shops or the CIO leaders and unions. They had two answers for Frey—denunciation of his tactics and continued concentration on the job of organizing the unorganized.

Said John Brophy, Mine Workers veteran who had become director of the CIO:

> Redbaiting, lies, slanders, raising the cry of "Communist" against militant and progressive union leaders, is nothing more than a smokescreen for the real objective of the people that use them. The real objective is to kill the CIO, destroy collective bargaining, destroy the unity

of the organized and unorganized that the CIO is building through the nation.

Walter Reuther, then a young organizer and officer of the
United Auto Workers, made a comment on Frey's performance:
Now the bosses are raising a scare—the Red Scare.
They pay stools to go around whispering that so-and-so,
usually a militant union leader, is a Red. What the bosses
actually mean, however, is not that he is really a Red.
They mean they do not like him because he is a loyal,
dependable union man, a fighter who helps his brothers
and sisters and is not afraid of the boss. So let us all be
careful that we do not play the bosses' game by falling
for the Red Scare. No union man worthy of that name
will play the bosses' game. Some may do so through ig-
norance—but those who peddle the Red Scare and know
what they are doing are dangerous enemies of the union.

The truth was, as everybody knew, that CIO top leadership
welcomed the help of all in the historic campaign of organizing
workers in mass production industry. This included Communists, who were among those devoting tireless effort in the front
lines of the struggle. The fact that Communists constituted
only a small fraction of the mighty army of CIO organizers did
not deter John Frey, Martin Dies, and his Un-American Committee from using this fact to whip up a Red hysteria in an
attempt to destroy the CIO.

II Frey's testimony, picked up at once by the
corporate enemies of industrial unionism, was broadcast to
workers and general public. The National Association of Manufacturers, monopoly's super propaganda arm, reached into the
till and financed the printing of a pamphlet in an edition of 2
million. On the cover was a caricature of John L. Lewis grip-
ping a picket sign inscribed: "Join the CIO and Build a Soviet
America." Copies went into mass production plants throughout
the country. Newspapers and news magazines, the reading matter of many working people, had a field day with Frey's stuff.

118

The mass media gave his work stunning display. Front pages, headlines, feature articles, editorials, and columns provided showcase after showcase for material based on what he had told the congressional committee.

CIO leaders and unions, unperturbed, went ahead with plans to hold their founding convention in the fall of 1938. The Committee for Industrial Organization—the first CIO—would be converted at that convention into the Congress of Industrial Organizations, a new house of industrial union labor. The leadership wasn't sidetracked by the Red Scare. Everybody stayed on the CIO train heading for further organization of the unorganized in mass production industry. When the delegates assembled at Pittsburgh in November of 1938 for the first constitutional convention of the CIO, they represented forty-one affiliated unions and "organizing committees" with more than 4 million members.

A million of these belonged to the eight unions whose leaders, three years before, had begun their fight for industrial unionism within the AFL. The other 3 million were in the young industrial organizations which had cracked the open shops of mass production. Their delegates predominated at the convention. Youth was their trademark. In the delegation representing the UE—by now the fifth largest union in the CIO—all the rank-and-file leaders were in their twenties or early thirties with only one exception, who was just over forty. Differences in age, however, were insignificant. Unity on the principles of industrial unionism made the old-timers, and the youth, one in spirit.

Together, they declared these principles: "To bring about the effective organization of the working men and women of America regardless of race, creed, color or nationality ... and to unite them for common action into labor unions for their mutual aid and protection." Furthermore, in reference to the people of the country as a whole: "To protect and extend our democratic institutions, and civil rights and liberties, and thus to perpetuate the cherished traditions of our democracy." These principles had been applied, and were being applied, in the field of economic and political action. In organizing. In campaigning. They had built the CIO.

III   John Lewis of the United Mine Workers, Philip Murray of the Steel Workers, and Sidney Hillman of the Amalgamated Clothing Workers were the logical convention choices to fill the three top offices of the Congress of Industrial Organizations. Lewis as president; Murray—formerly of the Mine Workers and now chairman of the Steel Workers Organizing Committee—as one of two vice-presidents; and Hillman as the other vice-president. That left open only the office of secretary. Delegates agreed that it should be filled on the principle of giving recognition to the new industrial organizations in mass production.

The largest of the new unions, the United Automobile Workers, was first in line. But the Auto Workers' delegation didn't wish to press its claim because the union was going through an early crisis in its leadership. Homer Martin, president by accident, and creator of such havoc that the membership was preparing to get rid of him, was no candidate the union's delegation had any interest in advancing even for the ceremonial position of CIO secretary. Next new union in order of recognition rank was the UE.

The three UE international officers, each serving an apprenticeship as a top union leader only because far more experienced UE unionists had moved aside in favor of youth, discussed how to handle the question of a UE candidate. They agreed that Emspak and Matles should meet with Lewis and ask him to support the president of UE for CIO secretary.

Lewis agreed to back Carey for the position. He advised discussions with the Auto Workers' delegation and also with Sidney Hillman of the Amalgamated Clothing Workers. Both responded favorably. Hillman, who volunteered to nominate Carey, said to the convention: "Of course there are many of the young organizations, and we could have nominated a great number of their leaders. But there is one organization that already stands out as having a most remarkable record of achievement."

Carey's nomination was seconded by UE director of organization, Matles, who said in part:

When we consider this nomination we can in no better

way express the difference between the old labor movement and the new labor movement. On the one side, a fear on the part of the leadership to trust the young people to go ahead; and on the other side, a leadership ready to push ahead the young people to become leaders themselves.

Carey made a brief acceptance speech, saying:
> Chairman Lewis, and leaders of the Congress of Industrial Organizations, I am certainly deeply grateful for this expression of your trust and confidence. I only disagree with one action of this convention. I cannot in my heart understand why I was given this great honor. But I assure you I appreciate it. And I pray that God give me strength to be worthy of your trust.

Another UE leader, General Secretary Julius Emspak, was designated to represent the union on the newly constituted CIO Executive Board, which would function as a ruling body between conventions, with each affiliated international union represented in its membership. As for the four officers, whose CIO positions carried no salary—they would be paid by their own unions—each was expected to continue devoting all time and attention to the organization whose members paid them for doing so. The weight of CIO leadership, however, as in the past, would be carried by John L. Lewis.

More than four hundred fifty delegates attended the CIO founding convention. They couldn't have been more confident of their future as militant industrial unionists banded together in organizations of a size and potential unequalled in the history of the labor movement. While none of the delegates had illusions about the nature of the opposition they faced, none had the slightest doubt that their solidarity and unity would overcome all obstacles. In just a few short years they had started to build a movement by now 4 million strong. What did it matter if mighty corporations, AFL craft union leaders, anti–New Deal politicians, and corporation-oriented newspapers and magazines were against them? Workers already organized in industrial unions had proven what could be done in the face of such opposition.

121

IV   As 1938 drew to a close the UE reviewed its two years of organizing struggle. From an industrywide point of view, the job was about half done. General Electric, even though under national contract, was less than 50 percent organized. Nevertheless, the very existence of the national contract was having its effect, serving as an attraction to workers in the unorganized GE shops, who could be assured of being covered by the contract terms if they decided to join in with the union.

Westinghouse, however, still following the Little Steel line of signing no contracts, was a different question. The legality of the Westinghouse position was being argued in the courts. There was no telling what the court's decision would be—or when it would be handed down. Throughout the Westinghouse chain, then, the UE pursued a course of persistent pressure in the shops. This was the course which the Westinghouse attitude—"We'll bargain but we will sign nothing"—made necessary. As time went by such Westinghouse policies proved a help rather than a hindrance to the union's organizing activities.

As in GE, about half the workers in Westinghouse had been organized—but without a contract or written grievance procedure. Thus constant stoppages, sitdowns, slowdowns, and piled-up grievances plagued production, as workers became steadily more militant and aggressive. So much so that the company began to get rumblings of dissatisfaction from various plant managers, who favored reaching agreements with the union if only to get on with the business of production. Westinghouse top officers had miscalculated. While Swope's GE agreement with the union had instituted orderly grievance procedure, the Westinghouse foremen and managers were up to their necks in snarls.

Frantically trying to arrive at memorandums-of-understanding on practices and policies, they were under daily siege by rank-and-file shop stewards and local negotiating committees. Since they were forbidden by corporate officials to sign even local agreements, every complaint had to be discussed separately. There was constant turmoil in the shops. Day by day the workers were consolidating their established locals—and organizing new ones. They gave Wesinghouse neither peace nor total war, just constant guerrilla action.

122

The UE strategy of "neither peace nor war" was being shaped and perfected primarily in the Westinghouse plant at East Pittsburgh, where a young organizer, Charlie Newell, had taken up the post of business agent at the request of the local. Local union leaders preferred to stay in the shop, working on the inside. But they felt they could use some full-time help. The international union, knowing Newell's talents as an organizer who could set up a first-class local union administration— and who would in short order be able to outmatch the management people in acquaintance with Westinghouse shop conditions—sent him to East Pittsburgh.

Charlie Newell, a skilled toolmaker, became one of the first volunteer organizers during the Metal Workers Industrial Union days in the early thirties. He was among those fired from Mergenthaler after being fingered by a company spy. As a shop worker he mastered the complexities of such matters as job classifications, job descriptions, wage-payment systems, incentive pay plans. Few in the union were his equal in this department.

The workers in the East Pittsburgh shop, not bound by a contract and operating a vigilant shop steward system that Charlie Newell helped establish, were free to conduct their flash stoppages and slowdowns. A rank-and-file committee, assisted by Newell, handled the bargaining. The people in the shop handled the on-the-job action. It was a combination that proved extremely hard for the company to deal with. All over the Westinghouse chain, the unsigned memorandums-of-understanding developed at the UE's East Pittsburgh organizing "laboratory" served as a model for workers who adopted similar guerrilla warfare tactics in their own shops.

V   Another "young veteran" of the UE, twenty-nine-year-old Ernie DeMaio, was on assignment in Ohio territory controlled by the electrical division of General Motors. Success at GM's electrical division, the remaining objective of the UE's plan for organization of the major fortresses of the industry, appeared to be a long way off. Four of the five GM electrical manufacturing plants, employing a total of about twenty-five thousand workers, were located in Ohio—the two largest, Frigidaire and Delco, securely settled as open shops in the heart of the company town, Dayton. By the end of 1938, only one small GM shop, with about five hundred workers, contained a recognized UE local union.

GM's "community control" system—its domination of the economic and political power structure of Dayton particularly —was only one reason for the extraordinary problems posed to the UE. The La Follette Committee had reported that in 1935 alone GM had paid out $187,000 to agencies supplying spies to companies bent on keeping union organization from getting off the ground in their plants. For years GM had been one of the chief industrial employers depending—most effectively— on this technique. What it cost was chickenfeed compared to the amount which could be extracted from a company by a militant union. After the Wagner Act, and the disclosures by the La Follette Committee, GM did exactly what the UE representative described in his 1939 appearance before the committee. When Matles said that the practice of industry using spies would continue to flourish unless new laws were passed, his remarks were based in part on the UE experience with the GM electrical division plants in Dayton.

GM did give up hiring outside agencies to furnish spies, finks, and informers. Instead, the company set up its own internal system, assigning supervisors to the task of soliciting workers to act as undercover operatives. The UE didn't have to do any guesswork about what was going on. From time to time the company would slip up and make overtures to the wrong person—an honest worker who passed the news on to union organizers.

Ernie DeMaio, then, knew well what the UE was up against in Dayton where the General Motors electrical division apparatus held a tight rein on people. He himself had been involved in other seemingly impossible organizing battles. He began his apprenticeship during the Depression, when he was barely out of his teens, as a volunteer organizer in the ranks of the Metal Workers Industrial Union in Connecticut. The first UE budget of 1936 provided for hiring four organizers. DeMaio came on the staff at ten dollars a week.

Three years later, after considerable experience in Ohio,

124

DeMaio described the situation in that state to delegates at the fourth union convention in Springfield, Massachusetts, in September 1939. Speaking in favor of a motion to hold the next convention in Cleveland, Ohio, DeMaio said:

> There are approximately one hundred and twenty-five thousand workers in our industry in Ohio. There are twelve General Electric manufacturing plants and two GE service shops, only one plant organized. Two Westinghouse manufacturing plants and two service shops—one organized. Four General Motors electrical division plants, only one small plant organized.

That was the picture. The delegates voted to hold the next convention, September of 1940, in Cleveland.

VI The officers' report to the 1939 convention stated the situation:

> Many powerful groupings of monopolistic and financial might in this country have too long enjoyed almost kingly privileges over the lives and welfare of millions of ordinary people to be in any frame of mind to relinquish these privileges without a stiff fight.... But labor can match their energy with more energy, their skill with greater skill. And above all, we of the labor movement have that matchless asset: solidarity. We know that the hearts of every working man and woman are stirred by this basic solidarity, which goes far back into history and far forward into the future.

Energy, skill, solidarity—how were these to be combined in an organizing campaign against the entrenched opposition of the electrical manufacturing industry in Ohio? Conditions called for more than rank-and-file activity in the shops, more than one full-time UE organizer, skilled and resourceful as he was. Additional commitments by the international union had to be made. The UE assigned five young organizers to work with DeMaio in Dayton. Like him, they were all seasoned union men, though still in their twenties. Among them were Dick Niebur and Bob Kirkwood, veterans of the 1938 Maytag lockout. In fact, four out of the five had been trained as organizers by the St. Louis UE leader, Bill Sentner.

In Dayton, the GM electrical division's Frigidaire and Delco plants operated on a three-shift schedule, requiring organization plans directed toward each shift—and beyond that, toward the separate divisions and departments of the plant. Inside organizing committees were set up in every sector. At the same time, because of the company terror in the shops—direct pressures from foremen and supervisors as well as the machinations of the spy system—house-to-house visits to the homes of many hundreds of workers were made by rank-and-file volunteer crews assisted by the UE staff organizers.

All in all, a different kind of strategy was employed than that followed at GE Schenectady and Westinghouse East Pittsburgh. In those plants, volunteer rank-and-file organizers were in a position to carry the ball, largely, on their own. But not so in the GM electrical division.

VII
Ohio looked like a long-range proposition in the fall of 1939. But something remarkable occurred over the next twelve months—the union's organizing campaign in Ohio made a clean sweep of the GM electrical division plants. Labor board elections and union recognition had been won in the two key GM Dayton plants, Frigidaire and Delco, as well as at other of the company's electrical division plants in Ohio and elsewhere, employing a total of twenty-six thousand workers.

This was a high point. The last citadel of what, only three years before, had been the open shop industry of mass production electrical manufacturing, was finally organized. UE success, moreover, had not been restricted to GM. In Ohio, and across the nation, workers in shop after shop of another giant, General Electric, had entered the union, bringing about seventy-five thousand workers under contract. Six thousand of them were in the plant at Erie, Pennsylvania, last major stronghold of the company to be organized. Not more than five thousand GE workers, scattered here and there in smaller shops around the country, still remained outside the union.

Much the same happened with Westinghouse, the other

126

giant. Labor board elections won, union recognition secured—though still without written contract—in plants employing about fifty-five thousand workers. Just two major Westinghouse plants as yet unorganized—and in one of them a UE petition for a labor board election was pending. As for the general organizational record reported to the 1940 convention delegates: forty-six out of forty-nine elections won by the UE, three lost in contests with AFL craft unions. The number of workers involved in the losses was three hundred six.

Two major factors accounted for an organizing accomplishment which, all in all, could be fairly called remarkable. One was the UE's practice, as in Ohio, of placing carefully selected organizers on the scene to prepare the ground for seeking union recognition. The other had to do with economic developments which made organizational breakthrough possible. In 1940 the depression clouds hanging over from 1938 had begun to lift. Sad to say, from one point of view, they were not blown away by peaceful reform measures of the New Deal but by the production demands of the expanding Second World War, in which the American people were to be involved before many months had elapsed.

As orders for military supplies and equipment began to flow into the offices of the corporations, workers were notified to return to the job. Very soon they felt the pressures of another economic consequence of war, which diminishes unemployment while inducing inflation. The cost of living started to climb. In hundreds of shops of the electrical, radio, and machine industry, the UE had established local unions or union leadership groups. It was the pattern of the mid-thirties all over again, but on a vastly enlarged scale.

The objective conditions created by war production contracts and cost-of-living pressures, combined with the groundwork laid by the organizational perseverance of the union, produced the results reported to the 1940 convention.

VIII   Immediately after the convention, in October 1940, the UE set in motion a campaign to increase the

127

wages of workers in the electrical manufacture and machine industry on an industrywide basis. Previously, as organization progressed, the union had conducted such campaigns plant by plant or company by company. Now, with organization extended throughout the industry, with local unions consolidating, with the international union on a firm base, it became feasible to broaden the drive for wage increases and to bring the union's economic program to bear on the industry as a whole.

The year 1940 had been one of UE success. But 1941 topped everything: renewal of the GE national contract; the first written national agreement with Westinghouse, and the first national contract with GM electrical division; also, national contracts with Phelps-Dodge and Electric Storage Battery; an agreement signed with Westinghouse Air Brake and Union Switch and Signal; more than one hundred sixteen thousand new members; and important wage increase patterns established in the industry, amounting to an annual total of $63.5 million—this apart from gains achieved in vacations, night bonus, and other improved contract provisions.

"The UE has made practical advances to a degree never before known in this organization," said the three international union officers in their report to delegates at the 1941 convention in Camden, New Jersey. They went on to summarize the particulars. Then they added a telling comment: "The wage drive in UE was coordinated with similar campaigns of other CIO unions in other major industries—and it was this general cooperation among CIO unions that helped materially in our own drive to secure these concessions from companies in our industry."

The UE, in short, was not alone. Its five-year steady advance from the founding convention of March, 1936—in organizing, striking, winning employer recognition, signing contracts, improving the welfare of the workers in its industry—were paralleled by comparable developments in other mass production industries, where new CIO organizations had been moving forward on a common front of industrial unionism.

Such cooperation contributed decisively to the success of the individual unions. Each had its own job to do for its mem-

128

bers and the workers in the separate industries. Each was self-governing, autonomous, free to determine its own economic and political strategies—and to have such respected by the sister unions. But together they were member organizations of a movement of militant industrial unionism, whose leadership had maintained a CIO unity and solidarity on which rested a truly amazing record of organization of the unorganized in basic mass production industry.

10
Millions Walk the Picket Lines

I In February 1941—the UE's peak year for or-
ganization and economic gains—international union President
Carey received a letter from the officers of a small local in
Pittsburgh, requesting an interpretation of the UE constitution:
Could the local bar members from running for local union
office on grounds of political belief or affiliation? Specifically,
"Nazis, Fascists, and Communists."

Simultaneously, another important development occurred in
the union. The officers of UE Local 201 representing workers in
the General Electric plants in Lynn, Massachusetts, were attending a meeting in New York of the union's GE Conference
Board. Led by Al Coulthard, the Local 201 representatives
made known to the leaders of other local unions in the GE
chain that they intended to place the name of one of their
members in nomination for UE president at the coming 1941
convention in September, opposing the re-election of Carey.
The Local 201 officers also informed the three top UE leaders
of their decision.

They explained that since 1937, when Carey had been asked
to remove himself from GE negotiations, they had repeatedly
urged him to apply himself to his day-to-day UE job and try to
learn it. Instead, they said, he had chosen to neglect his union
responsibilities, while using his title of CIO Secretary as a platform for headline hunting.

The Lynn local's choice for president of the UE was its own
president, Albert J. Fitzgerald, then thirty-four years old and a
charter member of the independent industrial union local in
Lynn GE since 1933. A Fitzgerald candidacy, proposed and
backed by a pioneer UE local from the second-ranking plant

130

in the GE chain, was bound to present a serious challenge to Carey. Everyone recognized it as such. And while it had absolutely no relevancy to the constitutional question suddenly thrown into the workings of the international union by the Pittsburgh local, Carey proceeded to make this question—which he and his supporters soon began to refer to as the "Commie issue"—the principal plank in his campaign for re-election as UE president.

There was immediate disagreement between the three top UE officers in February 1941 on the interpretation of the constitution called for by the inquiry from the Pittsburgh local. Carey took the position that the local union's plan, as proposed, did not violate the UE constitution. Emspak and Matles said it did. The three leaders submitted the question to the union's General Executive Board at its March 1941 meeting. Twelve of the thirteen members of the board—highest UE ruling body between conventions, made up of district presidents and the top officers—were present. They divided nine to two—the union president votes only in case of a tie—in favor of the constitutional position taken by Emspak and Matles.

Both groups, majority and minority, submitted written statements. Both these statements, dealing as they did with often-misunderstood matters of basic principle involved in rank-and-file unionism, are worth quoting from.

II   The majority statement declared:

When a worker joins the union, he joins as a member having full and uncurtailed rights equal to those of any other member. We do not have Class B status for any of our members. Merely to charge, or even to prove, membership in some political, religious or other organization, does not in itself justify disciplinary action. . . .

It is contrary to the democratic principles upon which our union, and our country, are founded, to deprive a member in good standing of rights and privileges because of his opinions or affiliations. In the elections held by local unions, each member has the full opportunity to submit facts and information to the membership for the purposes of showing that a candidate is, or is not, deserving of support. If after all this, the membership votes for such a candidate, then he must be accepted as the duly elected officer by both the majority that voted for him and the minority that voted against him.

These fundamental provisions which guard against discrimination among union members because of their skill, age, sex, nationality, color, religious or political beliefs or affiliations, are as old as the union itself.... Most of the founding groups of our union had a full and bitter experience with the kind of unionism which strayed from these principles. And it was exactly this experience which led to our constitution of 1936....

In view of these considerations we state: That the constitution, preamble, program and principles as outlined above constitute the foundation and source of strength of the UE. To tamper with them would be fatal to the union, just as tampering with the Bill of Rights in the national constitution would be fatal to the democratic institutions of the United States....

Any local by-law curtailing the rights and privileges of any member, on account of skill, age, sex, nationality, color, religious or political beliefs or affiliation, is inconsistent with and contrary to the international constitution of the UE and against the welfare of the union.

The minority statement did not endorse the barring of a member from office on political grounds. The two minority members said:

We heartily agree with that part of the international constitution which is recorded in the preamble and contained in the statement of the majority. We also agree that curtailment of the rights of members of UE will eventually lead to the suppression of the rights of members of the UE. We also agree that a member's religious or political beliefs should not be grounds for trial of a member by any organization.

Having said this, the minority went on to argue that, nevertheless, any UE local union had the right to put such a policy

132

into effect if its membership so desired. After the issue was decided, Carey told the board that his position was not subject to change unless and until the board's decision was upheld by the convention in September.

III   As soon as the board had made its decision, Carey and his supporters—inside and outside the union— charged that Fitzgerald's candidacy represented an attempt to impede UE local unions from keeping "Commies" out of local office. This turn of events could not help but remind many members of something Carey himself had experienced hardly more than a year previous. At that time, in January 1940, the Dies Un-American Committtee of the U.S. House of Representatives released its first report, based upon the 1938 "CIO Communist" testimony of "Colonel" John P. Frey and other witnesses. Carey—and one of his associates on the UE General Executive Board, Harry Block from the Philco local, a coauthor of the board's minority statement—were among those named as Communists in the Dies report.

On January 13, 1940, Carey replied to the report with a statement which included these passages:

> Our union is managed and administered by leaders who receive their mandate directly from the membership. . . . There is no control by Communist leaders in our international union. . . . Our union admits to membership without discrimination of any kind all those who find jobs in our industry. . . . We discriminate against no worker by reason of race, creed, color or political belief. . . . To deny any worker equality of participation would be a denial of democracy and the very life of unionism.

A vast majority of delegates at the September 1941 convention agreed with the Carey of 1940 and not with the Carey of 1941. They voted 792 to 373 in favor of the recommendation of the convention's constitution committee to uphold the General Executive Board decision on the question of constitutional interpretation raised by the Pittsburgh local union. They also voted—on the third day of the convention, customarily set aside

133

for election of UE top officers—for a new international union president, Lynn Local 201's candidate, Fitzgerald. He had been nominated by Al Coulthard, who described himself as a "comparative old-timer in this movement," member of one of the original seventeen UE local unions. Said Coulthard:

> No one man, no two men, no two men or women, but literally hundreds, have built our organization to what it is today.... "Minor-Leaguers" we are, of a rank-and-file organization. Albert J. Fitzgerald is just one of our "minor-leaguers." ... And I hope ... that we will always be "minor-leaguers," with control from the bottom to the top and back to the bottom.

Fitzgerald, who had served in Local 201 first as a rank-and-file member, then shop steward, then local treasurer, next local president—and who, at the time of his election to top office in the UE, was also president of the union's New England district —received 635 convention delegate votes. Carey, 539. Julius Emspak was nominated for reelection as UE secretary-treasurer by Leo Jandreau, business agent of GE Schenectady Local 301, Emspak's home local union. Carey seconded the Emspak nomination, saying: "I think I know Jules better than any delegate in this convention. I've had the pleasure of living with him and working with him." (Carey was referring to the period when he and Emspak, elected in 1936 as chief officers of the new UE, both then unmarried young men, had roomed together in New York.) "I sincerely hope," Carey went on, "that Jules Emspak receives the unanimous vote of this convention to assure the good continuity of the splendid organization we have all played a part in building."

Emspak's reelection was unopposed, as was that of Matles as UE director of organization. At Matles's suggestion, the delegates endorsed Carey for reelection to the post of secretary of the CIO. Not long after the convention, Fitzgerald, Emspak, and Matles visited CIO president Philip Murray in Atlantic City, where he was recuperating from an illness. In the presidential elections of 1940 John L. Lewis had broken with Roosevelt and supported Wendell Willkie for president. When Roosevelt was reelected, Lewis quit as CIO president and

134

Murray agreed with great reluctance to succeed him. Although Lewis proposed his old friend and protégé in the United Mine Workers as his CIO successor, their differences over Murray's support for Roosevelt left lifelasting scars on their association. Indeed, Murray's career as CIO president, haunted as he was by the huge phantom of Lewis, took turns that could only be explained by the shadow of Lewis upon him.

In Atlantic City the three UE officers advised Murray of the union's position in favor of Carey's reelection to the CIO secretaryship. And they urged the CIO president to help Carey find himself as a trade union leader by providing him opportunity to learn, under the experienced guidance of Murray, the things Carey had neglected to acquire during his five years as president of the UE.

IV At the September 1941 convention the officers' report to the delegates, as in the past, had been submitted jointly by Carey, Emspak, and Matles. While it dwelt primarily on the extraordinary advances of the union, and its plans for pressing forward, the report also contained some observations on serious events attendant upon developments of the Second World War. No one could foresee that three months later the attack of imperialistic Japan upon the U.S. military base at Pearl Harbor in Hawaii would occasion the country's entry into the war as a combatant. But already the deep involvement of the United States in the fight against fascism made it essential for the UE officers, in their convention report, to draw attention to significances affecting the labor movement and all the nation's people.

In June 1941, Hitler had ordered his mechanized Panzer divisions into action against the territory and people of the Soviet Union. The Carey-Emspak-Matles report referred to previous differences among the American people on attitudes to be taken toward the war in Europe. It summed up these differences by stating:

> Some said that the Governments of Great Britain and the United States, working in concert, would be able to

defeat the Axis powers [Nazi Germany, Fascist Italy, and Imperial Japan] without finding it necessary to include the Soviet Union in their alliance. Others said that, on the contrary, no alliance of powers from which the Soviet Union was excluded could be either stable or strong enough to crush Fascism.

Events, the report went on to say, had rendered these disagreements moot. They had lost all practical meaning. The report continued:

> Today there is no longer any basis for continuation of such a difference in opinion. ... Now, as before, each man and woman is fully entitled to his or her own opinion, including the opinion that he or she "was right all along." Only time and history can provide a really accurate answer to this question.

The officers mentioned in their report those groups which had previously differed:

> Certainly [they] now agree that the united might of *both* the British and the Soviet Governments, *backed by the United States and supported most of all by that hatred for Fascism which is bred in the bone of every worker*—such a combination can hardly fail to rid humanity once and for all of the very fountainhead of world Fascism, the Nazi Government of Germany.

The officers' recommended policy was approved by the 1941 UE convention delegates. Two months later the CIO convention approved a similar policy. The UE delegates also affirmed other sections of the report dealing with the course of action the union should pursue in guarding the rights and welfare of workers. The cause of "national defense" could well be used by employers and their agents in government as an excuse for ganging up on freedoms and conditions which CIO unions had struggled successfully to achieve. "We oppose and regard as injurious to the people of the United States," the officers' report stated, "all proposals in Congress which limit or curtail in any way the right to strike, or which impose compulsory arbitration."

136

The convention-adopted report took a stand against "premature intervention" by government mediators "for the purpose of diminishing the benefits that employees might gain through collective bargaining"; it urged labor representatives on wartime government mediation boards not to sign any recommendation which the CIO, or a CIO union, "deemed unjust or injurious"—and to condemn the use of the Army or the draft apparatus "to coerce working men into acceptance of unjust and unacceptable conditions of employment."

On the war itself, the report concluded by saying that "It is labor which will fight the hardest and the longest" against fascism. No idle rhetoric. In the following four years—from December 7, 1941, Pearl Harbor Day, to August 16, 1945, V-J Day—more than two hundred thousand members of the UE, among them many local union officers, union organizers, and an international union officer as well, served in the armed forces. The leadership situation in the organization during those years recalled words of the UE director of organization spoken as far back as the September 1939 convention, a few days after the Second World War began in Europe.

Remarking at that 1939 convention that the young leadership of the UE was "practically the greatest asset" of the organization, Matles reminded the delegates that this happened to be the case because old-timers had let "young fellows come to the front and finish the job that they, the older fellows, started." Entirely proper—the UE officer said—under the circumstances. But these seemed likely to be changed by the unpredictable demands the war might make on young men of the United States. And, he added, "we don't have a man on our organizing staff who is older than thirty years." In view of that, he suggested that it was essential for "our old-timers to polish up on the art of leading a union; and that the women among our membership be pushed ahead in these coming months—more than they have been thus far—in the leadership of our organization."

V   The preparations the union made in 1940 and 1941 for conducting its affairs in the event that necessity required U.S. participation in the fighting war, contributed in great part to the UE's record of performance during the almost four years of active war by the United States. New leadership came to the fore in the shops. The union won eight hundred thirty-one representation elections in plants employing about three hundred thirty-five thousand workers—and at the height of production and employment in the electrical and machine industry, UE contracts covered six hundred thousand workers in more than thirteen hundred plants. By 1943, the UE had become the third largest of all CIO unions, old and new, following in order of size the Auto Workers and the Steel Workers.

Among the most important of the eighteen hundred cases which the union argued before panels of the War Labor Board —machinery set up for handling wartime plant grievance and contract disputes between labor and management, wherein UE president Fitzgerald served as a representative of the CIO— was one which established the right of women workers to receive equal pay for equal work. When, in 1945, the board ordered GE and Westinghouse to cease pay discrimination against women workers, it marked a first breakthrough on this issue in mass production industry.

The positions on defeating fascism, and on guarding the rights and conditions of workers in the shop, which the union had adopted on recommendations made by the three top officers in their report to the 1941 convention, were maintained. President Roosevelt, Secretary of War Robert Patterson, and the GI newspaper *Stars and Stripes,* in their commendations of the war production record in the electrical and machine industry, attested to the caliber of UE support for the CIO "no strike" pledge. At the same time, when managements persistently tried to take advantage of that pledge, and of the patriotism of the workers, UE locals were compelled to engage in stoppages to put an end to violations of their contracts.

The corporations, however—historically accustomed to regarding war as their finest hour for profit opportunity—did not fail to take general advantage of their powerful position in the political economy of war production. Workers were in no such position, as the figures show. Their wages, governed by federal formula which corporate interests had a strong hand in fixing,

138

were not permitted to increase by more than 15 percent in the war years 1940 to 1945. Over the same period the cost of living went up 45 percent. Corporate profits were something else. In the six prewar years—1934 through 1939—they had aggregated $26 billion. But between 1940 and 1945, the war period, profits amounted to $117 billion—four and a half times what corporations reported in net profit during the preceding six years.

Much pressure was building up in the shops and in the homes of working class families. At war's end, August 1945, it was inevitable that there would be an economic confrontation between industry and the organized rank-and-file workers of the United States, squeezed almost unbearably by the constantly expanding cost of living. Industry's attitude in that confrontation was made explicit in November 1945 at the White House Labor-Management Conference called by President Harry Truman. (After the death of President Roosevelt in April 1945, Vice-President Truman succeeded him.) CIO proposals for immediate wage increases to make up the 30 percent loss in real wages and a demand for firm price controls across the board, were defeated by the combined votes of corporation executives and representatives of the AFL.

Already, the overwhelming sentiment for economic relief coming up from the rank-and-file of the three major CIO unions—Auto Workers, Steel Workers, and UE—had led to consultations among the union leaderships. In September, a UE national wage policy conference in Cleveland, attended by representatives from all local unions, approved a demand for a $2-a-day increase in wages. The Steel Workers were also pressing the $2-a-day demand. The Auto Workers in General Motors, headed by union vice-president Walter Reuther, demanded a 30 percent increase.

The $2-a-day demand of the UE and Steel Workers worked out to 25 percent in electrical manufacturing and 24 percent in steel. The flat $2-a-day demand of the UE and Steel Workers meant the same cents-per-hour increase for all workers, skilled and unskilled, while a percentage increase in the Auto Workers meant no uniform cents-per-hour increase for all workers.

Differences in the type of wage increase demand, however,

were insignificant as compared with the fact that organized workers in all three basic mass production industries were moving into a common struggle for a measure of economic justice—which they aimed to extract from the largest, richest and strongest corporations in the country.

VI   On November 21, 1945, the first strike in mass production industry began, when the Auto Workers under the leadership of vice-president Reuther shut down the auto plants of General Motors. Two CIO unions held contracts with General Motors. The Auto Workers represented the company's employees engaged in producing automobiles, while the UE contract covered workers employed in the GM electrical division, which produced refrigerators, electric motors, and other electrical equipment. At the time that the Auto Workers strike was launched, both the UE and the Steel Workers were approaching the critical stage in their negotiations with corporations in their industries.

On December 13, 1945, at plants of General Electric, Westinghouse, and the electrical division of GM, UE members voted by a seven to one margin for "strike action if necessary to win our demands." (The balloting was conducted by the government under the provisions of the wartime Smith Act.) GE and GM's electrical division came up with identical and unacceptable wage offers to the UE, while Westinghouse made no wage offer at all. The GE proposal to UE was presented in the following fashion:

One cold winter day in New York, not long before Christmas, the three top officers of the UE walked down the street from the union's headquarters to the GE tower on the corner of Fifty-first Street and Lexington Avenue. They had received an invitation to meet with GE president Charles E. Wilson, lately returned to the corporation from Washington where he had served as vice-chairman of the War Production Board. The UE officers found him at ease in the executive suite on the 45th floor. Wilson was seated at his desk, relaxing under the rays of a sun lamp. He told the union officials that GE was prepared to make an offer.

140

"The offer," said Wilson, "is ten percent or ten cents an hour." The UE officers reiterated the union's demand for a $2-a-day increase. Wilson made clear there was no room for discussion. The GE offer was being presented on a "take it or leave it" basis. "Mr. Wilson," said Emspak, "in that case we'll just have to leave it." The three officers bade Wilson good day and left him sunning himself. The meeting had lasted not more than thirty minutes.

The same 10 percent or 10 cents an hour offer was also made to the UE by the electrical division of General Motors and was rejected. Then the UE's strike coordinating committee, made up of members of local unions from Massachusetts to California, began final preparation for a test of strength between two hundred thousand workers and the three great electrical manufacturing companies. A strike date was set: after the Christmas and New Year holidays, January 15, 1946, 5:00 A.M.

In the meanwhile, President Harry Truman, making last-minute efforts to resolve the situation in the steel industry, recommended to the corporations and the Steel Workers a wage increase of 18½ cents an hour—$1.48 a day. (In 1972 dollar value the 18½ cents was equal to 41½ cents.) Steel Workers and CIO president Philip Murray first advised the Auto Workers and the UE of his union's intention to go along with the 18½ cents. He then announced this publicly. U.S. Steel, leading corporation in the industry, promptly rejected the Truman recommendation.

General Motors also turned down a wage increase recommended by a presidential fact-finding panel in the auto strike. Reuther declared that the panel's finding for a 19½ cent an hour increase was a complete vindication of the union's position. The state of UE negotiations remained unchanged. General Electric and the electrical division of General Motors continued to stand pat on their initial offer: 10 percent or 10 cents an hour. Westinghouse had still not made any offer.

The steel industry's rejection of the 18½ cents, and Murray's acceptance of that figure for the Steel Workers, had established the wage pattern ceiling—and the unions would now have to fight to reach that objective. On January 15, 1946, two hundred thousand UE members set up their picket lines across the nation at plants of General Electric, Westinghouse, and the GM electrical division. A week later, January 21, eight hundred thousand Steel Workers shut down the steel industry.

The CIO at that point was less than ten years old, five of those years spent in abnormal national wartime conditions. The three young organizations of workers in basic mass production were not only embarking on an action unprecedented in their experience—but also unprecedented for its scope and scale in American industrial history. How would they measure up?

VII The UE rank-and-file Strike Coordinating Committee, with every local union represented, concerned itself in late 1945—while negotiators kept vainly trying to secure a satisfactory settlement from the companies—with plans and preparations for the great strike. International union organizers, assigned well before the deadline to all plants in the chains of GE, Westinghouse, and the GM electrical division, were helping local unions to get themselves ready. Mass membership meetings discussed the issues. Local executive boards set up essential committees: picketing; strike kitchen; welfare; food for strikers' families; publicity and community relations; fund-raising; education; and entertainment.

Came the dawn of January 15. In New York UE headquarters—the old Vanderbilt townhouse on East Fifty-first Street just across from St. Patrick's Cathedral—word was anxiously awaited from the field. The organizers assigned to the plants across the nation were due to start sending daily reports —"a brief summary of the situation"—the moment the workers went out. Among the first received was that from UE Locals 506 and 618, General Electric, Erie, Pennsylvania. Dated January 15, 1945, it read:

> Picketing was scheduled to start at 6 A.M. but before 6 A.M. several hundred pickets had assembled at the various gates. As additional pickets arrived, they joined the moving lines. The temperature was down to twelve degrees with a strong wind. Fires were lit almost at once where pickets could warm themselves.

142

There are six picket lines covering all entrances on 24-hour schedules, with pickets on duty in eight three-hour shifts, a picket captain patrolling each gate and two picket lieutenants on each line. Mass picketing for one hour 7 A.M. to 8 A.M. and from 3:30 P.M. to 4:30 P.M. Tomorrow all committees will meet. The executive board will meet daily. Present arrangements also call for weekly membership meetings.

This was typical of the reports flowing in: Local 283—"All picket lines good"; Local 310—"About 200 pickets on duty"; Local 923—"Plant completely closed down"; Local 901—"Strike solid"; Local 301—"Morale good"; and so forth. Soon the reports began to contain news of a broader nature, reflecting the support the strike was receiving—in great part because of the active work of the local union committees—from people in the communities. A few samples of such reports:

"Beginning Monday we start getting hot lunches from restaurants we have contacted"; "Delegation of war veterans and local union officers went to see our congressman yesterday"; "Food committees doing good job supplying local union with food to distribute"; "Preparations being made for Town Hall meeting—mayor has agreed to act as chairman"; "Committee visiting merchants, businessmen, chamber of commerce—about forty women working on membership mailing—arrangements made for fifteen-minute radio program each Saturday"; "Veterans committee planning special picket duty in uniform"; "Today had meeting of about forty black members, held on same basis as meetings of vets, women, salary workers, etc.— good response—all volunteered for activity"; "Meeting tomorrow with township trustee, Red Cross, Salvation Army, to arrange for relief." So it went, in all sectors.

Nor was other trade union work neglected—such as organization of the unorganized. One report from an organizer in the field included this note: "Strike committee issued statements to press, and published stories in weekly strike paper, appealing to plant office workers to support strike and organize for their own protection." Then there were a few unusual communiqués, with a human, not to say humorous, touch: "Called to see police chief on matter of striker getting upset at city hall on relief application. Chief asked about our relief setup and ended up by donating $2 to our fund." And this one: "The only committee laying down on the job is entertainment. We are reorganizing it. Picket songs are going fairly well and we will have practice in singing at headquarters all next week to familiarize leaders with the songs." This, also: January 21: "Farmers in Schoharie County have decided to bring in a car-load of food and a live cow." January 23: "Today the farmers from Schoharie County delivered the live cow on the picket line and this event received quite a bit of publicity."

Farmers, war veterans, other labor unions, merchants, city councils, state legislators, congressmen, and senators, all played important roles in rendering assistance to the strikers in combat on the picket lines. Among city governments endorsing the UE strike and its objectives were those in Mansfield and Cleveland, Ohio; Lynn, Pittsfield, Springfield, Salem, and Taunton, Massachusetts; Bridgeport, Connecticut; Pittsburgh, Pennsylvania; Newark, New Jersey; Rotterdam, New York; Fort Wayne, Indiana; Fairmont, West Virginia; and Ontario, California. A group of fifty-five U.S. senators and congressmen said in a special public statement: "UE strikers deserve full moral and financial support in their grim struggle for a substantial wage increase and for a decent American standard of living."

VIII   The UE had struck the three giants of the industry—but had left RCA and most of the independent electrical companies operating. The Auto Workers, with General Motors shut down, kept its members on the job at Ford and Chrysler. The Steel Workers had closed down just about every mill and fabricating plant in the country, with the exception of one small steel company, Kaiser Steel, where the Steel Workers had settled for 18½ cents two days before the steel strike began.

Each union had its own reasons for adopting a particular strike strategy. In the case of UE, for instance, depending as it did on voluntary strike-support contributions rather than an accumulated strike-benefit fund, the members remaining at work would provide a financial base for assistance to the GE, Westinghouse, and GM electric division strikers.

At the same time, the UE hoped to create openings for settlement possibilities in nonstruck companies. The UE figured that Sarnoff of RCA might just recall the year 1936, when his policies had provoked a costly strike while RCA's chief competitor, Philco, was piling up profits. Perhaps now, having had ten years to ponder that experience, Sarnoff would consider stealing a march on his rivals, GE and Westinghouse, by settling with the UE before the strike enveloped RCA.

The first break in the 1946 CIO struggle came on January 26 in the auto industry, when Chrysler signed with the Auto Workers for 18½ cents. On the same day the Ford Motor company settled with the union for 18 cents. The next day, January 27, RCA and the UE arrived at an 18 cent agreement. The settlements with three companies which had not been shut down put immediate pressure on those companies whose million and a half workers—in steel, auto and electrical manufacturing—were fighting it out on the picket line.

At once the UE entered into intensive negotiations with GE, Westinghouse and the electrical division of General Motors. For two weeks these companies still refused to meet the wage pattern. The first to agree to do so was GM's electrical division, which signed with the UE on February 9 for 18½ cents. The next settlement came in the steel industry. On February 15 U.S. Steel signed with the Steel Workers union for the 18½ cents which the corporation had rejected before the strike. That left the UE still on strike in GE and Westinghouse—and the Auto Workers on strike in GM.

When the Auto Workers began their GM strike on November 21, 1945—two months before the start of the Steel Workers and UE strikes—Reuther had hoped that by winning a substantial increase from the largest auto company a wage pattern would be set for the rest of the auto industry. This, however, did not materialize. GM dug in its heels and refused to break away from the corporate alliance which had determined to cut the CIO down to size. In January one million CIO steel and electrical manufacturing workers joined the fight on the picket line.

After the Auto Workers settlements with Chrysler and Ford, Reuther decided to hold out for the 19½ cents which the presidential fact-finding panel had recommended in GM. When the company once again rejected this demand, Reuther broke off negotiations. The UE, with the agreement of Murray and Reuther, arranged a meeting with top negotiators of GM. It was held at the William Penn Hotel in Pittsburgh. Present were GM vice-president Harry Anderson and Lou Seaton, director of labor relations; President R. J. Thomas and Reuther of the Auto Workers; CIO president Murray and CIO general counsel Lee Pressman; and Matles, UE. Reuther and the other union leaders pressed for the 19½ cents, proposing that one cent of this be used to correct inequities in the wage rate structure at GM plants. Harry Anderson would not budge beyond the 18½ cents.

Days later, Philip Murray met with General Motors president Charles E. Wilson. (Because the GM and GE presidents had the same name and middle initial, it became the custom to identify GM's Wilson as "Engine Charlie" and to call Wilson of GE "Electric Charlie.") Murray and "Engine Charlie" of GM reached an agreement which included the 18½ cent wage increase and some improvements in overtime and vacation provisions. Reuther, who did not attend the meeting, declared the settlement a victory for the GM workers and later in 1946 defeated R. J. Thomas for the presidency of the Auto Workers Union.

Despite his public expression of satisfaction with the outcome of the strike, Reuther was deeply disappointed and embittered. He blamed the Chrysler and Ford settlements made by his own union, and the settlements of the Steel Workers and UE with U.S. Steel and the GM electrical division, for the failure to get the additional one cent from General Motors. This episode was the first of a series of developments over the next few years that produced a complete break in the relationship between UE and the Auto Workers. The break lasted for more than two decades. It was not until the winter of 1969–1970 that Reuther and Secretary-Treasurer Emil Mazey met with Fitzgerald and Matles and agreed to join forces in another nationwide strike struggle against a powerful corporation.

146

IX   On the same day of March 13, 1946, that agreement was reached in the GM Auto Workers strike, the UE settled with General Electric for 18½ cents. Actually, the GE strike could have been ended earlier had it not been for "Electric Charlie" Wilson's attitude toward GE's women workers, all of whom, grandmothers included, he called "bobby-soxers." Wilson, in 1946, sought to reverse the wartime labor board ruling on equal pay for equal work that UE had won. He finally agreed to the 18½ cent increase for men but insisted on only a 15 cent increase for women. The UE's stand on 18½ cents for all workers so irritated Wilson that he attempted an end run around the union.

Unable to grasp the fact that CIO unions were independent and self-governing in their decisions, Wilson flew to Florida— where Philip Murray was on vacation—on a mission aimed at securing the intercession of the CIO president with the intractable UE. Murray phoned UE president Fitzgerald in New York, suggesting that perhaps the three UE leaders could come to Florida to meet with him and Wilson. Fitzgerald in turn suggested that if Wilson wanted to negotiate, he get himself back to New York where the UE rank-and-file negotiating committee was meeting with the GE vice-president. After Wilson's return, settlement was rapidly reached on the 18½ cent basis, "bobbysoxers" included.

On May 12, Westinghouse signed with UE for 19 cents. The UE strike in Westinghouse was the longest and the last to be settled. There too, inequities in the wage rates of women workers was the issue which required extra time on the picket line to correct. The fact that UE settled with GE for 18½ cents did not prevent the 19 cents settlement with Westinghouse, one cent of which was used to correct wage inequities on jobs employing mostly women workers.

The 1946 strikes spearheaded by the three large militant CIO industrial unions eventually involved close to 5 million workers in the country. The labor movement leadership provided by these unions, the strength which they demonstrated, the example they set, the community and political support they were able to rally, proved beyond question the power and potential

147

of rank-and-file industrial unionism. The large unions, indeed, once they had won their own wage increase battles, threw their resources behind the strikes which other workers were conducting.

Many striking UE local unions, as a result of the contributions received from UE locals and districts whose members continued working—as well as from sister CIO and AFL unions and from people in the communities—found themselves, at strike settlement time, with strike funds left over in their treasuries. Thus they were in a position to help others, which they did, as the great strike wave rolled on and on through the year. The solidarity of workers and their allies among the people gave industry pause, to put it mildly. The corporations had counted on assets which appeared to them more than sufficient to overwhelm the workers.

In the first place, they had the $117 billion in wartime profits, a comfortable cushion on which to ride out strikes. Their wealth was such, moreover, that they didn't mind committing a little of it for anti-labor propaganda purposes. General Electric and Westinghouse were two of the big spenders. The corporations' supreme general staff, the National Association of Manufacturers, reported laying out $2 million in the first two months of CIO strikes in mass production industry. It seemed, too, that the public would be in a receptive frame of mind for propaganda implying that greedy "strike-happy" workers were responsible for the failure of consumer goods—in short supply during the war—to appear on the market between V-J Day in 1945 and the start of the strikes in 1946.

When the UE countered such "public relations" efforts of the corporations by exposing—on the basis of firsthand reports from UE members working in GE and Westinghouse warehouses—that the companies before the strike were deliberately holding back on consumer goods deliveries to force the government to abolish price controls, it helped to spike that corporation propaganda gun. All along the line, industry's confidence received rude shocks, for reasons pointed out by the UE after all the battles were over and the agreements signed. Said the UE statement:

> The people are indestructible. Industry's carefully laid

148

postwar plans to break the union movement failed. The conspiracy failed because labor unions such as UE took the initiative and demanded the right to a living wage. This conspiracy failed because in the heat of battle, rank-and-file labor was united—the CIO, AFL, and Railroad unions in many communities worked together. The conspiracy failed because labor was not alone. The townspeople were on labor's side.

From its early postwar battles, labor not only emerged victorious. Labor emerged conscious of its own strength when it is united in concert with its friends. But labor is also conscious that the fight has just begun for the right to a decent job, a decent home, freedom from fear, for peace and security. Defeated in the first battle, profit-hungry big business continues its war against unions and the people. Other battles loom ahead.

PART TWO

SURVIVING

11
Cold War on the CIO

I   A diagram of developments in the American labor movement in the quarter century following the Second World War—developments severely testing the rank-and-file principles of the UE—would have to start with an event that occurred on a small college campus in the midst of the great strikes. On March 5, 1946, addressing an audience at Westminster College in Fulton, Missouri—home state of President Truman—former Prime Minister Winston Churchill of Great Britain launched the cold war with a call for a political and military buildup by "English speaking peoples" to contain communism. Truman, seated on the platform, indicated by his presence, and by a cordial response to the Churchill remarks, his endorsement of the cold war proposition, upon which U.S. foreign policy was soon to be exclusively based and domestic policy oriented accordingly.

At that time the UE, preoccupied as it was with its major strikes, nevertheless took occasion to issue a statement calling attention to the grave implications for working people—and the whole people of the nation—contained in the policies which Churchill advised and Truman appeared to accept. Said the UE:

> The working people of America through their unions are carrying on the greatest wage fight in the history of our country, to prevent the monopolists from depriving them of a decent standard of living. With the same determination we must take the lead in the fight to prevent American monopolists from dragging the world into war. We must fight to take control of our people's destiny out of the monopolists' hands.

The issue over which the nationwide industrial struggles of 1946 had been fought was really a very simple one: standard of living. What the workers needed to provide a decent living for their families—and what they only in part received—was the difference between a 45 percent increase in the cost of living during the years of war and a 15 percent increase in wages over the same period. They felt that corporations with reported profits of $117 billion between 1940 and 1945 ought to be in a position to afford a decent standard-of-living wage for working people. That was the whole issue of 1946. Nothing more.

Organized workers were able to extract from the coffers of the corporations about half of what, in all fairness, they had coming to them. They had to fight like hell to get that, launching massive strikes backed by the support of community people. But it was enough to set off an explosion in the chambers where executives were guarding every last cent of corporate wealth produced by the workers. You would have thought the CIO had dropped an atomic bomb on capitalism itself.

Nothing could have come as more of a godsend to their worried minds than the cold war. It furnished them, for one thing, with assurances of continued riches from government military contracts. No longer, as in the past, need industry depend entirely on hot war to make a financial killing. Cold war, as correctly estimated by financial and industrial leaders, could do just as well if not better. At the same time, a cold war atmosphere was perfect weather for industry to resume full blast the offensive against the CIO which they had vainly conducted on two fronts: against the Wagner Act in the halls of Congress and against organization of the unorganized by propaganda use of redbaiting to divide and weaken CIO industrial unionism's advance.

It must be kept in mind that the labor movement had barely begun the job of organizing. Two-thirds of American workers were still employed in open shops. The CIO threat, as the corporations saw it, came not only from the demonstrated ability of its cooperating unions to win wage increases by solid strikes. It came, even more ominously, from the evident possibility that militant rank-and-file industrial unionism, united in the CIO, would go on to eliminate the open shop from its historic place on the American scene.

II   "Other battles loom ahead," concluded the UE statement issued in May 1946, after settlement of the big strikes. By the end of the year they were looming larger and larger. Among those who sensed the amazing advantage suddenly presented to industry by the cold war views of Churchill and Truman was "Electric Charlie" Wilson, GE's president. In October 1946, with congressional and senate elections near at hand, he remarked: "The problems of the United States can be captiously summed up in two words: Russia abroad, labor at home."

The National Association of Manufacturers planned to attack the labor movement where it was weakest—in the political arena. In 1944 the CIO Political Action Committee had assisted in the reelection of Franklin Roosevelt for a fourth term. But with the champion of the New Deal dead and gone, and his foreign policy for peace and friendship among nations scrapped by Truman's adoption of a program of militarism and belligerence, industry's strategy of concentrating its influence upon a Congressional coalition of reactionary Republicans and southern Democrats began to pay off. Soon after the elections of November 1946, all members of Congress received a booklet entitled *Labor Monopolies*, the gift of one John Scoville, formerly with the Chrysler Corporation but in 1946 employed by the "Committee for Constitutional Government." This was a propaganda outfit financed by ultrareactionary manufacturers, among them the Pews of Pennsylvania (Sun Oil and Sun Shipbuilding) and the duPonts of Delaware.

Scoville took credit for coining the slogan "labor monopoly." Maybe so. At any rate it began to get plenty of play in the press, at about the same time that another slogan, "communist-dominated unions," reappeared in a revival of the 1938 charge that "Colonel" John P. Frey had leveled against the CIO. The National Association of Manufacturers and the U.S. Chamber of Commerce made no secret of their goal. They were out after legislation which would not just undo the Wagner Act but also serve employers as an instrument for stopping the CIO. For that purpose they were willing to spend more millions than had been shelled out in 1946 in an effort to break the strikes of workers in mass production industry. Money was no object.

155

III "In our country, the period since President Roosevelt's death, short as it is, offers us many contrasts in government policy." So ran a sentence in the UE's officers' report to the eleventh convention of the international union, which opened in Milwaukee on September 9, 1946. Six hundred seventy-nine delegates on hand, representing two hundred sixty greatly enlarged local unions, constituted a barometer of the union's organizing momentum in the year since the Second World War had ended. The great strikes in which the UE participated in early 1946, the unity among CIO unions, the militancy of the workers, and the popular support their cause received in the communities, all pointed in the direction of continued success in organizing the unorganized—the task for which the CIO was born.

By 1941, when the United States entered the war, the UE's plans for establishing the union in the major companies of the industry—GE, Westinghouse, General Motors electric division, and RCA—had been realized. Throughout the war, in a period of full production and employment, membership in the organized shops showed a deceptive expansion, as did the memberships of other CIO unions in basic mass production industry. For example, at war's end, in August 1945, the "book membership" of the CIO had attained a high of about 6 million. On paper that looked good. But the immediate trend was downward, as the postwar layoffs began. Within three months after the surrender of Japan more than two hundred fifty thousand workers in the electrical manufacturing industry lost their jobs. The same pattern appeared in other industries. Overall, of course, this was something on which the employers were relying to keep wages down, only to have their dreams disrupted by the solid strikes of the workers.

One of the shifts in post-Roosevelt government policy to which the UE officers' 1946 convention report referred had to do with employment. The report called for a comparison:

> Contrast the new Economic Bill of Rights proposed by President Roosevelt one year before he died, a proposal hinged upon the right to a job and the right to earn a decent living, with the White House labor-management

156

conference of last fall called by President Truman, at which the earnings of American workers were barred as even a subject for discussion.

In spite of layoffs, however, and in spite of the demands made upon the union's energies and resources by the 1946 strikes, UE organizing campaigns proceeded without interruption. With the organization in the giant companies substantially secured, the UE had conducted campaigns among the smaller companies and individual shops. More than three hundred of these, containing upwards of seventy-three thousand workers, were organized between September 1945 and the Milwaukee convention of September 1946.

Although such a postwar organizing record was unmatched by any other of the thirty-nine affiliated unions of the CIO, the UE was not engaging in self-congratulation. The union directed major attention to the broad political nature of industry's developing cold war assault upon the labor movement, the CIO particularly. "We find," said the officers' report to the delegates at the Milwaukee convention, "that we must work and solve our problems in a situation of strengthened reaction." The economic security and political freedom of the American people, the report pointed out, had been basic New Deal considerations: "But today the chief concern of the government is the nourishment of profiteers."

Then the report proceeded to describe the character and significance of the cold war in terms of the position which American industry occupied in the world and the tendencies of policy which it was exhibiting at home:

> Victory over fascist aggression has not brought peace and security to the world. Attacks against the common people are taking place.... Exploitation, starvation and famine are almost the rule rather than the exception. A year and a half ago, the power of America was directed mainly toward the destruction of fascism and the strengthening of democracy, while today world peace is being played with by power-politics based on the underlying threat of our monopoly of the atomic bomb...
>
> Morally and politically, fascism spells suppression and

157

corruption. However, big business interests not only had no quarrel with the political system of fascism as such, but, as history has proved, big business was linked with the parent of that system.... The shock troops of big business even now would just as soon see such a system instituted in the United States.

IV Somewhat the same theme—though elaborated in more general terms—was struck by CIO president Philip Murray in an address to the UE 1946 convention. He told the delegates:

You are meeting at a time when our country if not the world is going through a period of confusion and bewilderment.... In the course of the past eleven years, you have made many magnificent contributions toward the well-being of the people you represent.... I am quite sure that [at this convention] you will of necessity direct your attention to issues of major moment influencing the destiny of our country and the welfare of its people.... You are part of the CIO. Your decisions oftentimes influence the judgments of the national body because of the tremendous interest you manifest in the progress of the movement.

Murray spoke warmly of the "splendid support" the CIO and he personally had received from the UE and its officers, who, he said, "have sustained and maintained and fought for all national CIO policies." The CIO, he went on, had been built upon a rock of understanding and knowledge—knowledge of the problems of the people. "So let no enemy of the CIO glibly get by with the argument that they are ever going to be able to destroy a movement like this. It's not in them. It can't be done."

Most of the delegates knew well whereof Murray spoke when he mentioned enemies of the CIO. But no one knew better than UE president Fitzgerald, who served as a CIO vice-president and had first-hand acquaintance with the heat being turned on CIO leaders by professional anti-communists in the

158

Truman Administration—many of them bankers from Wall Street or ranking executives from large corporations—and by other elements in the society, not least among them churchmen of the same Catholic faith as Murray and Fitzgerald.

Said Fitzgerald, as he rose to thank Murray for his remarks to the convention:

> I think that if every member of this organization, every member of the labor movement, knew the obstacles which a labor leader of the type of Philip Murray has met ... harried and hampered on every side by his enemies, by the big barons of industry, the financiers and bankers, yes, sometimes by fakers within the organized labor movement—and other times by the gentlemen of the press, who have such peculiar ways of slanting stories. . . . I think if our membership knew those things they would have even greater appreciation than they have for the work that President Murray has been able to accomplish.

Fitzgerald concluded with a reminder that another American —Franklin Roosevelt—had "stood up under those same kind of attacks and faced those kinds of people." The UE president said "we know that CIO president Murray will have the courage, and the determination, to carry on with his work and defeat his enemies."

The personal note in Fitzgerald's remarks about Murray was somewhat unusual. But Fitzgerald, deeply concerned about the pressures that were bearing down on industrial unionism— menacing its forward progress in organizing and collective bargaining, posing dangers to solidarity within the CIO—had good reason to believe that much depended on the way Murray would go.

The labor movement had two general alternative choices for meeting its problems in what the UE officers' report called "a situation of strengthened reaction." Taking its cue from the militancy which rank-and-file workers had demonstrated in the great strikes of 1946—and from the victories won by unions working in concert—the CIO could decide to fight on its own ground, the ground of organizing the unorganized, of confronting industry as a united force, and of mobilizing the people politically against reaction. Or it could decide to give a little ground to the enemy by acknowledging a need to seek absolution from the "communist-dominated" propaganda with which the U.S. Chamber of Commerce, the National Association of Manufacturers, their agents in government and the mass media, the AFL craft union stalwarts, and other elements as well, were deluging the country in a cold war climate.

Crucial decisions would, no doubt, be made at the upcoming CIO convention in November. The UE leadership was hopeful that the still young forces of industrial unionism would decide to stick together, fighting on their own ground, letting nothing stand in the way of unity and aggressive organizing. Murray's attitude under pressure would be a key factor in the verdict the CIO would render on its future. That was why Fitzgerald spoke as he did at the UE 1946 convention.

V   On November 15, 1946, two days before the scheduled opening of the CIO convention in Atlantic City, Philip Murray called together the executive board of industrial unionism's house of labor. He appointed a special committee of six: Walter Reuther, recently elected president of the Auto Workers; Milton Murray, president, American Newspaper Guild; President Emil Rieve, Textile Workers Union; the Transport Workers president, Mike Quill; Ben Gold, president of the Furriers Union; and Abram Flaxer, president of the United Public Workers. Murray assigned this committee responsibility for working up a resolution on what he referred to, in his opening convention remarks, as "wild and wholly irrational statements . . . that this great big mighty trade union movement was communistically dominated."

Said Murray, further, in introducing the resolution prepared by the committee: "Propaganda disseminated throughout the nation, particularly in the newspapers, created in certain sections of our country a kind of hysteria over the subject. And in the course of the last congressional elections, many aspirants for public office, taking advantage of these representations, denounced and slandered this movement to win votes at the polls." The CIO president declared that the resolution, answering "all the villainous, slanderous abuses," would portray the CIO as a movement "interested in the logical aspirations of all true trade unionists in the United States of America."

Murray next, in a paraphrase of the language of the resolution on which he was about to request an immediate vote, said that the CIO "does not care to be bothered with, and it will not tolerate, interference not only from the Communist party, remember, but other political parties. . . . There should be no misunderstanding about that." The resolution itself, after preliminaries about the CIO goals of organizing workers to protect and improve their wages, hours and conditions of employment, contained this final paragraph:

> In pursuit of the principles set forth herein, and adopted by the CIO Executive Board, we the delegates to the Eighth Constitutional Convention of the Congress of Industrial Organizations resent and reject efforts of the Communist Party, or other political parties and their adherents, to interfere in the affairs of the CIO. This convention serves notice that we will not tolerate such interference.

The convention, at Murray's request, approved the statement without debate.

VI   Actually, the convention discussion on organization of the unorganized—the only subject to which UE delegates had ever addressed themselves on a CIO convention floor—amounted to a debate on the relevance of the "communistically dominated" question to the objectives of the CIO. In June 1946, when the CIO executive board decided to undertake an organizing campaign in the open-shop American South, the UE contributed one hundred thousand dollars to the cause. George Baldanzi, Textile Workers vice-president, was in charge of that union's southern organizing drive. He and the Textile Workers president, Emil Rieve, had been in the forefront of the effort to have the CIO pass a "resent and reject" resolution aimed at absolving the organization of the "communistically dominated" propaganda charges. They contended that they couldn't organize in the South unless the CIO so declared itself.

The first speaker in the discussion, UE director of organization Matles, said:

> I think those of you who know something of the organization which I represent will at least agree with me that we are getting our share of this propaganda in organizing campaigns. In the year ending in July 1946, the record shows that our organization participated in three hundred and twenty-one labor board elections. And 84.1 percent of those elections covering seventy-three thousand people were won by our organization. And by way of comparison, and since we always like to engage in friendly competition as far as organizing work is concerned, I would like to say that this percentage of UE victories constitutes the highest percentage secured by any labor organization in CIO or outside of CIO.

Matles, who was speaking on behalf of the UE delegation, remarked that "the damnable slander of communism as a line of propaganda against us started, to the best of my knowldege, on the same day the CIO was founded." After his mention of the UE's 1946 organizing record, in the face of the intensified "line of propaganda" in the postwar period—and the launching of the cold war—he went on to outline the union's position on the principles which had governed and should continue to govern the fundamental work of the CIO. He said:

> I am not here to kid you that this campaign of slander, and bigotry, and attacks upon our organization played no role. But I am here to state that the answer to that problem is the same as we have used in the early stages of our campaign. No one in our movement can hope to build his own organization by trying to outdo the American Federation of Labor or the company unions in bigotry and propaganda. . . . I am telling you from our own experience, when you are confronted from that angle you take on the fight without any compromises.
>
> And you take on the fight to organize simply on the proposition that this CIO movement of ours believes that all men are created equal—and we propose to fight

for that principle. . . . And if we continue to organize this movement of ours on that principle, then the overwhelming majority of the unorganized workers will rally to us. They will join us. And our ranks will be tremendously increased.

I am speaking on this question because, as far as I am concerned, nothing that this convention can do along philosophical lines will satisfy us. I am concerned about organizing the unorganized. And I am concerned to see the kind of program adopted by us, and the kind of cooperation instituted among affiliated unions of CIO, that will rekindle the enthusiasm which existed among us in '37 and '38—during the years of the greatest organizing effort. I say that is the answer. If this convention can accomplish that, if we are united, and fighting back, and if we ourselves do not indulge in doing or saying anything that will result in the loss of a single election by any CIO unions then the victories in labor board elections will be much greater than they are today.

I would like to say another thing here that may not be very popular. Our staffs that were engaged in organizing work in '37 spent fewer man-hours in the swivel chairs than they are spending today. I say we have to get out of the swivel chairs down to the factory gates—and give those people an organizing campaign that will bring results.

Of the eight or nine speakers who participated in the discussion on organization—the most extensive debate of the convention—none took issue with the remarks of the UE leader. CIO president Murray, closing the debate, spoke of the situation in the automobile, steel, and electrical manufacturing industries where hundreds of thousands had been laid off following the war's end. He said:

With respect to the organizing activities of the UE, it suffered substantial losses in membership following V-J [victory over Japan] Day; that fact being attributable to the reconversion and dismantling of many plants of which the union formerly assumed jurisdiction. That organization's membership has steadily grown, and con-

163

tinues to grow, because there is an earnest desire on the part of the officers and members of that organization to make it a bigger organization, not only numerically speaking, but more influential in other respects.

VII Murray also made mention of the "steady growth" shown since the close of the Second World War by the other two major CIO unions, the Steel Workers and the Auto Workers. The organizational progress of the three leading unions, however, did not touch upon the central problem facing the CIO as a whole. If the 1946 convention proved anything at all, it proved that the CIO was in serious trouble. There were still 30 million unorganized workers in the country. Only three hundred fifty thousand of these had been organized by CIO in the twelve months preceding the 1946 convention—20 percent of them organized by UE.

Partial explanation for this trend could be found in the experience of much of CIO leadership during the course of the war years. Industrial union leaders, rubbing shoulders in the giddy Washington scene with "big government" and "big industry" figures, were being transformed—although most of them hardly knew it—into "labor statesmen." The power of the establishment was subtly domesticating them.

Not only did such occur in the case of certain older CIO leaders, who had emerged from the AFL framework. Some of the more fiery young leaders of the industrial union uprising of the 1930s had also begun to sniff the sweet smell of success and status. They were drifting in high circles, farther and farther away from the rank-and-file. Just the day before the CIO 1946 convention opened in Atlantic City, signs of the new life style of hitherto rank-and-file oriented union leaders indicated the effects that "labor statesmanship" was having upon them.

A luxurious hotel suite occupied by the president of one of the smaller of the new unions was the setting for a caucus of a number of leaders, called to discuss the grave questions facing the CIO and how best to preserve it as a militant industrial union movement.

The three UE officers arrived, sat down and waited. There

164

seemed to be some delay. All at once the doors to the suite were flung open, a white-jacketed bartender rolled in a mobile unit and proceeded to set up shop, offering from the store of booze just about anything that could be desired in that line. While the party got going, two waiters wheeled carts loaded with fancy food delicacies into the room. No such scene could possibly have taken place at the 1938 CIO founding convention in Pittsburgh. Obviously, great changes had occurred, seriously undermining the defenses of militant industrial unionism.

Just a few months previous to this, at the UE's Milwaukee convention, Philip Murray had asked rhetorically: "Do you know why our thirty-nine international organizations have built up a mighty, mighty labor movement known now as the CIO?" And he answered himself by saying:

> Because the officers ... of these organizations ... live close to the people. They live with the people. They live with the shop stewards, and live with the committees, and they live with the local union officers. They understand the people's problems and they fight for the people.

His characterization of CIO leaders was apt if applied to the early years. By 1946, however, CIO leaders, for the most part, no longer lived the lives of the rank-and-file. Many of them were well on the way to leading the lives of the AFL business unionists, whose paragons of ease, respectability, conduct, income, and material satisfactions were those who dwelt in the executive offices of big industry. Much of CIO leadership, indeed, was in no better shape than the AFL craft union leaders to organize the unorganized, let alone defend industrial unionism against its enemies. Already, in the eyes of millions of organized and unorganized workers, the CIO was becoming indistinguishable from the AFL.

VIII

Murray's "resent and reject" resolution, far from sheltering the CIO against the gathering storm, served only to increase its tempo and ferocity. John Scoville—self-proclaimed originator of the "labor monopoly" slogan—may have been small stuff. And his Committee for Constitutional Government, though well-heeled, relatively uninfluential in the land and in Congress. But the National Association of Manufacturers, the main force blowing up the "labor monopoly" storm, was something else.

Founded in 1895, in response to a late-century surge in the membership of organized labor, the association over the years had fought on behalf of open shop industry against every campaign of workers to form unions. At the time of its cold war offensive aimed at the CIO, the association, consisting of close to seventeen thousand affiliated companies, was dominated by about sixty of the largest. Its 1947 budget, totaling more than $5.5 million, had allocations of about $4 million for public relations and selling "free enterprise," as well as hundreds of thousands of dollars assigned to "legislative activities" and "government relations."

Even while the November 1946 CIO convention was trying to conciliate reaction by pleading "non-communist" purity, a bill to curb "labor monopoly" and require government certification of the "non-communism" of labor leaders was being prepared—as Congressman Donald O'Toole of New York later said —"sentence by sentence, paragraph by paragraph, page by page, by the National Association of Manufacturers." This was the Taft-Hartley bill, so named for Senator Robert Taft of Ohio and Congressman Fred Hartley of New Jersey, both Republicans.

Next to Taft, the senator who had most to do with shaping the bill and steering it through Congress was Republican Joseph Ball of Minnesota. At the December 1946 annual convention of the National Association of Manufacturers, Ball, as featured speaker, promised that Congress would deliver the goods. In January 1947, as the 80th Congress convened, he said of the proposed legislation: "It will bear down most heavily on unions. I see no point in trying to dodge that fact." And Taft, in April of the same year, remarked: "The bill is not a milk-toast bill. It covers about three-quarters of the matters pressed upon us very strenuously by the employers."

What were some of these? In a pamphlet, *Industry's Law Against the People*, issued by the UE near the time of the law's

166

passage in June of 1947, a number of them were summarized. "The whole emphasis of the law," the pamphlet pointed out, "is on keeping people out of unions—what the National Association of Manufacturers calls 'the right not to join.' The Wagner Act protected the right of workers to organize their own unions without employer interference. The Taft-Hartley Act does the reverse." That was the number one objective of Taft-Hartley—to bring to a dead stop organization of the unorganized.

Other objectives included the fragmenting of industrial unions in the shop and the weakening of active shop steward systems, the very basis of rank-and-file unionism as practiced by the UE. "Colonel" John P. Frey, who for twelve years had been maneuvering to cripple the Wagner Act, bragged of the part he and his associates had played in getting Taft-Hartley on the books. They had ample cause to pat themselves on the back. The law encouraged the breakaway of craftsmen and professional workers from industrial unions. Also, it encouraged workers to bypass shop stewards and take up their own individual grievances with management. And although corporations had enjoyed considerable success so far in their own political action—the Taft-Hartley law itself constituting key evidence—they took no chances on the future. The law forbade unions to contribute to campaigns for federal office. Corporations were forbidden, too—but, as the UE pamphlet commented: "Politicians favored by the corporate interests somehow have never lacked for funds." Nor have they since.

The law also sanctioned court injunctions against unions, thus nullifying the New Deal Norris-LaGuardia Act of 1932—and enabled employers to file million-dollar damage suits against labor organizations. Built into the bill was an institutionalization of redbaiting. Organizations of working people, and officers of these organizations, were placed by the Taft-Hartley in "second-class citizenship" status. All union officers on every level were required to swear to "non-communist affidavits." If they did not so swear, their unions could not use the facilities of the National Labor Relations Board, could not appear on the ballot in labor board elections, could not be certified by the board as bargaining agent in an organized shop.

IX The CIO Executive Board met shortly after the law's passage. All the board members, from every affiliated CIO union, pledged that they would let the Taft-Hartley Act affidavit wither on the vine. They would not humiliate themselves and their memberships by signing the "second-class citizen" non-communist affidavits. They would not use the facilities of the labor board. So they said at the time. They intended to ignore that discriminatory provision of the act and render it a dead letter.

Taft-Hartley went into effect in August 1947. On October 13 of that year the CIO convention opened in Boston. In the sixty days which had passed since the solemn pledges given at the Executive Board meeting in June, a number of CIO union officers had signed the Taft-Hartley non-communist affidavits. That was the CIO situation. It was also the situation in the AFL, which assembled in convention at the same time three thousand miles away in San Francisco. By further coincidence, resolutions on Taft-Hartley reached the two convention floors on Tuesday, October 14.

In San Francisco, when it seemed evident that the AFL was going to go along with Taft-Hartley and its non-communist affidavits, delegate John L. Lewis of the Mine Workers, whose organization had rejoined the AFL, delivered a speech in opposition, saying in part:

> I represent an organization whose members believe they pay their officers to fight for them, not to deliver them into slavery. . . .
>
> How much heart do you think you will give the members of our organizations out in the industrial centers of this country when they see their great leaders, with all the pomp and ceremonials of a great convention, kneeling in obeisance before this detestable and tyrannical statute? Do you think that will encourage them?

While Lewis was speaking on Taft-Hartley in San Francisco, a UE leader was doing likewise at the CIO Boston convention. This was the second fight undertaken by the UE in the postwar years at a convention of the CIO. But the issue was identical—organizing the unorganized. In 1946 the UE director of organization, speaking in the atmosphere of the "resent and reject" resolution, had warned of the need for CIO leaders to "get down from the swivel chairs and down to the factory gates to conduct an organizing campaign that would bring results." In 1947 the UE officer spoke in a similar atmosphere, created by the procession of such leaders as those from the Textile Workers, Auto Workers, and Shipyard Workers who had signed the Taft-Hartley affidavits.

That so-called CIO southern drive, a year and a half old by the date of the 1947 convention, had cost hundreds of thousands of dollars contributed by many CIO unions—and gotten next to nowhere—especially in textile shops. Rieve and Baldanzi were maintaining their union's perfect record of having organized only a handful of workers in the south since the Textile Workers' inception as a CIO union, although they had signed the affidavits—so they said—to cleanse their union for acceptability in the south.

X   Although a number of CIO unions decided to comply with the Taft-Hartley law and sign the affidavits, Murray's Steel Workers, the UE, the West Coast Longshoremen, and a number of other unions, were sticking by their executive board pledge to boycott the Taft-Hartley board and the non-communist affidavit provision. This was the CIO picture in 1947 as UE director of organization Matles rose to present his union's challenge to those who were surrendering to Taft-Hartley:

> I don't believe that we can go out and say, on the one hand, that the Taft-Hartley law is intended to cut our throats and that we intend to change the Congress and abolish that law, but in the meantime we will sneak in through the back door and be there the first in line, so then maybe a given employer will cut our throats just a little bit! ...
>
> The newspapers today in headlines listed the unions that are in the [Taft-Hartley] line-up. It reminded me of an employer announcing the results of a back-to-work movement.

169

No International Union should or can dictate to another what the policy of that International Union shall be. But before we lead our members down the path to hell, let us ponder on what we are doing; let us understand we are sitting here, six hundred of us, ninety percent of us paid officers or representatives of our respective unions, sent here to find ways of protecting the interests of our people. We are here on their payrolls. They provide us with many necessities of life and with some of the comforts they, themselves, don't have. . . .

We don't believe that you can start out today and lead men into submission, step by step, that you can lead them to submit to their employers day by day, but in November 1948 they will spring to their feet and will replace the Congress. They won't do it. . . .

As far as UE is concerned, I cannot predict what we are going to do next year. I don't claim that we are not affected by what you do. We are greatly affected by that. We don't say we are such great heroes that we will do it ourselves.

But we will not rush to that Taft-Hartley line-up for the simple reason it is not a chow line. It is a line where they are dishing out poison. If we are ever found in that line we will be found in the rear, and we will be squawking like hell; we will tell our people we are there because we were compelled to be, because there were too many ahead of us.

Once again, as in 1946, there was no rebuttal. No leader of any union who had signed the affidavits defended that position. And once again, too, as in 1946, Philip Murray himself made the last contribution to the debate, saying:

Some of the organizations attached to the Congress of Industrial Organizations may file and qualify with the Taft-Hartley board. There is certainly nothing which prevents those organizations from exercising that right if they want to. . . .

Whether the action is good or bad is not for me to prognosticate. I cannot predict. I'm like Jimmy Matles. I do not know.

170

Murray told the delegates that the Steel Workers had decided not to sign and that the union had no intention of changing its mind very quickly. Then he concluded: "Time, circumstances and conditions are matters that are always of some importance in these considerations."

XI Political mobilization against the Truman program of cold war, which had created an atmosphere for passage of Taft-Hartley and for other repressive governmental measures, had for many months been centered upon the activities of Democrat Henry Wallace, who had been vice-president under Roosevelt from 1940 to 1944. At the time that Churchill made his momentous Fulton, Missouri, speech in March 1946, Wallace was serving as Secretary of Commerce in the Truman cabinet. He took issue with the Churchill recommendations for a military approach to the solution of international questions—and endeavored to persuade Truman to return to the Roosevelt postwar plans for world peace through an effective United Nations organization.

This soon made Wallace one of the first governmental casualties of the cold war. After submitting his resignation from the cabinet—demanded by Truman—Wallace embarked on a public-speaking campaign, his constant theme the hazards he foresaw in the abandonment of Roosevelt's foreign policy and the substitution of the Churchill-Truman policies of cold war and militarism. The UE invited him to speak to delegates at the September 1947 Boston convention. Wallace, for the first time addressing representatives of organized labor since he had been forced out of federal government, told them: "Our enemies are all those who talk war instead of peace. Every congressman, every brass hat, every columnist and every commentator who preaches the inevitability of war, and who slyly hints that we should drop bombs now, is your enemy and the enemy of your children. They cry Communism but their real fear is democracy."

The former vice-president, who had served in high places in the New Deal in the thirties when workers were organizing their industrial unions, refreshed the memories of UE delegates

171

with updated references to those days, which now seemed to have belonged—as they really did—to a bygone era:

> Our enemies will tell you that they agree with your objectives—but that you must get more reasonable leadership. They will tell you that almost all of you are fine citizens but that they can't work with you until you get rid of the troublemakers among you. These are the same lines of propaganda they used ten years ago when CIO was first started. Don't let the enemy call the signals. One of the old "robber barons," just before the turn of the century said, "You don't have to worry about the workers if you can keep them fighting among themselves."

Wallace said he intended to continue working within the Democratic party, "unless and until I am convinced that this Administration is committed to out-redbaiting the redbaiters and to fomenting a final war." In that case, he went on, if American voters were given no opportunity by Democrats or Republicans to declare themselves politically against war, loyalty purges, overseas shipments of arms, and depression, "they are still entitled to a voice and they shall have a new party of peace and liberty."

XII   At one point in his remarks, Wallace said: "When Roosevelt died, Wall Street moved in." Wall Street had "moved in" long before Roosevelt died. The UE convention delegates also had something to say on this subject:

> Scarcely a week goes by without announcement that some new Wall Street banker has been placed in a position of power over the domestic or foreign affairs of the nation. ... Do the men of big business who have set out to squeeze the American people dry have any other purpose toward the people of other lands? Do the men who would suppress the liberties of America work for freedom abroad? ...
> It is folly to expect that men under the domination of the monopolists will put into practice either at home or

172

abroad the policies of our late President, Franklin D. Roosevelt.

We must drive these men out of Washington as an essential first step in redirecting the foreign policy of our country toward building a peace which is stable and secure, because it rests upon the common interests of common people in every nation.... We declare to the people of the world that we will not make war upon them, nor burn them alive with atom bombs to enforce the re-establishment of international monopolies.... We call upon our countrymen to join us in our fight to take the government out of the hands of Wall Street and redirect it to the interests of the people. That is the road to peace.

Both Wallace and the UE convention delegates made reference to a new domestic phenomenon which cold war policies had produced—the "inquisitors, spies and informers [who] creep through our government, our cities and our factories." Said Wallace: "The loyalty purge is not confined to the employees of the federal government. Members of UE, and members of other unions, are now faced with the horrors of inquisition." Before the next year was out, the members of more than one UE local union did indeed face those horrors. How one militant rank-and-file local dealt with them, we shall now see.

12

"Injury to One...
Concern of All"

I   On July 1, 1948, in the huge South Philadelphia Works of the Westinghouse Electric Corporation, a thirty-one-year-old design engineer was accosted by two officials—one from the company, the other from the U.S. Navy. They informed Frank Carner, an active member of UE Local 107, that he had been found to be a "poor security risk."

Within fifteen minutes, Carner had been further notified that Westinghouse was placing him on "leave of absence" without pay; that he had the "right of appeal" from unspecified charges before a military board, that he must leave the plant at once. Two armed security guards escorted him to the gates.

Union representatives immediately demanded the reinstatement of Carner. Company officers, at a meeting attended by Navy brass, said that no reinstatement would be considered unless Frank Carner was able to "clear himself." They took the position that a letter from the Navy dated June 24 justified what the company had done.

This letter had been addressed to Carner, care of Westinghouse, whose officials had chosen to deliver it on the first of July as the design engineer was being removed from the plant. The letter began:

> This is to advise you that the Westinghouse Electric Corporation has been directed to deny you access to classified matter pertaining to Navy work or access to restricted areas in which Navy work is in progress.

The union opened up action on two fronts: (1) it filed a grievance charging violation of contract, in that no prior notice had been given to Local 107 of the company's intention to separate a worker from his job; and (2) it also began to pre-

174

pare an "appeal" on behalf of Carner before a military board. (This second task was incredibly difficult. No specific charges had been made, no "evidence" offered. Furthermore, the procedure of requiring a person to "prove his innocence" was a complete reversal of basic American due process of law.)

While the union was going forward on these fronts—with Westinghouse Corporation in regard to the grievance; with the federal government in regard to the "appeal"—lightning struck again in the turbine plant. On July 12, a thirty-four-year-old sheet metal worker was given the same treatment Carner had received.

At 10:00 A.M. two security guards walked up to Herb Lewin at his bench. Not many minutes later he was on the other side of the plant gates, in possession of a letter containing the language the Navy had used in the Carner case. Also, like Carner, he had been told by the company he'd have to "clear himself" before being considered for reinstatement.

Once again, the union committee immediately approached Westinghouse plant management. Strong protest was lodged against the manner in which Lewin and Carner had been hustled out of the shop. The union demanded that the two men be returned to their jobs without delay. Westinghouse stood pat. Nothing doing. At this point the executive board of Local 107 went into emergency session in the union hall.

Sitting in at the meeting was John Schaefer, a man in his early fifties who was a skilled pipefitter on turbines. He was known among the six thousand members of Local 107 as an unassuming but militant leader, not given to wasting words. At that point, 1948, he had worked in the Westinghouse plant for twenty-five years.

Lewin had been marched out of the plant at ten in the morning. The union-company meeting on the matter had been brief. The executive board had gone into session about 11:00 A.M. Discussion by the Local 107 leaders proceeded. Everyone had a say. John Schaefer, as was his nature, said very little. Finally, however, when it was evident that a common sentiment prevailed, Schaefer summed it up:

"Well, fellows, it is clear that we can't let them get away with it."

175

A motion was carried unanimously to present the cases of Carner and Lewin to an emergency membership meeting on a baseball field within the plant gates at 2:00 P.M. It was then shortly past noon. The local officers and division stewards returned to the plant. They passed the word: meeting at two, on the field, flagpole area.

II This was enough to alert many members of UE Local 107 that something urgent was up. From the early days of the organization, the ball field had been the rallying ground in a crisis—and union leaders had traditionally reported to the rank-and-file from the flagpole vicinity. Word of the meeting quickly circulated beyond the plant. By the appointed hour when thousands of workers had assembled, reporters and photographers could be seen atop a freight car on the siding serving the plant, overlooking the ball field. Bosses were peering from the windows of executive offices not far away. All eyes on the meeting. Production had stopped.

It didn't take long for the executive board to make its report. Nor did it take long for the union members to arrive at a decision: They demanded that Carner and Lewin go back on the job—the demand to be supported by an immediate stoppage of work. The membership instructed the union leaders to serve immediate notice on management of the mass membership decision, made without a dissent.

Late in the afternoon UE Local 107 issued a news release. It went out to Philadelphia and other area papers and radio stations. Also to the wire services. It read in part:

> Two union members have been denied the right to work. They have been removed from their jobs in direct violation of the UE-Westinghouse contract, deprived of their livelihood without charges, without evidence, without cause.
>
> The company has completely broken faith with the 6,000 people in this local union . . . completely disregarded the individuals involved, and has broken the contract absolutely. This action not only places the job of

every individual in jeopardy, but is the beginning of a potential blacklist in industry that will prevent those individuals on it from ever being employed anywhere!

The next day, July 13, another union news release reported:
> An emergency meeting between the International officers of UE, and officers of the Westinghouse Electric Corporation has been arranged for tomorrow morning in Pittsburgh [Westinghouse headquarters] to discuss and resolve the issue that resulted in the protest demonstration at the Lester plant of the Westinghouse company.

UE Local 107 officers, UE international officers and officers of Westinghouse convened in Pittsburgh on July 14.

For two days the meetings continued. On July 16 a statement was released. It had been drawn up and signed by representatives from Local 107 and by executives of the South Philadelphia Works. It read:
> The situation involving the involuntary leave of absence of two employes from the Aviation Gas Turbine Division of the South Philadelphia Works was discussed at the National level.
>
> The company will immediately take action on the problem of finding work for these two men in the South Philadelphia Works.

III   A short while later, UE Local 107 prepared and published for its membership a twenty-page pamphlet reviewing and analyzing the intense struggle. The First through Tenth Amendments to the U.S. Constitution—the Bill of Rights—were reprinted. And on the front cover, below a photograph of the inscription on the Supreme Court building in Washington—"Equal Justice Under Law"—Local 107 led off with this:
> American trade union workers in the South Philadelphia Works of the Westinghouse Corporation in Lester, Pennsylvania, sounded a significant note for the preservation of basic democratic rights in the United States on Monday and Tuesday, July 12 and 13, 1948.

177

Hear this! Americans with very few exceptions for the past two years, have not remembered their heritage, and have to some extent become mentally inactive. We have indulged in the luxury of permitting others to make the decisions, others to do the fighting, while we sat back.

For the first time in a long time, Americans have fought back and won! That's what makes this story different. Plain people in the face of much opposition stood up and were counted when they recognized their civil liberties threatened. We haven't been hearing about this kind of thing lately, especially in the trade union movement.

The union pamphlet concluded this chapter in UE 107 history with a message:

The membership of UE Local 107 sincerely hopes this incident will serve both as a warning and a lesson.

We must not forget that any arm of government, be it a military or a civil agency, is subject to the will of the people and answerable for its actions to the people.

We have the right to question. We have the right to challenge without fear, without intimidation, without economic sanctions being applied against us.

Let's not lose that right by default!

IV Frank Carner and Herb Lewin, obscure workers in a Westinghouse plant, were singled out for loss of livelihood under the authority of Presidential Executive Order 9835, issued March 22, 1947, signed by Harry Truman, and covering 2 million workers in plants with government contracts. The Truman "Loyalty Order," as it was generally called, predated by almost three years a speech by Senator Joe McCarthy in Wheeling, West Virginia, in which McCarthy made headlines all over the country by charging that the Truman Administration was infested with "Reds" and "poor security risks."

This was the origin of the period when wild accusations,

persecutions, and sacrifice of the rights and jobs of hundreds upon hundreds of persons came to be defined as "McCarthyism." McCarthy himself did not invent it in 1950. He merely picked up a Truman-made model that was already on the market, stamped on the McCarthy brand name and promoted it for mass consumption—ironically using the Truman administration as his political victim.

Part of the agreement reached in Pittsburgh on July 16 obliged the Navy to come up with whatever it was that had led the government to put the finger on Carner and Lewin. The only item eventually cited was that both men were members of the Socialist Workers party, whose political philosophy derives from Leon Trotsky's teachings.

This was nothing new to many members of UE Local 107. Carner and Lewin had never made any secret of their political conviction. No radical of any sort in that local ever held back on his ideas. Carner and Lewin were particularly assertive, often to the point where other workers grew tired of hearing them expound. As active trade unionists, Carner and Lewin were far from the most popular men in the plant.

But neither the degree of their popularity, nor the nature of their well-known political opinions and affiliations, affected in the slightest their status as union members to be defended under the contract and under the UE constitutional principles of "uniting all workers in our industry . . . regardless . . . of political beliefs." Nor did it affect their title to civil liberties guaranteed in the U.S. Constitution—as UE Local 107 emphasized by including the Bill of Rights in its pamphlet on the struggle to reinstate Carner and Lewin to jobs in the plant.

As time went by, Carner took a job in another shop. Lewin stayed on. Neither he, nor anyone else in the South Philadelphia plant, were restricted or interfered with on "security" grounds during the worst days of the cold war and one of its domestic by-products, McCarthyism. Not even when the workers of UE Local 107 were called upon to build the *Nautilus*, first atomic-powered submarine. As one member said: "You can hardly get more 'classified' than that." The point the united membership had made on July 12, 1948, turned out to be a lasting point.

V One final note on the case:

Corporations are often pleased to have the excuse of "super-patriotism" to deal harshly with workers and with unions. In regard to their own "patriotism," they are not always so "super." The Westinghouse turbine business record shows this. Indeed, between 1939 and 1959, according to a finding of federal courts, Westinghouse was engaged in a price-fixing conspiracy in that very line of work: making and selling steam turbines. In 1961, Westinghouse, GE, and twenty-seven other companies were convicted under the antitrust laws. A total of 25,632 claims for damages was filed against them by municipalities and electric power suppliers, including the Tennessee Valley Authority.

The UE was one of the few international unions in the country which fought to defend its members from persecution at the hands of the military-industrial complex. Carner and Lewin were not the only workers in UE plants to get the "poor security risk" treatment during the cold war-McCarthyism period. Memberships of other local unions held strong protest meetings, fought the cases through the grievance procedure, took them into court—and most of the time, lost out. Local 107 members, however, the only workers to shut down a plant on the spot, taking on Westinghouse, the U.S. Navy and Truman's "Loyalty Order" all together, were able to win. History might have been very different if others in that tragic era had done the same.

VI What is the explanation for the characteristics which this particular local union displayed not only in 1948 but on many another crucial occasion? It is interesting to discover that the roots of Local 107 go deep into the soil of working class struggle in our history as a people. It proves to have been a union nourished in its earliest beginnings, long before any real trade union organization appeared, by principles of democratic, aggressive struggle imparted by just a few workers with deep convictions.

A quarter-century before John Schaefer attended that emergency executive board session of the local, he had hired on, at the age of twenty-six, in the South Philadelphia Works. The year was 1923. Another postwar period, by the way, when union-busting in a manufactured climate of "Red" hysteria was going strong. The working class organization in which Schaefer had already been seasoned, young as he was, had been hit perhaps harder than any other: He was a member of the IWW, the Industrial Workers of the World.

Schaefer walked into the shop with the tools of his two trades—pipefitting and teaching—in hand. Essentially the Wobblies—a nickname for those who, like Schaefer, carried the small red membership book of the IWW—were teachers. Although they filled this role as leaders of epic strikes, their steady mission, as they viewed it, was to spread the gospel of militant industrial unionism among workers on a day-to-day basis in the shops. They were rank-and-file-oriented, by practice and philosophy. And they had a well deserved reputation for being incorruptible.

On his first working day, John Schaefer came in early. He placed IWW literature on the benches and machines of workers who had not yet arrived in the shop. It was Wobbly procedure to follow up such distributions by talks and discussions with individuals, for the purpose of organizing a group of committed IWW members—who in their turn would help to carry on the work of class-struggle education.

For ten years in the South Philadelphia plant the Wobblies, other militants, and a handful of just plain solid rank-and-file trade unionists conducted a pioneering effort of organization. During that decade, the Wobblies themselves numbered a couple of dozen at the most. There were many obstacles facing them. Nevertheless, the small band of IWW members never became discouraged. They continued meeting, talking, and reading up on all kinds of subjects. They passed out literature, made their presence felt in the shop. Militant industrial unionism was their theme. No one could have known they were helping to plant seeds of UE Local 107, this handful of fellows. But that turned out to be the fact of the matter. They and their allies—others with radical or strong trade union beliefs—laid the groundwork of the local.

VII   In the 1920s in the South Philadelphia plant of Westinghouse, most of the IWW group were recruited in the shop by John Schaefer. Others, like Schaefer himself, had already had Wobbly experience. He was twenty years old when he joined the IWW in New York City. Too young to vote, he was nonetheless deeply interested in politics and he regarded as a hopeful sign the election of two Socialist party candidates to the state legislature.

Then he picked up the newspaper one evening to read that the elected representatives were not going to be allowed to take their seats because of their political convictions. He was disgusted with the undemocratic nature of such a thing. How could the people ever bring about changes through political action if the candidates they elected were barred from representing the people? Youth can be very quickly disillusioned, especially idealistic youth such as Schaefer, when they get their eyes opened to hypocrisy and trickery within the workings of the political system.

He went out for a walk to turn some thoughts over in his mind. As chance would have it, he came upon a lighted storefront window displaying the IWW newspaper, which declared that the only way for workers to fight with the ballot box was to fight it with an ax. That sounded sensible to him, feeling the way he did. He stopped inside for a talk with the men sitting around the room. He went home that night with a lot of IWW ideas in his head and much literature in his pockets.

That was how John Schaefer became a Wobbly at a very young age. Later, he participated in some maritime and transport strikes, also some textile strikes. He began to live, as the IWW itself had lived since its inception in 1905, from battle to battle.

VIII   In 1933, AFL Federal Labor Union 18872 became the official name and number of the Westinghouse industrial organization at South Philadelphia. During the next three years, several factors contributed to the direction in which this union was to go. For one thing, there was the growing split inside the AFL between the advocates of militant industrial unionism and the representatives of craft-business unionism, until on September 5, 1936, the CIO unions were suspended from the AFL.

Also, after a while, the craft-union business agents showed up in South Philadelphia. Their objective was to carry on the traditional AFL practice in regard to federally-chartered local unions: to capture for the different craft unions the skilled workers and let the remainder of the workers shift for themselves. Then, in March 1936, nine months before the eight CIO unions were suspended from the AFL, the UE was founded.

On a Saturday afternoon, November 7, 1936, AFL Federal Local 18872, by unanimous vote at a well-attended membership meeting, transformed itself into UE Local 107. This action was reported and commented upon in the next issue of the *Union Advocate*, official news organ of the Westinghouse Industrial Union.

Under a banner headline: "EXIT 18872—ENTER LOCAL 107, U.E."—part of the account ran as follows:

> Why has the Westinghouse Union decided to affiliate with U.E. rather than retain its connection with the AF of L?
>
> Our membership is strongly in favor of industrial unionism—every worker in a plant in one union. The U.E. stands for INDUSTRIAL ORGANIZATION.
>
> Secondly, as a Federal union we are isolated from other locals in our industry. There was no connecting medium which enabled us to work together for the fulfillment of common aims. This need is adequately met by the U.E.
>
> Every organized plant of both the Westinghouse Company and General Electric is affiliated with the U.E.
>
> The above reasons, among others, seem to the members of the Westinghouse Union sufficient to more than justify the momentous step taken.

The same November 1936 issue of the *Union Advocate* carried a slogan on its masthead: "An Injury to One is the Concern of All"—a motto of militant industrial unionism dating all the way back to the nineteenth-century Knights of Labor, and adopted in the twentieth century by the Wobblies.

Twelve years later, in the Carner-Lewin case, there was a remarkable demonstration of how the meaning of this IWW-inspired sentiment could be realized in the organized rank-and-file militancy of a UE local union. Many influences were at work in the formation and development of Local 107. But the imprint of the Wobblies was engraved in the beginning. It certainly had its effect. Just as the organization of the UE had its effect upon IWW people. Would Wobbly Jim Price have ever dreamed, for instance, when he was riding the rods, organizing harvest hands, leading strikes at the side of famous IWW militants, that he would in time become the paid business agent of a local union?

IX   Jim Price—or Pricey, as all his friends called him—had been, like Johnny Schaefer, a Wobbly long before he arrived at the Westinghouse shop in South Philadelphia. He had been in the leadership of the IWW. When he first showed up in the shop he looked as if he had just dropped off a freight train, as he may well have done.

Pricey cut quite a figure. Maybe soaking wet he could have weighed all of ninety-five pounds. He always wore a blue work shirt and a crumpled hat. A shop wiping rag served as his handkerchief. He'd tell you he couldn't count the number of times he'd been in and out of jail, often for exercising his right to free speech. The fight for free speech was an IWW specialty.

When Pricey became business agent of UE Local 107, his IWW code and conscience had no reason to bother him. He received as business agent exactly the same rate of pay he had been getting in the shop as a skilled worker—UE constitutional policy.

Pricey didn't believe in spending all his time sitting behind an office desk. That was not his idea of how the business agent of a rank-and-file industrial union operated. Every morning, at the start of work, he was in the shop, roaming around, talking with this one and that one. He kept in touch with the people

184

and the problems first hand. Pricey always new what was going on.

Eventually he assumed larger responsibilities in UE. He was elected president of District 1 in Eastern Pennsylvania. But his pay, of course, grew no larger. All the new job meant to Pricey was the obligation to serve on another level of the union with the same loyalty to the rank-and-file as was expected from a shop steward, business agent, or local union officer. Being district president carried with it membership on the General Executive Board of the International UE. He came to New York for quarterly meetings of the board. After a session was over, Pricey would disappear. He was off to visit with some of his old Wobbly friends.

One of these happened to be Elizabeth Gurley Flynn, a former IWW leader known widely for her militancy and her ability in working class struggles. Pricey knew her well. They had both been arrested and jailed in the same IWW strikes. He seldom left New York without making a call on her. By the 1950s, when Jim Price was coming into New York for board meetings, she had long been in the forefront of the Communist party.

The country was up to its neck in the cold war in those days, with the "Red Scare" going full blast. But no fears deterred Pricey from going to see Elizabeth Gurley Flynn. Nor did he keep this to himself. She was his good friend.

X   A younger veteran of the Wobbly movement, Ed Boehner, arrived at the turbine works and UE Local 107 a few years after serving as a GI in the Second World War. Before the war, Boehner had been a harvest stiff along the west coast, which was still IWW breeding ground. Boehner enlisted in the organization. Later he located in Seattle, hoping to help organize a working class political party. Activists there whose allegiances were locked into established radical parties didn't approve of any new ventures. Stymied, Boehner rode the rods to Chicago, where he dropped into IWW national headquarters. When he mentioned he might be heading for Philadelphia, he was told to hunt up a Johnny Schaefer at the Westinghouse South Philadelphia Turbine Works. Schaefer was fond of telling the story:

> Boehner found me but by the time he did he'd landed a sweat shop job in a box factory and I couldn't budge him out of it. He said conditions were so bad there, the people needed help. Finally on my own I filled out a Westinghouse application for him, and I shoved it in front of him for him to sign. I got him to do that at least. Next, I handed it over to the employment manager at the plant.

Nothing happened for a while. When Schaefer made inquiries, the employment manager told him that Boehner seemed to be a bit low on experience in machine shop work. He didn't appear particularly qualified by his record as a migrant agricultural worker, landscape gardener, hod carrier, and soldier. Schaefer would recall further:

> I kept pestering the employment fellow. I laid the cards on the table. I said I knew it wasn't Ed's lack of experience was keeping him from being hired, because they were filling unskilled and semi-skilled jobs right then. I said they were only keeping him out on account of me recommending him.

At last the employment manager threw in the towel. "All right, John," he said to Schaefer. "I don't know how much Boehner will be worth to us but I guess he'll make you a good shop steward. Send him in tomorrow." Thus Ed Boehner came to work at Westinghouse in 1950.

By the time of a 1955–56 lockout, and fifteen years later a tough 1970–71 strike, Boehner had made many a contribution to the Local 107 Publicity Committee. He had a bent for writing. All during these struggles he helped prepare the daily lockout and strike bulletins and news releases. Also, his picket duty card was punched out completely, showing perfect attendance. It was reproduced in an issue of the *UE News* as a sample not of how Ed Boehner personally, but Local 107 members generally, were meeting their rank-and-file union responsibilities on the line at the plant gates when the UE was engaged in crucial battles.

186

13
Organized Workers Split Asunder

I   The struggle which UE Local 107 had conducted, in the Carner-Lewin episode of mid-1948, signified that the political developments against which Henry Wallace warned at the UE's September 1947 convention had proceeded apace. The American people, as Wallace had speculated at the 1947 UE convention, were being left no significant political choice between the foreign policies of the two major parties. A new national political party headed by Wallace was founded —its program calling for a return to the progressive domestic and foreign policies of Franklin Roosevelt—at a convention in Philadelphia in the summer of 1948. Delegates, who named it the Progressive party, nominated Wallace as candidate for president of the United States in the elections scheduled for November of that year.

Back in January 1948 CIO president Philip Murray had convened the organization's executive board for the purpose, among others, of issuing a declaration against the formation of a third major political party in the United States. By this time —three months after Wallace's appearance at the 1947 UE convention—the political handwriting was on the wall. A bipartisan front of Truman Democrats and reactionary Republicans—led in the Senate by Republican Senator Arthur Vandenburg of Michigan and, in the Truman Administration, by corporation lawyer Secretary of State Dean Acheson and international Wall Street banker and lawyer Republican John Foster Dulles—had agreed upon a foreign policy of cold war which permitted the two major parties to exclude the voting public from expressing a preference for any alternative to such policy. At that point, late in 1947, Wallace made his intentions known to help form and lead a new political party.

After a majority of CIO executive board members at the January 1948 meeting approved a resolution condemning the creation of any new political party, Murray then said this was CIO policy and he expected all unions to abide by it. Fitzgerald, a CIO vice-president, and Emspak, executive board member, argued and voted against the resolution, as did ten others. The two UE officers took the position that traditional CIO autonomy guaranteeing international unions the right to come to their own political decisions was being violated by the resolution and Murray's interpretation of its binding effect upon affiliated CIO organizations.

Just about two months earlier, at the 1947 CIO convention, Murray had used the autonomy rights of affiliated unions to justify the course being followed by some union leaders who decided to sign the Taft-Hartley non-communist affidavits. This decision, he said, was their autonomous right. The UE took the same stand at that CIO convention. Its delegation asked only that union officers think very carefully about the interests of their members and unorganized workers before rushing into the Taft-Hartley trap. But the UE nevertheless agreed that the CIO constitution guaranteed each union the right to decide for itself. Now, in January of 1948, on the question of political action decisions, Murray revoked the autonomy provisions of the CIO constitution which he had only a short time ago supported.

Fitzgerald and Emspak represented the UE on the CIO national Political Action Committee. Fitzgerald had served there since 1944. When Sidney Hillman's death left a vacant seat on the committee in 1946, Murray appointed Emspak to fill that vacancy. Both UE leaders, in a letter to Murray early in 1948, withdrew from the committee, which was proceeding to enforce upon CIO unions the political policy adopted by the CIO executive board in January.

At that time, Murray had declared that the policy against a third party in no way implied endorsement of any other party or candidate. But by summer the executive board had changed that. It endorsed Harry Truman for a second term and all CIO unions were then instructed to toe the line for Truman. The UE said that as an autonomous organization it would make its own political determinations.

188

II   The union maintained that position at its convention of September 1948—two months before the presidential elections—when a political resolution reached the floor. Fitzgerald, Emspak, and Matles, each as an individual, had endorsed the Wallace candidacy. They explained that their views on the dangers of war in the Truman-Dulles policies and on the threats which militarism presented to the liberties and welfare of the people, left them no other choice. At the same time, when the political resolution was being discussed by UE convention delegates, the officers supported its declaration that the union would endorse no presidential candidate, leaving to UE districts, locals, and members the independent right for political decision and action in 1948.

Said Fitzgerald: "The resolution confines itself to two very specific points: one, the right to free political expression in this country, the right of officers, districts, locals, and members of this organization to be for whatever political candidate they want to be for President." He went on to remark that, at the convention, he would oppose a resolution to endorse Wallace, Truman, or anyone else, because of the wide division of political opinion "not only within our organization but within the labor movement and among the people of the country."

Fitzgerald's second point was that endorsement of a candidate for president could have no "other possible effect on this organization than to weaken it in the coming year." He said that the international officers would "continue to urge that the CIO leave its autonomous international unions, their locals and their members to decide these things for themselves . . . and not engage in reprisals against us because we do not permit them to regiment us politically either in this country or within the CIO."

Fitzgerald remarked that he had admired Phil Murray in 1940 when Murray, asked by John L. Lewis to withhold support from President Roosevelt, had told Lewis "to go to hell," that no one was going to govern Murray's political thinking. Added Fitzgerald: "My answer today to anyone who is going to try to govern the political thinking either of myself or any member of the UE can best be expressed in the same words that Phil Murray used in his answer to John L. Lewis." The

1948 UE convention resolution, endorsing no candidate for president, passed by a delegates' vote of about four to one.

III Truman's reelection in November 1948 put the CIO leadership in a jubilant mood as its convention assembled on the twenty-second of the month in Portland, Oregon. In his opening remarks, Murray proudly told the delegates:

> Together with others we won that election and saved America. I do not mind reminding the delegates that the CIO as a labor organization was about the only union in the United States that stuck its neck out in this fight. . . . We put all of our effort and our might, together with the expenditure of legitimate monies, toward the election of President Truman and a liberal Congress. And we won. The people won. Thank God for that!

Murray, the picture of confidence, outlined CIO political objectives which he identified as the "Truman program." Among these he listed "repeal of the vicious Taft-Hartley Act, . . . restoration of an excess profits tax upon the greedy industries, . . . an all-out attack on monopolistic control in the United States, . . . ample social security," and full employment. Then he opened up on Henry Wallace and Wallace supporters in the CIO, although he refrained from mentioning the UE. Instead, he directed his attack, with its strong cold war redbaiting overtones, against the leaders of several smaller unions which had supported Wallace, hitting them in their weakest spot—their failure to have done very much organizing of the unorganized in their jurisdictions. But their deficiencies in the organizing field were as nothing compared to the sorry record of such ranking redbaiters as Rieve and Baldanzi, leaders of a "pure" union, the Textile Workers.

Murray's neglect of the Textile Workers leadership in his tirade against those who he said weren't doing an organizing job was accompanied by another omission. He said nothing of such former rank-and-file militants as Mike Quill of the Transport Workers or Joe Curran of the National Maritime Union. Small wonder. They had "seen the light," abandoned their independence and joined Murray's CIO establishment in its political position as junior partner in the Truman-Dulles cold war program.

IV   Murray's convention remarks gave rise to a torrent of redbaiting from the floor. This brought Fitzgerald to his feet for the first time at any CIO convention, to say:

> For the life of me I cannot understand why you people, representing an organization which has done so much to abolish bigotry and intolerance in this country, carry on the way you have carried on here. Not that you do not have a right to disagree, to express your viewpoint, but some of you seem to take it upon yourself to deny others the right to carry out their honest convictions. It made me sick at my stomach yesterday, when Abe Feinglass [of the Furriers Union] was speaking.... One does not have to support Abe Feinglass to feel deeply hurt when he hears expressions coming from the lips of a few delegates: "Why doesn't that dirty Jew sit down?"

Then Fitzgerald went on to say:

> Let us be honest about some of these things, delegates. Phil Murray feels safe when he turns his back on me. I have no aspirations to hold any other office in CIO... or in this country. I am not trying to further my own ambitions.... To sacrifice my individual rights, my honest convictions, for any office whether it be in a labor union or any place, would require more of a price than I am willing to pay.

When Murray succeeded John L. Lewis in 1940 as CIO president, he was very much troubled by anxieties about future moves that Lewis—who was far from forgiving toward people such as Murray who had crossed him—might make in the labor movement that would adversely affect the CIO. In those years, Murray could count on the support of the leadership of the three largest unions: his own Steel Workers; the Auto Workers' president R. J. Thomas; and the UE officers, for whose support he had expressed his appreciation at the UE convention in 1946.

In 1946 Reuther won the presidency of the Auto Workers, defeating R. J. Thomas after Murray had gone to great lengths to help get Thomas reelected. Thomas's defeat produced another figure—this one inside the CIO—to haunt Murray. The CIO president often talked with UE leaders about the "little redhead" who, Murray felt, was out to further his own political ambition. Murray resented what he regarded as Reuther's efforts to create a public image of himself as the CIO's new dynamic spokesman and leader.

Thus Murray continually sought to maintain a working relationship with leaders of the UE. As late as November 1948, during the CIO convention, Murray in a "gesture of good will" sent his protégé, Secretary-Treasurer David McDonald of the Steel Workers, to inform Fitzgerald that McDonald had been designated to nominate the UE leader for reelection as a CIO vice-president. Fitzgerald, with thanks, declined. He said it was customary for him to be nominated by his UE fellow officer Emspak and that, if it was all the same, he preferred to keep that tradition alive.

V   After the 1948 CIO convention, the UE leaders, still in Portland, once again sat down with Murray to talk things over. One extremely important topic was on the agenda: the raids which sister CIO unions, principally Reuther's Auto Workers, had been conducting on UE shops. As far as the UE was concerned, the Auto Workers' raids offered reason for speculating on why Reuther, having pledged to boycott the Taft-Hartley board, had proceeded to sign the non-communist affidavits in 1947. Shortly after this, Auto Workers' raids began on UE locals in Hartford, Connecticut, and Brooklyn, New York. The Auto Workers, in good standing with the Taft-Hartley board, followed a strategy of petitioning the board for elections in UE organized shops, wherein the UE would be barred from appearing on the ballot.

The CIO president gave every indication of his disapproval

of these raids. He agreed with UE leaders that it was Reuther's way of settling old scores with the UE, dating back to 1946 when UE settled with the electrical division of General Motors before Reuther signed with GM in the auto industry.

Speaking with Murray, the UE leaders put the case to him much as Matles had discussed the raiding situation only two months previously, at the UE's 1948 convention in New York. Matles had then said to the UE delegates:

> What we are talking about here is whether CIO shall survive or die. If the practice of pure and simple cannibalism is not stopped, the CIO cannot survive. That is the issue. . . .
>
> This union has contributed almost $2.5 million to help other CIO unions. Every penny, and every penny that went into the organizing of UE, came out of the pockets of the members. This union has been organized out of the sweat and blood of its members. We are saying, let the CIO take care of a simple proposition. Let the CIO condemn raiding and order all raiding unions to stop.

When UE leaders repeated these sentiments to Murray in conversation in Portland right after the CIO convention, they emphasized that the UE membership was of no mind to go on paying dues to an organization at whose hands they were suffering. It would be plain foolishness to finance their own union's destruction.

Murray said he would do everything possible to stop the raids. He promised that no CIO staff person, no one on the CIO payroll, would lend assistance to raiding. If anyone did, he would be disciplined. But as the months went by, the increasing cold war commitments of Murray and the CIO took precedence over the need to keep CIO united in pursuit of its original working class objectives. Indeed, in 1949 the raids got worse. The Auto Workers expanded theirs. The Communications Workers took off on the UE. In Canada, Murray's own Steel Workers began chipping away at the UE's thirty thousand members—and when, in July 1949, the Steel Workers' officers signed the Taft-Hartley affidavits, it was the signal for Steel Workers' raids on UE locals in the United States. All of which, as could be expected, opened wide the doors for the AFL craft union leaders. The Machinists, IBEW, Sheet Metal Workers, Pattern Makers, and others, plunged into the raiding game.

VI By the time of the UE's 1949 Cleveland convention, after twelve months of intensified raids everyone recognized that the union was compelled to take the distasteful but necessary defensive measure of qualifying for appearance on the ballot in elections conducted under Taft-Hartley auspices. The UE was the last CIO union in the Taft-Hartley lineup. The siege guns of the raids dictated the choice. The convention delegates therefore authorized officers of the union to sign the non-communist affidavits required by the employers' law of which other unions were taking such self-interested advantage. It was a bitter pill to swallow.

Once more, however, the UE resolved to test to the limit CIO procedures for protection against raids. The 1949 UE convention delegates directed the union's general executive board to "secure written assurances" from CIO president Murray that affiliated organizations which had issued charters to shops organized by UE would withdraw the charters; that if they didn't, the CIO president would file charges against them; that any CIO payroll person promoting raids be fired; and that in the event such written assurances from Murray were not forthcoming, the UE board "withhold capita tax from the CIO."

Between the UE convention of September 1949 and the CIO convention in November of that year, the union received no assurances from Murray that raiding would be stopped. The UE, with its membership of three hundred twenty-six thousand, then ceased paying per capita dues to the CIO and decided to disassociate itself from CIO by not sending its delegation to the November convention—a decision announced to news reporters at a press conference.

CIO leadership, clearly, had not expected such a UE decision prior to the convention. The nonappearance of UE delegates infuriated Murray, Reuther, and others. As the convention

194

opened up, they hastily mounted the rostrum to declare the UE "expelled." They launched into harangues denouncing the "communist-dominated" UE for "cowardice in not having the guts to come to convention and face the CIO delegates." Entrenched leaders, it seems, suffer from the same habit as the old open-shop employers when a worker used to quit his job only to be told, "You can't quit in this place. You're fired."

It was all reminiscent of the original CIO days, when the eight AFL unions of the Committee for Industrial Organizations, headed by John L. Lewis with Murray by his side, told the AFL craft union crowd to go to hell and simply did not show up at the AFL 1936 convention after the AFL high command had ordered them to disband the CIO. The AFL convention had suspended these unions "in absentia." Twenty years in the future a similar event would occur in the AFL-CIO involving Walter Reuther and the Auto Workers.

Scarcely had the UE been "expelled" when the CIO established another union with jurisdiction in the electrical, radio, and machine industries. James Carey, CIO secretary who had been voted out of office in 1941 as UE president, was installed by Murray as head man of the new CIO union. This as yet had no locals and no members, being simply at the time a chartered creation of the CIO. Murray then sent out a quick call to all UE locals, asking them to name delegates to come to a convention on November 28 and put the stamp of authenticity on the new union in their industry. Murray's call, issued in the midst of the CIO convention, went like this:

> Because of the deliberate refusal and failure of the United Electrical, Radio and Machine Workers of America to function as a trade union, established to improve the economic well-being of its members, the Congress of Industrial Organizations has revoked the charter of the UE.... The Executive Board has issued an international union charter to the International Union of Electrical, Radio and Machine Workers, CIO.

VII   In almost all the literature dealing with the relationship between the UE and the CIO, it has been assumed

195

—even by scholars as well as journalists—that the UE was simply "expelled" from the CIO at a certain point in history because the union, being "communist-dominated," had taken unacceptable positions on foreign policy. The record tells an entirely different story.

On only three occasions—from the founding of the CIO in 1938 until the UE left in 1949—did the union or any of its leaders express disagreement on the course the CIO was charting for itself. Each of these occasions fell in the period of the cold war: 1946, 1947, and 1948.

In 1946 the UE took the position that CIO efforts to absolve itself of cold war redbaiting at the hands of corporate and government forces would not strengthen but weaken campaigns to organize the unorganized. In 1947 the UE argued exactly the same in urging a solid CIO front against caving in to what CIO president Murray referred to as the "vicious Taft-Hartley law." And in 1948, UE differences with CIO revolved around the right of autonomous CIO unions, their leaders, and members, individually or collectively, to take any political position or support any political candidate they chose. When CIO unions unleashed raids upon UE as a punishment for political nonconformity, it led inevitably to a UE decision to withhold per capita tax, send no delegates to the 1949 convention, and withdraw from the CIO.

UE's fight within the CIO from 1946 through 1949 was based entirely on trade union principles, on its right to take independent positions on all questions affecting its membership. Only years later did history provide comments on the wisdom of the cold war program which, from the moment of Churchill's Fulton, Missouri, speech, the UE opposed as being harmful to the interests and welfare of working people, not to say the whole people of the United States.

In 1964, when the UE was among the first labor organizations in the country to urge an immediate end to the U.S. military intervention in Indochina, this was far from a popular stand, although consistent with UE policy on world peace stated time after time since the cold war began. But only a few years after 1964, the president of the United States—in a journey to the capitals of the two largest Communist powers

on earth, the People's Republic of China and the Soviet Union
—initiated a process of peaceful coexistence which everyone
came to agree paved the way for ending the U.S. military intervention in Vietnam.

The president was Richard Nixon, the year 1972. In 1946,
when the UE was calling for international peace and friendship, Nixon, as a candidate for Congress from California, was
launching a political career based almost exclusively on cold
warmanship and redbaiting, which carried him to Congress, to
the Senate, to the vice-presidency in the Dwight Eisenhower
administrations, and then to his position as chief executive of
the country. In 1972, however, he soft-pedaled his redbaiting
and cold warmanship. Indeed, his friendly trips to Peking and
Moscow, his new stress on the need for peaceful coexistence,
became his principal claim upon the American people for votes
to reelect him in 1972—votes which he received in substantial
number.

It was exactly the appeal for peace that Henry Wallace made
to Americans while addressing a UE convention in 1947 and,
in 1948, as a candidate for president. What was his fate then?
Having been first driven from the Truman cold war cabinet,
Wallace's peace campaign brought him slander and persecution
to a point little short of his being labeled a traitor. And the
UE, it must be said, came in for much of the same. But in 1972,
few of the former outspoken cold warriors and redbaiters said
a word in criticism of President Nixon's sudden switch in favor
of peaceful coexistence. How times change. How people and
moods change with them. And what short memories some find
it convenient to possess.

VIII   As soon as the 1949 CIO convention
ended, Murray met with Gwilym Price, president of Westinghouse, and then with General Electric's Charlie Wilson. These
meetings between the heads of the great corporations in electrical manufacturing, and the president of CIO, were planning
sessions for a supreme strategy which was aimed at annihilat-

ing, in short order, the UE. From its ashes, the strategists anticipated, would emerge the new union Murray had chartered, the
International Union of Electrical, Radio and Machine Workers, which came to be known as the IUE.

The first move made by Murray, Price, and Wilson involved
use of that legislation which the corporations' legal hands had
prepared for the Congress to pass in 1947: Taft-Hartley. Under the New Deal Wagner Act, superseded by Taft-Hartley,
only workers could petition the National Labor Relations
Board to conduct an election in a plant for collective bargaining representation rights. Following normal procedure a union
would present the petition, which had to be supported by evidence, in the form of signed membership cards from at least
30 percent of the workers in a plant. Taft-Hartley kept these
requirements for unions. But it extended to employers the right
to petition the labor board—without any evidence at all—
for elections by the workers, an anti-union procedure which
the CIO had strongly condemned in 1947. But in 1949 these
"employer rights" came in handy for the CIO.

The plans called for Westinghouse and GE to petition the
Taft-Hartley board to hold elections in their plants. Then the
CIO and all its allies would go to work on the people in the
plants to get them to switch to the CIO. On April 14, 1949, a
GE officer addressed the Pittsburgh Personnel Association at
the William Penn Hotel in that city. He said: "Our fight to get
out from under the domination of the left-wing UE, we expect
to consummate this year."

That came from W. B. Merihue, General Electric's manager
of employee and community relations. Some years later a top
GE lawyer spilled the beans completely. In 1952, testifying before a Senate Committee, he said: "We took Mr. Carey off the
hook by filing our own petitions for an NLRB election. This,
under NLRB rules, made it unnecessary for the IUE–CIO to
show any membership at all." Three years in the future, on
November 25, 1955, Westinghouse president Price undertook
to correct the impression that GE had beaten his company to
the punch in landing a haymaker on the UE. He said, "Westinghouse was the first company to file petitions with the National Labor Relations Board."

198

IX The anti-UE strategy employed by the CIO, the corporations, and the government—operating as a team—started with a telegram from the CIO to every company with which the UE held a contract. The wire told the companies to cease recognizing the UE and its contracts in the plants. This had its intended effect. Following the lead of GE and Westinghouse, many other companies followed suit. Immediate chaos reigned in the thirteen hundred plants from Vermont to California where the UE had bargaining rights. Shop steward systems, and local union grievance committees, could no longer function as usual.

The abrupt cancellation of company contracts with the UE did more than introduce disorder into the plants. It also disrupted membership dues payments to the union. Most of the contracts contained a "dues checkoff" provision, meaning that the company paymaster office, upon written authorization from members, deducted union dues from their checks and forwarded a total amount each month to the UE locals. With that system suddenly terminated it could be expected that the union would have financial difficulties.

The UE reestablished the old system of dues payment, with shop stewards collecting the dues by hand from each member, while officers and organizers adopted an austerity program in regard to their union salaries. No such austerity prevailed in the CIO. Its larger unions, such as the Steel Workers and the Auto Workers, poured thousands upon thousands of dollars into the war on the UE. And the CIO itself contributed to the cause of the IUE, which of course had no members or funds of its own when it was first chartered by the CIO as a new union in the industry.

Adversaries of the UE in this cold war era were, indeed, legion. Not only the CIO, its executive board, its unions and their leaders; not only Charlie Wilson of GE, Price of Westinghouse, and a host of lesser companies of the industries; not only President Truman—ensconced in the White House, commander-in-chief of the political forces of the executive branch—the Department of Defense, the Department of Labor, the Department of Justice, the FBI, Army and Navy Intelligence, and Secretary of the Air Force Stuart Symington, former head of Emerson Electric in St. Louis . . .

Not only these. There were also the AFL craft union chieftains; congressional and senate committees; the Un-American Committee, which under four different chairmen, Democratic and Republican—depending on which party held the majority in the House of Representatives—hauled before it time after time rank-and-file UE members, local union stewards and officers, district and international officers; the Joe McCarthy Committee, the Eastland Committee, and the Butler Committee of the Senate; the Kersten Committee of the House; the Subversive Activities Control Board, finally so discredited by Supreme Court decisions regarding its unconstitutional functions that it was left high and dry with no work to do while its members continued to draw big salaries . . .

Not only these, either. There were also U.S. Senators Jacob Javits from New York, Hubert Humphrey from Minnesota, Paul Douglas of Illinois, Congressman and later Senator John Kennedy of Massachusetts, and, after his Air Force secretaryship, Senator Symington of Missouri. There was the Association of Catholic Trade Unionists—whose major area of concentration during its lifetime was the UE, where about 50 percent of the union membership was Catholic—aided and abetted by many priests preaching the gospel of anti-communism every Sunday and visiting the homes of UE members in order to swing them out of the UE and into the CIO.

Their message coincided with that contained in innumerable newspaper reports, editorials, columns, magazine articles, radio and television broadcasts, public speeches—all constantly defining the UE, without the slightest evidence, as "communist-dominated" and refering to it as "expelled" for that reason from the CIO.

The strategy of those who in late 1949 undertook to destroy the UE aimed to get the job done speedily. The signal for such actions had been given by none other than President Truman himself. In a message to the IUE–CIO in 1949, which was reprinted and disseminated by the thousands in the plants of the electrical, radio, and machine industry, Truman wrote:

200

Please extend my cordial greetings to the officers and members of the IUE–CIO. I wish them every success. . . . In keeping with their dedication to the democracy which has served our people so well through the years, they will always oppose subversive activities in and out of the labor movement.

Hubert H. Humphrey, then a Democratic senator from Minnesota, added his political bit. Said Humphrey to Murray's CIO Union:

As a member of the United States Senate, I would seriously question the award of any sensitive defense contracts to plants whose workers were represented by an organization whose record leaves doubt as to its first allegiance. . . . The UE leadership leaves considerable doubt.

The signficance of Humphrey's remark cannot be fully appreciated without knowing that about half of the entire membership of the UE was employed in plants which held government military contracts. What Humphrey was offering the CIO union Murray had created was material with which it could go to the workers and tell them, in effect: Leave the UE or lose your jobs. That was exactly the message the workers received. It could not help but shake many of them loose from the UE. They were naturally frightened.

X   A typical operation against the UE would go like this:

After a company, in response to the CIO telegram of request, had cancelled its contract with UE, then a petition would be filed with the Taft-Hartley board for a plant election. The Taft-Hartley board obliged. An election date would be set and Murray's new CIO union given a place on the ballot. The company would then permit CIO representatives free run of the plant to carry on a campaign on the inside.

On the outside, the big guns were wheeled into position. Usually a congressional committee, such as the House Un-American Committee, scheduled "hearings" to coincide with the preelection period. Rank-and-file members, shop stewards, local union officers, organizers, and staff representatives were called to appear before the committee. This had several consequences, among them: (1) it "set up" UE people to be fired under Truman's "Loyalty Order" of 1947, which hung like a guillotine blade over every plant with government military contracts; and (2) it provided sensational material for local newspapers.

These consequences in turn produced others: The firing of union people served as a warning to workers as to what might happen to them if they stuck by the UE. The daily front page newspaper headlines about the "Red UE," meanwhile, sank into the consciousness of the community, causing anxiety and fear in the families of workers, and alienating individuals and groups which had come to the support of the UE in the strikes of '46.

Agents of the Association of Catholic Trade Unionists—ACTU, as it was called—found themselves in a brand new ball game. Its missionaries would engage in an intensive home visiting campaign of UE members of the Catholic faith. Their activities were coordinated with Sunday sermons by priests from the pulpits, a sample of which, in the exact words delivered shortly before one plant election, is the following:

> We consider that you have a moral duty to vote in this election and to vote not to uphold Communism. The leaders of the UE support the attackers and persecutors of Archbishop Stepinac, Cardinal Mindszenty and the heroic priests and nuns and Catholic people behind the Iron Curtain. The people over there cannot vote against Communism. You still can."

As an election campaign against the UE reached its pitch, in the final week or so, big wheels of the CIO and the Truman administration rolled into town. Phil Murray himself, Walter Reuther, Emil Rieve, the "reformed" Mike Quill and Joe Curran, CIO director of organization Alan Haywood, these and many others at last had left their swivel chairs and come to the factory gates. And to mass meetings. Not, however, to organize the unorganized but to disorganize the already organized. Side

202

by side on the platform with them would likely be congress-men and senators—or Truman's secretary of labor, Maurice Tobin, whose principal assignment for quite a while was to act as a "staff CIO organizer" in campaigns to exterminate the UE in this plant or that. He often appeared at factory gates to appeal from the stump to UE members to switch to Murray's union.

An operation of this scope and strength, conducted in the general atmosphere of cold war and Korean War hysteria in the country, and directed at a single independent and em-battled union, was bound to take its toll upon the UE. It did. The rank-and-file organization suffered great losses. Its days, weeks, months, and years were filled with crisis. And although the UE was never crushed, the unity and solidarity of the workers in the industry were shattered, as all kinds of unions, CIO and AFL, grabbed what they could of the membership spoils of the war upon UE.

XI   At the 1948 CIO convention, when the leadership celebrated the Truman victory, Murray had referred to the "bounden duty" of the CIO to secure certain political aims: repeal of Taft-Hartley, an excess profits tax, the break-up of monopolies, "ample" social security and pension laws, industrial expansion for full employment. These were some of the measures, Murray said, "in which we manifest an interest." That was about all the CIO could do: manifest an interest. Congress paid no attention. Industrial unionism and the work-ers of the country were losing out on the economic front and the political front.

Nothing makes sadder reading for a labor leader who partici-pated in the terrible struggles of that epoch than the record of the CIO during the "dirty decade" of McCarthyism in the fifties. The cold warriors played a tune and the CIO danced to it, while the house of militant industrial unionism went up in flames until, at last, there would be nothing left but a flimsy frame of the old solid structure.

This period set a high mark for a display of exceptional

political class consciousness and action on the part of the corporate class of the United States—just as it set a low mark for so many leaders of the working class. They did more than give up the ghost of class struggle without a whimper. Hooked by the drug of redbaiting, they themselves became pushers for the interests of the class against which workers had organized to protect and defend themselves. It is, indeed, a sad record to review.

14
McCarthyism and
Humphreyism

I What is also somewhat sad to review is the role played by any number of politicians who wished to be all things to all voters—liberal, pro-labor, cold warrior, and "patriotic" anti-communist at one and the same time. A specimen of this breed was Senator Hubert Humphrey of Minnesota, the *Drug Store Liberal,* as he was described in the title of a book about his political career by two authors, Robert Sherrill, Washington correspondent of *The Nation* magazine, and Harry W. Ernst.

In 1945, as Humphrey started on his political career in Minneapolis, he solicited the support of UE—the largest union in the city—when he ran for mayor. Upon his election he appeared before a meeting of UE members to thank them personally for the major role they played in his successful campaign. Again, in 1948, UE supported him when he ran for the U.S. Senate. In 1952, at the height of the Korean War, with McCarthyism riding high and Humphrey coming up for reelection, he undertook to chair a ten-day series of hearings on labor legislation proposed by such companies as General Electric and Westinghouse—and supported by the allies of the corporations in the Pentagon.

Not long before the hearings, the magazine *U.S. News and World Report,* published by David Lawrence—who some years later also published a book by GE's champion of anti-unionism, Lemuel R. Boulware—had printed a lengthy question-and-answer interview with Humphrey. The senator said a great many things in that interview, not all of them easy to follow. As *Drug Store Liberal* points out, Humphrey "is quite capable of promising everything to everyone, and as a consequence one side gets misled and hurt. It is lying in a way, but it is Humphrey's way, so it is not quite lying."

Still, in some places in the magazine interview, Humphrey was quite clear. He said: "It could be a matter of public policy and could be a matter of public law ... that even if that union—following a line which one is able to identify as the Communist line—gets a majority, it shall not be given bargaining status in terms of a collective bargaining contract." This really summed up the kind of legislation that Humphrey, with the "advice and counsel," as he put it, of seventy-five eminent people in the country, including a number of management people, was soon to consider at the hearings. Stripped down to essentials, the Humphrey propositions amounted to government licensing of unions as proposed by such industry spokesmen as GE's Boulware.

II   UE representatives had not been included within Humphrey's list of "eminent people" whose advice the Senator sought. Nevertheless, since the UE had been mentioned a number of times in the *U.S. News and World Report* interview, since Boulware was "eminent" enough to be consulted, and since the proposed legislation would be a serious blow to democratic unions, the UE asked to testify. On July 8, 1952, UE Washington Representative Russ Nixon and Director of Organization Matles appeared before the one-senator subcommittee. Said the UE's Nixon:

> It is the position of the UE that all of these proposals, regardless of form, whether under existing or proposed new legislation, which would establish government controls depriving workers of their free choice of selection of their own bargaining agent, or of their free choice in selection of union officers, or which would deprive individual workers of full protection from discrimination because of their political views, or which would limit the right to strike, are profoundly antidemocratic and are a major weapon of the anti-labor forces seeking to destroy the free, effective American trade union movement.

206

On the morning of July 8, 1952, Boulware of GE had said to Humphrey at the hearings: "In recommending legislative action on this problem we have been beset by certain misgivings—as would any good citizen when suggesting that the liberty and freedom of others be curtailed." On the afternoon of July 8, Matles made an effort to let Humphrey in on where Boulware was leading the senator: "All that Boulware wants," said Matles, "is to get you started on the road just as he has with Murray, Carey and others. He has used them. He has split the union. He made millions of dollars out of that for GE."

The UE officer also pointed out to Humphrey that the committee had heard testimony from a "damnable liar" in the person of one John Small, chairman of the government's Munitions Board and former president of Emerson Radio, who had said: "There is not the least bit of doubt that if the policy of the Soviet Union called for strikes in various industries in the United States, then the leadership [of UE] would subjugate the membership to a strike." Matles produced a clipping from *The New York Times*, dated June 12, 1941, which reported that of all strikes in industries holding military contracts from January to June 1941—before the Soviet Union was attacked by Hitler—not one strike had involved the UE; and that of more than 2 million man-hours lost in labor disputes in war industry, the UE was responsible for none. *Drug Store Liberal* comments that Humphrey was left "remarkably speechless" at this point.

III   Although Humphrey complained that Washington reporters were paying almost no attention to his hearings, Sherrill and Ernst observed that perhaps that was just as well from the point of view of Humphrey's political image, because he proved to be, they wrote, "no match" for the UE representatives. They might have better said for the union's principles, which were presented to Humphrey in the following exchange.

> *Matles:* I suspect, Senator, that if you were in the Senate for sixteeen years and somebody were to discuss whether you constitute a danger to the United States of

America, you would fall back upon your record of sixteen years of service in the Senate of the United States.

Senator Humphrey: That is correct, sir.

Matles: That is correct, and I would like to say the following: that today there isn't a union in the country that exceeds the UE in its essential democracy. It is because of this essential and basic democracy of the UE that it is under serious attack.

It was well for us in 1936 and for several years after, when the CIO was formed, that there were other large organizations who proceeded on that foundation and fought as hard as we did to preserve those democratic principles of the organization. And when they hit us, we were able to share in the fight and share alike. Now one after the other has caved in under attack and has surrendered some of these principles. Senator, we have to carry now a larger share of the load.

Our organization in the preamble of its Constitution states:

> "We form an organization which unites all workers in our industry on an industrial basis, and rank and file control, regardless of craft, age, sex, nationality, race, creed or political beliefs, and pursue at all times an aggressive struggle to improve our conditions."

That was there in 1936, and never a period or comma has been changed. Now, who is twisting, who is turning, who is adjusting himself, who is adapting himself, who is working on the basis of expediency? Those who stand by this principle and refuse to deviate, or those who have deviated and abandoned and surrendered?

Year after year within the UE attempts have been made in various forms to persuade the membership to weaken the basic UE principle that every member of the union has equal and unalienable rights and privileges of membership. Year after year, in convention after convention, the representatives of the UE membership have overwhelmingly rejected every effort to abandon or weaken this principle. The issue has always been placed

208

as the issue of communism, although that has been to place it falsely.

The issue is the unity and democracy of UE and its continuation as an effective, fighting organization, controlled by the membership. This is the strongest possible insurance that the membership will continue to control this union and that no group, political, religious, fraternal, national or any other, will ever be able to dominate the union.

IV   As a parting shot, the UE provided Humphrey with another perspective from which to take a view of what *Drug Store Liberal* called his "blind and foolish venture." The UE said:

> Had the members of this union declared that war profiteering is fine; if our members had put their stamp of approval on the tax-price-wage squeeze that is wrecking the country's living standards; had we called for atomic war, for $60 billion arms budgets, for distributing America's wealth to corrupt dictators like Franco and Chiang Kai-shek—we would not be under attack and charged with endangering the country's security.

As the appearance of the UE representatives drew to a close that July afternoon, the last day of the hearings, Humphrey remarked how anxious he was to get off to vacation in the Thousand Lakes region of Minnesota, his native haunts. The UE officer said that the senator should indeed go home and relax.

"I say that you can sleep at ease," said Matles, "from the standpoint of any union or any group of working people being a threat to the United States of America. That does not exist."

Hubert Humphrey never came forward with any government licensing legislation of unions. He didn't have to. Eisenhower and the Republicans were elected in 1952 and they did the anti-labor legislative job with the Brownell-Butler Law—named after Attorney General Herbert Brownell and Republican Senator John Marshall Butler of Mayland—for which Senator Humphrey voted aye.

V   Humphrey's hearings of 1952, however much they were designed to serve the interests of the corporations, had the excuse of being concerned with legislative proposals. No such excuse could be offered by the various inquisitorial committees of the Congress, chief among which were the House Un-American Activities Committee—in business since 1938 when Kentucky "Colonel" John P. Frey, president of the AFL Metal Trades Department, pioneered redbaiting of the CIO before the committee—and that one-man outfit of the Senate consisting of the senator from Wisconsin, Joe McCarthy. How ironic that McCarthy, who perverted Senate investigating procedures not only in regard to the labor movement but across the board of the whole society, should have supplanted Robert La Follette, whose committee in the late 1930s had followed legitimate senate functions and procedures in its investigation of corporate spies and strikebreakers hired to smash labor unions.

The La Follette recommendations for new laws to deal with this corporation racket got nowhere. And by the early 1950s, his successor in the Senate, McCarthy, was himself conducting the racket in the name of the government. McCarthy shaped up as a walking conglomerate of unionbusting devices for which corporations formerly had to shell out plenty. Now, with McCarthy, they got the service for free, on taxpayers' money. As for McCarthy, he got headlines and votes as the outstanding professional redbaiter in the cold war time when he had lots of competition. McCarthy and the corporations teamed up well together, each with an individual objective in view: profits for corporations, votes for McCarthy. In 1953 they were joined by a surprising third party, CIO leadership. Here's an example of how the three-member team operated.

On November 17, 1953, the *Lynn* (Mass.) *Daily Evening Item* carried two streamer headlines across the top of its front page. Headline number one: "NLRB ORDERS GE UNION POLL." Just below: "MCCARTHY DUE TO QUIZ LYNN WORKERS ON RED TIES." The news story began:

> The National Labor Relations Board will conduct an election among some 13,000 General Electric workers in

210

Lynn and Everett "within 30 days" to determine and designate the union or unions which will represent the employees as bargaining agent. Coming almost simultaneously with the Washington decision was an announcement in New York last night by Senator Joseph R. McCarthy (R.-Wis.) that he and his Senate Investigating Committee will hold a closed hearing in Boston tomorrow at 11 A.M. on security policies and alleged Communist infiltration at GE's Lynn and Everett plants.

The phrase "coming almost simultaneously" was appropriate for handling the connection between the two items of news. There was a lot of "coming almost simultaneously" in those years. Almost every time the UE was involved in an important NLRB election competition with the CIO, almost every time there was an important UE strike, you could depend on one of those investigating committees of the Congress showing up "almost simultaneously" with a pocketful of subpoenas, ready to make headlines about the "UE reds."

VI   Back in 1950, the CIO union created by Murray with the cooperation of General Electric and Westinghouse had captured bargaining rights from the UE at the Lynn GE plants. Very few campaigns against the UE matched this one for redbaiting from high and low. Murray himself appeared on the scene, as did Truman's secretary of labor, Maurice Tobin. Senator Humphrey pledged to do all in his power to keep government contracts away from the Lynn plants as long as the UE, bargaining agent since 1936, remained as the workers' union.

Even with all this, and much more besides, the contest was close. The CIO union took control by the margin of only a few hundred votes among more than ten thousand cast. By mid-1953, when the Korean War ended, the influence of Senator Humphrey wasn't required to prevent government military orders from reaching the plants. A period of slack between hot war and the next cold war round of military contracts provided GE with the opportunity to stage an "economy" drive—laying off many workers, cutting piecework prices, introducing intensified speedup. Conditions in the plants were such that in addition to the several thousand Lynn GE workers who had stayed loyal to UE, other workers by now had second thoughts about the wisdom of the choice made in 1950. Both groups asked the UE to seek another NLRB election. The UE did so. Its petition to the NLRB made the news which appeared in the *Lynn Item* on November 17, 1953.

Enter McCarthy and the terror of McCarthyism, which had been epidemic in the country for more than three years, striking down diplomats, generals, scientists, teachers, factory workers, labor leaders, public officials, and, indeed, anyone and everyone, the Democratic party included, that McCarthy chose to redbait for his own political advantage. While he was going strong, he swooped down on the workers in the Lynn GE plants to lend his powers to the CIO and the company. McCarthy's aim was to spread fear and terror among the workers to keep them from voting for the UE.

VII   On November 18, in a federal courtroom in Boston, nearest large city to Lynn, McCarthy held "closed hearings." These private sessions were one of his favorite settings for inquisition. To quote a Lynn GE worker summoned before him, "McCarthy is prosecutor, judge and jury [and] no defense counsel may speak, no [stoolpigeon] witness be cross-examined." The next day, November 19, McCarthy staged televised hearings. The *Lynn Item* reported that a "self-styled undercover man for the FBI . . . declared he knows of 30 Communists in the Lynn GE plants." He named two. They were promptly suspended from their jobs by the company. Both were UE members active in the campaign to bring UE back. On November 20, IUE Local 201 announced that two other workers, members of IUE who had appeared at the closed hearings, would be brought up on charges by the CIO union and, if found "guilty" of invoking their constitutional rights when grilled by McCarthy, expelled from the union.

For the past seven years, ever since the 1946 CIO convention when Murray had sponsored the resolution to "resent and reject the interference of the Communist party or any other political party" in the CIO, many of its unions had been inserting clauses in their constitutions permitting McCarthy-type persecutions in the labor movement long before McCarthy himself appeared on the political horizon. It cannot be repeated too often that the differences between UE and the CIO rested fundamentally upon one simple issue: union membership rights and privileges for any worker in the industry, bar none—the UE position—or union membership rights and privileges restricted by political or any other qualifications—the CIO position. That's all there really was to it.

VIII　　The two Lynn workers fingered by the "self-styled" undercover man were immediately suspended by the company. The two other workers summoned to a CIO hearing were expelled by the union and then suspended by the company. Four other Lynn workers were suspended. It was only the opening gun. Soon, suspension of workers at GE plants in Schenectady, Erie, Syracuse, Fitchburg, Louisville, and Bridgeport brought the total to twenty-eight. The "undercover" agent, dug up by McCarthy for the televised Lynn hearings on November 19, had said he not only knew of a lot of "reds" in the Lynn plants but also in other GE plants, such as Fitchburg, where he had previously worked.

That night of November 19 the Worcester (Mass.) *Evening Gazette*, published not far from Fitchburg in the central part of the state, ran a report which was headlined: "FITCHBURG WITNESS HAS 34-YEAR POLICE RECORD." The report began:

> Fitchburg, Nov. 19—William H. Teto, 53-year old former Fitchburg resident, was recognized by Police Chief Carlisle F. Taylor as Teto appeared before the McCarthy committee in a televised hearing from Boston this morning. Chief Taylor stated Teto is the same man who had made court appearances here on several counts of larceny by check.

213

The report went on to say that Teto had been arrested six times between 1933 and 1940 for larceny by checks and, in 1921, after World War I, had been arrested twice—once by Chief Taylor—as a soldier absent from the Army without official leave.

In the *Boston Post* of November 21, a "high Department of Justice official" was quoted as saying that Teto was "never enrolled as a full-fledged undercover agent." He simply "volunteered" his "information," the *Post* reported. On November 24, the Massachusetts Commission on Communism and Subversive Activities, also anxious to get into the act, answered that it expected to hear from "volunteer" Teto. But he didn't show up. The *Item* reported that he was down in New York "still meeting" with McCarthy and his aides, then preparing the ground for a New York hearing the next day, November 25, at which the UE director of organization was due to appear.

IX   This had come about in an unusual way. In the first place, neither the McCarthy nor any of the other inquisitional committees ever made a practice of going after UE rank-and-file workers and local union leaders, while leaving top union leaders alone. Quite the contrary. The top leaders were customary prime targets, as the UE leaders knew from experience. This was not the case in November of 1953. McCarthy avoided calling the UE leaders to appear before his one-man inquisition.

The international officers discussed this union situation. They figured there was only one thing to do: demand that McCarthy confront an international officer. Rank-and-file workers in the shops were bearing the brunt, being mowed down by McCarthy while the UE leadership on this occasion was left sitting on the side lines, untouched. Because the McCarthy tactics were clearly aimed at defeating UE in the NLRB election in Lynn, it was decided that UE director of organization Matles, directly involved in the Lynn campaign, take on McCarthy.

The union sent a telegram to McCarthy demanding that Matles be subpoenaed. Nothing happened. No reply. The UE's

214

general counsel got on the phone to McCarthy's aide-de-camp, twenty-six-year-old "committee chief counsel," Roy Cohn, to ask about the subpoena. Cohn was unclear on the matter. The attorney challenged Cohn to issue a subpoena or he would tell the press that he refused. That did the trick. The subpoena arrived. By the time it did, a union statement had been drafted, which Matles handed to McCarthy the moment the hearings opened. It said in part:

> Your purpose in Lynn has been to interfere in a coming NLRB election. The purpose of your bogus spy-hunts is to assist GE. In Schenectady, A. C. Stevens, plant manager, sat with you in your secret sessions where you attempted to browbeat and terrify workers in the Schenectady plant represented by UE.

The union's international leadership had agreed that the proper method of dealing with McCarthy lay in taking the initiative right off the bat and trying to hold it. The senator opened up in his customary style. No sooner had he and Cohn glanced at the statement than McCarthy asked Matles: "Are you a Communist?"

The answer: "My [Taft-Hartley] affidavit answers that. It shows I signed five non-communist affidavits in the last five years and these affidavits carry a five-year jail sentence and ten-thousand-dollar fine if falsely signed."

The hearing was being held in a federal courtroom in Foley Square in downtown New York. McCarthy had assumed the judge's seat behind the usual elevated bench. Off to one side, at a table, sat Cohn. Matles and UE counsel—who was allowed only as an observer—were seated at another table in the well of the courtroom. The UE had requested a public hearing. It was more of an "invited-guests-only" affair. In the front row of the spectator section were arrayed a dozen or so women whose appearance—and the small red-white-and-blue flag emblems pinned to their bosoms—gave them a Daughters of the American Revolution aspect. They, or women like them, showed up at many a McCarthy hearing, clucking and beaming at every hard swing of the executioner's ax.

Matles's response to "the" McCarthy question didn't satisfy

the chief inquisitor, who kept repeating it in ever-heavier tones. Said Matles:

> You are using the same kind of threats you use to scare working people in Lynn and Schenectady. You have been running around to Schenectady and Lynn. You have had a lot to say about spying and sabotage. When you accuse us of that you are lying, Senator McCarthy. You are a liar.

At this point McCarthy, who had been pounding away on the judge's bench with a gavel, sprang from his chair and rushed headlong down into the courtroom. He was purple. Matles kept right on talking:

> You are doing a dirty thing, going to Lynn and Schenectady for the General Electric Company, terrorizing and browbeating decent working people. I tell you to stop it.

By now McCarthy had arrived within a couple of feet of Matles, glowering over him. Cohn had moved to a chair at the table where Matles now stood up, eyeball to eyeball with McCarthy. He was ordered by McCarthy to sit down. He said he would do so when McCarthy returned to his seat behind the bench. McCarthy finally went back there and, after he sat down, Matles did too. Said McCarthy, "I want to set you straight on the purpose of this executive session. We've got a lot on you. We wanted to give you a chance to clear yourself."
Matles replied:

> You've got nothing on me, not a damned thing. You've been trying to frame me on my non-communist affidavits for three years, the pair of you, and you haven't done it. Let me ask you a question: Are you a spy? That question is as good coming from me to you as coming from you to me.

It was the last straw for McCarthy. Enraged, he banged his gavel for the final time and dismissed the witness. Before leaving, however, Matles had a question for Cohn: "What are you doing around here? I see you lost Schine." (David Schine, a twenty-five-year-old "special assistant" to McCarthy and a wealthy playboy type, had just been drafted, very much against his will, into the Army.) Matles went on, "I put in my time in the Armed Services, Cohn. What are you doing around here?"

Cohn said, "Do you want me to tell you?"

"Yes."

McCarthy felt obliged to come to the aid of his chief counsel. "You don't have to answer that, Roy," he said, as if he were a lawyer advising a client to plead the Fifth Amendment, the use of which by witnesses before McCarthy usually got them fired from their job or indicted for "contempt" of the committee, or both. A few moments later the executive session, which had lasted about fifteen minutes, ended. That night there was a meeting held in Lynn so that the workers could receive a blow-by-blow report on the UE-McCarthy confrontation.

X   General Electric proclaimed its official Fifth Amendment firing policy on December 9, 1953, one day before the election at the GE plants in Lynn. The announcement of *General Electric Policy No. 20.4* was printed on the front page of all the company's plant newspapers in the form of a news story, which started: "The General Electric Company today announced that it will immediately . . . suspend employes who refuse to testify under oath . . . when queried in public hearings conducted by competent government authority." There was a great deal of talk in those days about the imminent danger of overthrow of the government by force and violence. While this was ridiculous on the face of it, and while no one associated the danger with the policies of such corporations as General Electric, it has to be said that *GE No. 20.4* effectively overthrew a section of the U.S. Constitution within the domain ruled by the GE company.

The *Berkshire Eagle,* published in Pittsfield, Massachusetts, location of a large GE plant, was quick to point this out editorially: "GE has proclaimed that [the Fifth Amendment] has been repealed as far as the company is concerned. . . . We dislike to see it being repealed by means not provided by the Constitution itself." In York, Pennsylvania, *The Gazette and Daily* commented in an editorial: "When one of the largest

217

corporations in the United States declares that it will suspend any employe who fails to meet the standards of inquiry set up by Senator McCarthy's investigating committee, it is due time, in our opinion, for all Americans to take notice . . . of a most vivid contemporary illustration of the decline of freedom."

General Electric explained that *No. 20.4* was being promulgated for patriotic reasons. The statement signed by GE president Ralph J. Cordiner included these observations:

> In the event of a sudden national crisis, national preparedness requires that all General Electric employees should be free of any real question of disloyalty . . . [there arise] grave doubts concerning the possible danger to the safety and security of company property and personnel whenever a General Electric employee . . . asserts . . . that he might incriminate himself by giving truthful answers concerning his communist or his possible espionage or sabotage activities. . . .

> Such conduct by General Electric employees also undermines the confidence of the government and the public that the vital productive facilities of General Electric will be fully and immediately available to the country in time of national crisis. In addition, such employees damage the reputation and good will of the company . . . and generally impair the morale of all employees.

XI   One UE response to *General Electric Policy No. 20.4* was UE *Publication No. 285.* It was headed "GE's Lawbreaking Record" and began:

> Printed below is a short outline of GE's record of criminal and civil convictions in the past few years for violations of the United States anti-trust laws. . . . No GE official has ever been penalized by the company for his part in the corporation's long, lawbreaking record. The record of cases given below goes back only to 1940. There were many others in earlier years.

Among the listed items of GE's history as a defendant in federal courts were: a criminal conviction on charges of defrauding the U.S. government on cable used on Navy ships; a criminal conviction on charges of faked competitive bidding on electrical devices—and another conviction on charges of conspiring for noncompetitive bids on streetlighting equipment; conviction on charges of restraint of trade in incandescent and fluorescent lamps; conviction on charges of price fixing (in 1944 under wartime price controls) in fuse cut-outs. UE *Publication No. 285* also recorded that twice in 1945, with the war coming to a close, General Electric made pledges to the U.S. government to stop its participation in illegal international "cartels." The company promised it would cease being a party to a division of the world market in electrical equipment—and it wouldn't participate any more in an association for "cartel deals" (international monopolies) with Nazi, Swiss and British firms.

No GE policy statement about such seeming reflections on the "reputation and good will of the company," not to speak of what they might have contributed to the undermining of "the confidence of the government and the public" in General Electric, was ever issued. It did not appear, either, that Cordiner or any other GE official felt that criminal convictions of the company could have the effect of "generally impairing the morale of all employees." It was only the workers' assertion of their rights under the Constitution which would, apparently, to quote Cordiner again, "subject [the company] to serious embarrassment." Cordiner's *GE No. 20.4* of 1953, with its explicit declaration of intent to discriminate against certain GE workers, was just the opposite of the explicit nondiscriminatory provisions of Swope's *GE Q 105A* of 1935, which had figured so importantly then in achieving the first UE contract with General Electric.

XII   The next day after the proclamation of *GE No. 20.4*—December 10—the IUE retained bargaining rights at the Lynn plants in an election won once again by only a few hundred votes. The team of McCarthy, CIO leadership, and corporation, by inquisition and terror, had managed the deal. But just barely. Anyone who lived through such times knows that it was very much out of character for people to resist the terrors of McCarthyism to the extent shown by the working people in Lynn GE. Wherever McCarthy turned in those years he swept all before him—until his luck finally ran out. The fact that he did not rout the workers in Lynn was not because of any lack of effort on his part, or on the part of his colleagues—the company and CIO. It was, rather, due to the solid rank-and-file corps of UE members in the plants, who refused to buckle, and to the day-by-day trade union work of UE staff people such as International Representative Don Tormey, born and bred in Massachusetts, who was a key person in this action at Lynn GE.

In the early thirties, Tormey worked in several Massachusetts machine and metal shops before he joined the union's staff in 1941. Highly skilled as an organizer, negotiator, and writer, his specialty was to take on all comers in open debate. In such encounters he had few equals. It was then that his deep convictions, and his knowledge of the historic struggles of the working class, stood the union in good stead. The pressure was on Don Tormey every day of the election campaigns in Lynn during the dirty decade of McCarthyism. He took it and he dished it out, playing no small part in mobilizing the resistance movement of thousands of Lynn workers against McCarthyism at the GE plants.

XIII Cordiner's *GE No. 20.4* repealed the job rights of many workers who had exercised their constitutional rights before one government investigating committee or another. The GE policy called for immediate suspension of any worker who thus availed himself of constitutional privilege. Then the jobless worker was given a ninety-day grace period, within which he could get his job back by surrendering his rights under the U.S. Constitution and by appearing as a "cooperative witness" before a committee. Failing that, the suspension automatically became a discharge. The worker was fired and blacklisted from further employment by the company.

The implications of the *GE No. 20.4* were emphasized by UE General Secretary-Treasurer Emspak in a message sent to all union locals soon after the Lynn election of December, 1953. The message opened with this paragraph:

Dear Brothers and Sisters: In order to guarantee the winning of the Lynn election recently for the CIO, the General Electric Co. released the text of its new employee relations policy the day before the election. However, this new statement of policy by GE goes far beyond any momentary trick to confuse its employees on the eve of an election. In issuing this new policy, GE has taken a dangerous step down the road leading to the open-shop, to the return of the hated blacklist and to the complete destruction of industrial unionism.

Among the first of local union UE leaders to be suspended and discharged was John Nelson of the Erie Plant, UE local 506, who had worked there—except for a period of service in the Army—for thirteen years. His experience stretched from that of rank-and-file worker in the shop, shop steward and local union president, through years of membership on the UE–GE Conference Board and on the committees which negotiated national contracts with the company. He happened to be, like many another UE leader, a devout Catholic. All of Nelson's children, he made certain, received their early education in Erie parochial schools.

When he was haled before the inquisitional committee headed by Senator John Marshall Butler—coauthor of the union-busting Brownell-Butler Act of 1954—John Nelson, at age thirty-seven, headed a key UE local union in the GE chain. Next to Schenectady and Lynn, the Erie plant, with its normal force of six thousand production and salaried workers organized into two UE local unions, constituted a major objective of the groups which were out to get the UE. They went after Nelson because he was one of those who stood in the way of getting the union.

The UE took the Nelson and other cases to court, bringing charges against GE of breach of the union contract, violation of constitutional rights, and conspiracy with the McCarthy Committee. Specifically, the union cited the clause on dismissals in the UE national contract with GE, which according to contract could discharge a worker only for just cause. A union press release at the end of trial in Washington, D.C., reported:

There was not a single word of testimony to indicate

221

that John Nelson, or any of the other workers suspended and discharged by the Company, had engaged in any wrongdoing whatsoever. Quite to the contrary, the Company was forced to admit that workers had their right to avail themselves of their constitutional privileges—but, if they did, the Company would discharge them.

The UE counsel, having subpoenaed two McCarthy committee representatives, had opportunity to ask one of them this question:

> Mr. Anastos, did you and Mr. Roy Cohn enter into arrangement with Mr. Stevens and Mr. LaForge, representatives of the General Electric Company, on or about late October or early November 1953 at the Mohawk Club in the City of Schenectady to the effect that General Electric employees would be called before the [McCarthy] committee and that the company would suspend and then discharge any such employees who asserted any constitutional right or privilege as a reason for declining to answer questions relating to so-called communist associations?

The witness refused to answer the question, citing privilege under two Senate resolutions. He was not compelled by the court to reply nor was he held in contempt for refusing.

The union's case was first heard in November of 1954. Then began one of those familiar slow legal progressions through the various courts of appeal. More than thirteen years later, on December 12, 1967, UE president Albert Fitzgerald addressed the following letter to General Electric:

> Mr. Philip D. Moore
> Manager Union Relations
> General Electric Company
> 570 Lexington Avenue
> New York, N.Y. 10022
>
> Subject: *Cordiner Policy 20.4*
>
> Dear Mr. Moore:
> In December 1953, Ralph J. Cordiner, then president of the General Electric Company, issued Policy 20.4 call-

222

ing for the discharge of any GE employee who invoked the protections of the Bill of Rights of the Constitution and refused to submit to an inquisition by Senator McCarthy, the UnAmerican Committee or similar committees. Under this policy the General Electric Company discharged 28 employees, with many years of service, members of UE and other unions. Under this policy the livelihood of these employees was destroyed and their reputation irreparably injured in their communities.

UE fought this policy from its inception on the ground that it was an arrogant invasion of the Constitutional rights of its employees and the Union's right of collective bargaining. Among those discharged was John Nelson, president of UE Local 506, Erie GE. UE took the Nelson case to the courts for the purpose of compelling GE to abandon this policy. The case dragged on and by 1960, while it was still pending in the Federal court, John Nelson died at the age of 40. We were compelled to abandon the case.

The Supreme Court yesterday struck down the statute that gave the right to the Defense Department to bar workers from employment on the ground of political affiliation or association. In the case of the GE employees, the General Electric Company did not even claim any political affiliation or association as the ground for discharge. They were fired solely because they invoked their rights under the Constitution.

During our last contract negotiations in 1966, UE declined to execute a letter of agreement that would continue to exclude the Cordiner policy from the areas of collective bargaining, grievance procedure or arbitration. Furthermore, UE again insisted that the Company wipe this infamous policy from its books.

Today, we were advised by the Company that it had, in effect, already abandoned this policy sometime subsequent to our contract negotiations in October 1966. But the injury that was inflicted on the victims of Policy 20.4

cannot be cured by quietly dropping it. The Company cannot ignore or erase the damage that was done to these employees and their families.

We are asking that the General Electric Company promptly correct the injustice to these employees and their families. Merely to drop this infamous policy without making the necessary amends would only permit another Cordiner sometime in the future to put into effect Policy 20.4.

Very truly yours,
/s/ ALBERT J. FITZGERALD
General President

AJF:K

No reply was ever received to this letter. No amends were ever made by the General Electric Company.

XIV The McCarthy Committee was only one of a number of congressional committees engaged in inquisitional business on behalf of such great corporations as General Electric. Years after McCarthy had passed from the scene, having suffered one of the few censure actions ever taken by the Senate against one of its club members, another committee came to the rescue of Westinghouse. The tactics of this committee in 1960, as far as open collusion with employers went, beat even McCarthy.

Chairman of the Senate Committee on Internal Security at that time was Senator James A. Eastland of Mississippi, famous for his open encouragement to governments of southern states to defy the Supreme Court 1954 decision against segregated schools. On March 15, 1960, the *Baltimore Evening Sun* carried a news item about an Eastland operation in that area. The first few paragraphs said:

> The chief investigator for the Senate Subcommittee on Internal Security today began an investigation of Communist influences in a labor dispute at the Westinghouse Air Arm plant in Anne Arundel County.
>
> The labor dispute involves the question of which of

224

two electrical unions will represent 1,200 workers at the plant. The unions are the United Electrical Workers Union and the AFL–CIO International Brotherhood of Electrical Workers.

March 25 has been set as an election date for settlement of the dispute between the two unions.

The excuse given for the arrival at the Westinghouse plant of two subcommittee staff agents was that the company held government contracts for "top secret" work involving airborne military electronics programs. It was the same old McCarthy line—with a new twist. Instead of official hearings in a federal courthouse to which UE members would be subpoenaed and then browbeaten, the Eastland gang just moved right into the plant.

On March 15, the two committee agents set up shop in offices provided by Westinghouse executives. With the election ten days away, Westinghouse management delivered one worker after another to Eastland's representatives in the private quarters management had supplied. "Star-chamber-session" is the phrase historically used to define such proceedings. It simply means that the selected victims get the third degree under circumstances in which everything is on the side of the inquisitors. The intention is to scare the living hell out of people.

After the Eastland committee-Westinghouse collaboration team had finished its work on UE supporters, the company distributed—two days before election—a long letter to its employees which began with redbaiting and finished with such sentiments as these: "Westinghouse deals with many reputable unions, and we do not play favorites. In this election, our position is simply that we oppose the UE."

The company, however, was taking no chances on missing the opportunity afforded by the visit of the Eastland internal security investigators. On March 24, 1960, with the election coming up the next day, Westinghouse ran a large ad in the *Baltimore Sun* addressed "to Westinghouse employees and the general public" and calling for "defeat for the UE." The ad was headlined: "WESTINGHOUSE CANNOT TAKE CHANCES WITH NATIONAL DEFENSE."

The Eastland Committee of Baltimore of 1960, just like the McCarthy Committee in Lynn of 1953, did its assigned job— Eastland for Westinghouse, McCarthy for GE. The effort of the UE to win bargaining rights at the Air Arm plant was defeated. The company got the union that it wanted. This was not the last of the three-pronged attacks conducted against UE by the team of corporation, AFL–CIO leadership, and congressional committee. But it was one of the worst.

15
The Ninety Thousand

I   Between 1949 and 1955—years of cold war, of McCarthyism, of hot war in Korea—AFL and CIO leaders were preoccupied with overseas missions on behalf of whatever administration happened to be running the show in Washington. They sought to influence unions and union leaders in other lands, persuading them to support the foreign policy emanating from the White House and the Department of State.

By 1955, for all practical purposes, the AFL and CIO were one in everything but name. The CIO had long ago ceased to worry about organizing the many millions of the unorganized. It had settled down. Its membership of about 4 million was almost exactly what it had been in 1938, while CIO affiliates for the most part adopted the old AFL practice of administering their affairs in business unionism fashion. AFL leaders were more than willing to talk "merger" with CIO leadership at this stage of the game. The AFL high command regarded the word "merger" as only a face-saver for CIO leaders, whose industrial unionism—which leaders of the AFL had rejected and fought twenty years before—was no longer an obstacle in the way of admission to the AFL.

Everybody said it was a great idea. Prominent Republican and Democratic figures, from President Eisenhower and Secretary of State John Foster Dulles to presidential candidate Adlai Stevenson, couldn't find words enough to praise the "statesmanship" of the labor leaders who were planning to bring the AFL and CIO together. Someone coined the phrase "the new mighty mainstream of labor" which received popular currency not only in the conventional press but also in liberal and left journals. The Communist party and other radical groups hailed the merger as new hope for the labor movement.

227

UE leadership pointed out that a ceremonial joining of hands by AFL and CIO officers had little to do with meeting the needs and aspirations of rank-and-file workers. The UE took the position that the "merger" merely formalized the CIO surrender of its early militant industrial union principles, long since abandoned in practice. This view of "the mighty mainstream" carried little weight with those who felt the UE's days were numbered, since it seemed inevitable that the cold warriors would soon put the union out of business.

II   This did indeed seem possible. A Republican-dominated Congress had passed the Brownell-Butler Communist Control Act in 1954, intending, along with other objectives, to close the loopholes in the Taft-Hartley Act of 1947. The Brownell-Butler Act constituted a new device of repression to be employed against such a trade union as the UE, which had the audacity to remain in existence with one hundred forty thousand members—in spite of everything its enemies had been able to level against the organization. The Subversive Activities Control Board, established by the Brownell-Butler Act, aimed to put the UE in a position where it would be stripped of bargaining rights in all the plants where it had contracts and represented the workers.

This could be initiated by a board "finding" that a union had aided "communist-front" groups within a prior three-year period—or that its leaders "had consistently identified with communist groups within the prior two years." Once such a "finding" had been made the basis for successful Justice Department prosecution of a union, the organization would, in effect, have its citizenship rights revoked. In that way a trade union could be barred from appearing on the ballot in plant elections in an effort to win or regain bargaining rights.

In December of 1955 the Subversive Activities Control Board finally got the Department of Justice to file legal proceedings against the UE, charging it with being "communist-infiltrated." The case was set in motion toward trial. No trial was ever held. Finally, in 1959, four years after the charges were filed, the Department of Justice went into federal court and asked permission to withdraw the case against UE. The union opposed this government maneuver and demanded instead that the federal court dismiss the charges, so that in the future the government could not use them for further harassment. The union won its point.

Final outcome of the case of the Subversive Activities Control Board against the UE symbolized the outcome of every one of the hundreds of wild charges flung at the UE over the years. Not one officer at any level, not one rank-and-file worker, not one staff representative or organizer was ever charged or tried for violating laws having to do with the security of the United States. Nor was a single government contract ever withheld or removed from any plant because workers were represented by UE. As for legal moves that were made against the union and its leaders and members—moves such as that of the Subversive Activities Control Board, grand jury proceedings, contempt citations, denaturalization actions and so forth— these added up to a complete zero. They came to nothing whatsoever, none of them.

Still, they served some of the purposes of UE enemies. In 1955 the stratagem of the Subversive Activities Control Board, coupled with the AFL–CIO merger, produced the second most serious crisis affecting the UE in the 1950–1960 span which many members will always refer to as the "dirty decade."

III   The terror unleashed against the membership of the UE in the first half of that dirty decade had sown much fear and confusion among the rank-and-file—some workers swayed by the "Red Scare," others panicked by the prospect of losing their job if they stuck with the union. In 1955, however, the remaining one hundred forty thousand members had been tempered in the fight to preserve their UE. There was no panic. The latest government endeavor to destroy the union was regarded by the 1955 membership as one more serious challenge, which they braced themselves to meet. The AFL–CIO merger? UE rank-and-file workers in the shop

229

couldn't have cared less. Their attitude generally was: "So what else is new?"

It therefore came as a shock to some of them when a number of UE field leaders whom they had learned to trust in battle suddenly advised them the union was finished. Four union district presidents, plus about thirty international staff people and local union business agents, prevailed upon many locals to give up the UE and go elsewhere. The defectors could not agree among themselves on a particular AFL–CIO union and therefore split the locals up three ways: to IUE, IAM and the Auto Workers. Claiming that it was just impossible for the UE to survive as an organization any longer against the powerful government threat posed by the Subversive Activities Control Board, the defectors urged members to seek haven in the AFL–CIO.

One reason this was persuasive to a substantial number of members lay in the militant reputation the defectors themselves had developed over the years as fighters against redbaiting propaganda leveled at the union. Indeed, all of them had been labeled "Communist" more times than could be counted. Now, at the very moment the government had selected to charge the union directly with being "communist-infiltrated," they had decided to run for AFL–CIO cover, taking with them those members in whom they had built up confidence in their leadership qualities.

A very strange turn of events. They were recommending affiliation with unions whose officers and staffs, in raiding attacks upon the UE, had cried "Communist" the loudest against these particular UE field leaders. It can well be understood that the AFL–CIO unions might be willing to use any possible means for ripping off chunks of the UE membership. But how were they able to secure the cooperation of hitherto staunch UE leaders?

Some of the defectors, unlike the membership, had simply panicked when the Subversive Activities Control Board placed the union in its bombsights. Others confused the AFL–CIO "merger" with legitimate rank-and-file unity in the labor movement. Still others, weighing their own future jobs and careers in trade unionism, figured the hour had struck to make a fast getaway from the embattled UE. All in all, the defectors were able to carve about fifty thousand members out of the union, leaving the UE, surrounded on every side by enemies, with a last-ditch garrison force of approximately ninety thousand.

It seemed to almost everybody concerned with the labor movement that the UE had no alternative now but to throw in the towel. But even though the union had been drastically reduced in size, it still retained in its composition of membership and leadership the major elements of the broad coalition on which it had been originally based—and which had formed its strength at all times, no matter what its numbers. This was a coalition consisting of trade unionists "irrespective of skill, sex, race, or political beliefs." Some were conservative in outlook, some moderate, some had more radical inclinations and ideas. They held on, united in defense of the principles on which their union had been founded. Grouped in the front lines under fire in 1955 and the immediate years thereafter, they preserved the organization in day-by-day struggle.

IV The first constitutional convention of the AFL–CIO took place on December 5, 1955, at the Seventy-first Regiment Armory in New York City. Assembled were the top leaders of the two organizations who assured themselves they were participating in one of the greatest events in the annals of the American trade union movement. While they so congratulated one another that December day, AFL–CIO members were involved in several strikes, including one of fifty-five thousand UE and IUE Westinghouse workers. The delegates to the AFL–CIO convention acknowledged the strikes with a resolution which said: "The AFL–CIO and all its affiliates pledge their support and that of their membership for all legitimate strikes." At the time of this resolution's passage, several AFL unions with membership in Westinghouse plants, whose leaders were voting in favor of the resolution, had failed to join the UE and IUE strikers. Their members remained working.

Once the strike resolution was adopted, the next order of

business by sheer coincidence was a "presentation of rings." The chair recognized Tom Murphy, delegate from the bricklayers' union, who, mounting the rostrum, addressed the delegates as follows:

> During the two or three days of this convention I have read in the papers that it has been called a marriage. In most instances a marriage symbolizes an exchange of gifts or at least an exchange of rings between the interested parties.
>
> I would like to take this opportunity on behalf of the Bricklayers and Plasterers International Union to present this ring first to President Meany. The principals in a marriage ought to be joining hands rather than me. I am appearing here probably as the officiating clergyman without benefit of portfolio.
>
> I will now also call President Reuther to the platform to receive the same token of our esteem and affection.
>
> President Meany and you, President Reuther, on behalf of the organization which I am proud to represent, I thank you very much.

After the AFL–CIO leaders had completed their ceremony, concluded the convention, and departed, Westinghouse workers all over the country continued to walk the picket lines outside the plants for another three months. The merger had not softened up the company. But no matter. The workers had their own unity to take care of in the traditions of the working class rank-and-file. Especially was this so in the case of the six thousand workers in one Westinghouse plant. They were among the ninety thousand UE members who in late 1955 composed the invincible resistance force of the union.

It fell to the lot of the members of that militant organization in South Philadelphia, UE Local 107 at the Westinghouse turbine works, to demonstrate what rank-and-file unity was all about in that dark year. The companies—thoroughly confident by now that the 1955 defections from UE, the attack by the Subversive Activities Control Board, and the AFL–CIO wedding announcement, had so weakened the union that it was ready to be finished off—prepared to move in for the kill. Local

232

107, with its outstanding record for unity and solidarity, its deeply rooted traditions of militance manifested spontaneously whenever the need arose—as in the Carner-Lewin struggle of 1948—was selected by Westinghouse to suffer the fatal blow.

V   On August 12, 1955, this local union received a short note from the chief plant management official. Of all the local unions in the Westinghouse national chain, UE 107 was the only local to get such a notice:

> Gentlemen:
>
> My purpose in writing you at this time is to advise you . . . that effective as of midnight, October 14, 1955, the Company is terminating all local supplements covering the hourly and salaried employees of the South Philadelphia Turbine plant and all . . . understandings between foremen, supervisors, or other management people —and officers, stewards or representatives of the local at any level.

For seventeen years, "supplements" had formed part of the contractual relations between union and company at the turbine works. Such was also true at other individual Westinghouse plants. Ever since 1941 the UE had traditionally negotiated a national agreement with Westinghouse covering wages, hours, and conditions in the corporation's nationwide chain. Because each separate plant, however, had its own special problems, these were covered in local "supplements" to the national agreement. Termination of the "supplements," then, as announced by the company, would destroy a pattern of conditions in the plant established over years of bargaining.

What would replace them? For quite a while, management replied in general terms. All jobs, for example, would be redescribed and reclassified. And a completely new wage payment system would replace the one that had been in existence since time immemorial at the turbine plant.

The new wage payment system would provide for a 50-cent-an-hour wage cut, on the average, plantwide—a 20 percent pay cut for some of the most highly skilled workers in electrical manufacturing, whose average annual income, under the master plan, would be reduced to $3,900. The company also proposed that "the wage payment plan in effect will be measured day-work. . . . The company may apply individual or group production standards."

People who have never participated in collective bargaining in basic industry may have difficulty in understanding the tremendous import of these few words. The members of the negotiating committee, however, understood that "measured day-work" posed a speedup threat for six thousand workers, while the phrase "the company may apply individual or group production standards," spelled out Westinghouse intention to set aside the union's right to protect its members against speedup unlimited.

As the October 15 deadline approached in South Philadelphia, the local union negotiators could note no sign of change in the company position. On the contrary. The turbine plant's industrial relations officer put it this way: "We will tolerate no interference from the union. We do not intend to be saddled by the union pointing to past practices."

VI At midnight on October 14, 1955, workers of the second shift walked out through the five main gates of the enormous turbine plant. The union pickets took up their posts. They, and their union brothers and sisters from all three shifts, remained on picket duty for two hundred ninety-nine days—from the end of the World Series of 1955 almost to the finish of the 1956 pennant races. Many of the baseball fan members measured the duration of the strike in exactly that way.

A UE Local 107 pamphlet, the *Westinghouse Lockout*, which provided a day-by-day history of the struggle, concluded with these diary entries of 1956:

> *August 5:* General Negotiating Committee mails letter to membership notifying them of a special meeting the night of August 7 at Broadwood Hotel (in Philadelphia). Members are informed: "You will be given a copy of the proposed new agreement at this meeting."

234

August 6: General Negotiating Committee and company sign settlement agreement and new contract—subject to ratification by the membership. James J. Matles, UE director of organization, calls agreement one in which "there are no victors and no vanquished. It is a settlement between equals."

August 7: After meeting more than eight hours on August 6 to review the terms of the settlement, the Local 107 Executive Committee meets again for most of this day.

August 7: The membership discusses and debates the new agreement for over four hours at the membership meeting at the Hotel Broadwood.

August 8: At 1:00 A.M. in the morning, after 299 days of lockout, the tally of the secret ballot vote is announced. The vote is 2,167 to 539 for ratification of the new agreement. The lockout ends.

In the early morning hours of August 8, 1956, at the same time that the local agreement was approved, the Local 107 membership also ratified acceptance of a previously negotiated national Westinghouse contract. Since this provided a general wage increase throughout the Westinghouse chain, the workers of 107 had participated in winning a general wage increase; defeated the scheme to cut local wage rates by means of a new pay system at the turbine plant; defeated the scheme to terminate their local supplements; defeated the scheme to institute uncontrolled speedup and measured daywork.

But there was still another issue which, as negotiations reached the final stages, assumed a very important position in the list of items to be settled. During the lockout, Westinghouse fired fourteen members of Local 107, most of them leaders of the local. When the negotiators, months later, began to agree on some of the economic issues, the question of the fourteen became more and more the key to complete settlement. The union committee held off from discussing it until the last two weeks of the lockout. Why was that?

Bargaining tactics provides the answer. The committee felt that if it proceeded to discuss the fourteen before economic agreement seemed within grasp, Westinghouse would have little incentive to compromise on the discharges. If, however, the committee went beyond the stage of "within grasp," and wrapped up the economic issues, then the jobs of the fourteen the company was holding hostage would be in extreme jeopardy. The fourteen discharges, the toughest and last issue to be settled, were all lifted.

VII   Probably the most crucial episode of the 299-day confrontation between the membership of Local 107 and the Westinghouse Corporation was initiated on February 17, 1956. The company brought charges in county court against forty leaders of Local 107 who had been active on the picket line. Accused of having violated the injunction which the same court had handed down on the previous December 2, their trial began on February 27. Company testimony was provided by agents who had been posted in a third-floor office building observation post, equipped with spy glasses, movie camera, and tape recorder.

The "case of the 40" became the "case of the 26" on February 29, when the presiding judge handed out a total of twenty-two thousand dollars in fines against twenty-six of the leaders —and a five-thousand-dollar fine against Local 107. The union was given until March 2 to pay the fines. It not, the twenty-six leaders would be imprisoned "for an undetermined period of time." Among them were most of the members of the general (negotiating) committee and the officers of Local 107. They, and other members, got together and talked it over.

All of them, mindful of both the plight of their families and the interests of the membership, discussed these two concerns. It soon was agreed that the payment of the twenty-two-thousand-dollar fine would be a serious loss which the company was hoping to inflict on the limited relief resources of the union, paving the way for repeated use of the tactic so that union relief funds would be used not to feed the families of strikers, but to pay fines.

Then they talked about the effect that their going to jail

would have on their own families—their wives and children. They mentioned the support they had been getting on the home front. Their families were with them, one hundred per-cent. Would their going to jail hurt the morale of the families? It remained for John Schaefer, as happened at the executive board meeting in the Carner-Lewin case, to help all of them reach a decision. He was among the twenty-six under sentence.

"I've been getting along pretty well with my wife, Maggie, over the years," said Schaefer. "But I just have a notion that if I ducked out of going to jail at a time like this, I'd be in bad trouble at home." They decided unanimously to go to jail in-stead of paying the twenty-two thousand dollars in fines.

An account in the *Philadelphia Bulletin* described the morn-ing of March 2:

> Union members began assembling near the courthouse about 9 A.M. an hour before the deadline set by the judge for payment of the fine.
>
> Some of them began marching around in a large circle, carrying signs, one of which read: "Negotiate, Westing-house."
>
> The workers had been marching in the rain a short time when the county sheriff appeared and served notice they couldn't continue in that manner.
>
> The demonstrators then broke up into two stationary lines, each facing the other to form sort of a corridor leading to the steps of the courthouse.
>
> Then the defendants, who had been waiting under store awnings about a block away, started marching four abreast down South Avenue. (Wives walked with them.)
>
> As they swung onto the pavement and passed between the two lines of union members, loud cheers went up from the workers, who broke into "Solidarity Forever," a union song. The defendants filed into the courthouse and were placed in the basement cellblock. Shortly after-ward, they were taken to the county prison nine miles away.

A few hours later, with all but one member of the negotiat-ing committee safely behind bars, the company proposed resumption of bargaining. For the previous six weeks, Westinghouse had refused to negotiate. But now management said it was ready to do so. Company spokesmen suggested that the union had no option but to appoint a new negotiating committee. They intimated that Westinghouse was prepared to get going toward a resolution of the differences between union and company.

Local 107 promptly replied to the company's proposition. If the company was sincere about the resumption of bargaining, it could: (1) dispatch its negotiating representatives to jail to meet with the union committee, or (2) since it had put the union leaders in jail, no doubt it could get them out so that they would be free to negotiate.

Once again, a Westinghouse tactic boomeranged. The membership remained solid as ever. The labor movement of the area, the mayor of Philadelphia, the congressman in the district, the county commissioner, and people at large, condemned the company and backed the union.

VIII   On March 8, the Delaware County AFL-CIO Joint Labor Council sponsored a "town meeting." As UE Local 107's diary recorded, "It was historic. Under one roof was represented the entire labor movement of Delaware Valley. Over seventy-five union leaders were on the speakers' platform." The people at the meeting declared in a resolution: "The struggle of these workers shall go down as one of the proudest pages of all labor in Delaware Valley."

Two hours before the meeting started, the twenty-six jailed leaders had been visited by UE international officer Matles, who was on hand to lend help to Local 107 during the lockout. People in jail are allowed to meet with their attorneys. So, for the purpose of this visit, Matles assumed the role of an attorney.

He found twenty-five of the twenty-six lodged in one large cell equipped with double bunks. John Schaefer was walking around thoughtfully, pondering the whole situation. Among those with him was George Baker, one of Schaefer's old friends and close companions in all the struggles at the turbine plant.

Every few minutes a prison guard, making the rounds of the cell blocks, would pass close by. Whenever he did, all he heard was "lawyer" language: writs, habeas corpus, contempt of court, things like that. As soon as he was out of hearing, the jailed leaders got an earful from Matles about the state of the lockout, how the rank-and-file was holding up, the great rally scheduled to take place that very evening, and so forth.

Then Matles went to see the other member of the jailed leadership, laid up in the infirmary with bursitis. As Matles climbed the narrow stairs, the guard escorting him took a quick look around and then whispered, "Watch yourself now. Be careful what you say to him. They got his bunk bugged."

When it came time for all the twenty-five prisoners downstairs to say goodby to their "attorney," he shook hands with each one of them. The last handshake left a piece of crumpled paper in his palm. Outside, Matles examined it. The paper contained a message to be read to the workers at the meeting that night. The last six words of the message said: "Carry on! Don't worry about us."

About two weeks later, minutes before an order was expected from the Pennsylvania Supreme Court directing release of the jailed twenty-six—an order requested by counsel representing UE—they were freed on order of the county court judge. "Our going to jail," said the report made to the members at the ratification meeting on August 7, "and our membership carrying on in the same effective manner, was the turning point in our struggle."

Among those who had stepped forward to help the membership "carry on" was a worker who had been one of the pioneer IWW band active in the turbine plant in the twenties. He was Howard Dietrich, a former president of the local. He resumed that job, temporarily, while the leaders were in jail. "Howard was at the union office twelve and fourteen hours a day," a member recalls. "When the fellows were freed, Dietrich went back to rank-and-file picket duty."

Two weeks after the strike ended, the Local 107 executive committee prepared for publication in the *UE News* a report for the entire UE membership, saying in part:

When the gates swung open again on August 8 they were opened by more than the 6,000 UE Local 107 members. They were reopened by the entire labor movement of the Philadelphia-Delaware County area, and by a host of friends and neighbors in the communities.

IX   Among the friends and neighbors were thousands who had responded to what Local 107 members called "Maggie's plan." Maggie Schaefer had a full-time job at the SKF ball-bearing works in Philadelphia, where she was a leader of the local union of AFL–CIO Steel Workers. But like many other wives of the workers of Westinghouse turbine, she also involved herself in extra duty on the lockout front. Maggie headed the women's committee of the lockout. One day, when the winter was rough and spirits a bit low, the women got talking about how to give things a lift. Maggie came up with an idea.

For many weeks, various groups of Local 107 members had been circulating out to the gates of shops and plants in the Philadelphia area, collecting contributions from other workers to support the 107 cause. The support had been steady and generous. What Maggie proposed was to broaden the approach by going to neighborhoods, house by house, appealing to working people in their homes to give what they could to the support of the members of Local 107 and their families.

An unusual idea. Whether it had ever been tried anywhere in similar circumstances, no one knew. At least no one had ever heard of it. Some were worried that if it didn't come up to expectations, it would be a setback for the morale of the Local 107 membership. Was it too risky?

Maggie didn't think so. Her own enthusiasm for the project was so contagious that she convinced the lockout leadership to give it a try. Soon residents of Philadelphia, first in one section, then in another, were finding on their doorsteps or in their mailboxes a leaflet headlined: "HELP WESTINGHOUSE WORKERS." Its text read:

> Dear friend: This is the fifteenth week of the Westinghouse lockout.

240

Six thousand workers are still solidly resisting the attempts of the Westinghouse Company to force us to take an average 20% wage cut and destroy our union conditions. This would mean a yearly loss of $7,000,000 in purchasing power in our area.

We feel that this fight is important not only to our own families but to the families of all working people in this area. A major wage reduction in any one industry can and will ultimately affect the working people in all industries and the merchants who depend on the wages of workers for their sales.

For this reason we are appealing for public support. We are soliciting foodstuffs as well as money contributions to aid our people over this difficult period.

Tomorrow we will be here to solicit your support. Anything you care to contribute—can or coin—will be appreciated.

The leaflet was signed: Workers of Westinghouse UE Local 107.

Several weeks later a reporter from the *UE News* went from international union headquarters in New York to Philadelphia to have a look at "Maggie's Plan" in action. He wrote:

The response to the program of the Local 107 community relations committee—one of the most extraordinary operations in labor history—has astounded even the most experienced labor leaders in the area.

The *UE News* account recorded that in the initial stages of the program many thousands of dollars worth of food—and several thousands in cash besides—were donated. Rank-and-file members, going house to house in a neighborhood the day after a leaflet was distributed, found people sympathetic and as generous as their means allowed.

X   "All of labor is watching you," the *UE News* reported one woman saying as she welcomed a collection team into her home. Perhaps she hit it right. Not just as far as UE

Local 107 was concerned. The life of the entire UE was on the line in this crucial period of its career. Attacks from without, defections from within, a total membership of ninety thousand, a national strike of members throughout the Westinghouse chain—and then, after that was settled, the protracted struggle at the Westinghouse turbine plant in South Philadelphia where the company had given every evidence of trying to break through toward eventual elimination of the UE from the entire industry. All of labor may well have been watching the UE. All of labor—and a lot of others besides.

What they were observing was a clue to the union's survival: "democratic unionism guaranteed by a broadly participating rank-and-file in all phases of the struggle." The quote is taken from the report to the whole UE membership issued by Local 107's executive committee after the settlement at South Philadelphia. Said the report, further: "UE Local 107 members can never forget and will be forever grateful that it was the UE international union, UE locals and members throughout the country who gave first, gave the most and were our firmest and most reliable source of support throughout the 299 days— when not one scab entered the plant." Just as the solidarity of Local 107 members behind their jailed leaders marked a turning point in the lockout struggle, so the solidarity of UE members across the country behind Local 107 marked a turning point in the UE's struggle for survival.

"Our victory," declared the local union's report, "is a victory of unity." The unity had extended from the rank-and-file membership of Local 107 to the other workers in the Westinghouse chain to "all our brothers and sisters of UE." It had extended into other labor organizations in the area, particularly the AFL–CIO of Delaware County, and into the people of the community. Could all this be regarded as the first step in UE's long march back to a place in the ranks of a reunited militant labor movement? There is reason to look at it that way. Especially when the parallels are drawn with an event of unity many years later as the UE, together with other unions in the industry, challenged the General Electric Company and its "take-it-or-leave-it" labor relations policy, known as Boulwarism.

242

PART THREE

FIGHTING FOR UNITY

16
GE's Take-It-or-Leave-It

I   When GE's Charles Wilson resumed the presidency of the company in late 1945 soon after the end of the Second World War, he brought with him a newcomer to General Electric management, Lemuel R. Boulware. Wilson had become acquainted with the aptitudes and views of Boulware when both were serving with the War Production Board, Wilson as vice-chairman, Boulware as his assistant. For Boulware the opportunity to join GE represented a step up into bigtime industry.

Then in his early fifties, with the air of a successful salesman, Boulware had proceeded in a business career through stages as an accountant, purchasing agent, comptroller, factory manager, marketing manager for Easy Washing Machine Company, general manager of Carrier Corporation, and general manager of Celotex. Very little on the surface of this experience suggested the eventual role he was to play in GE's postwar operation against workers and unions. Indeed, his initial assignment with General Electric—vice-president in charge of its wholly owned subsidiaries—appeared to indicate that Wilson wished to add Boulware's executive assets to the company in a routine management position.

Developments of early 1946, however, thrust Boulware out of the subsidiaries sideline and into something crucial to the whole company. Wilson gave him the job of studying and analyzing what had gone wrong—from the GE point of view—with its efforts to contain the UE drive in 1946 for wage increases aimed at making up a measure of the income losses the workers had suffered during the war period. Some years later a report drawn up by a trial examiner of the National Labor Relations Board on GE's collective bargaining conduct provided some illustrative quotations from Boulware's analysis of the 1946 UE strike. It had been, in GE-Boulware perspective, "little short of a debacle" and a "somber event" for company management, which received a "jolt" from the fact that the strike had "been broadly supported, not only by the employees but by many segments of the community."

Just as the strike itself had pulled Boulware away from overseeing GE's subsidiaries, so his report of that "somber event" led Wilson, in 1947, to create a title for his former wartime assistant in keeping with brand new company duties to which he was now assigned. Boulware became vice-president of "Relations Services." As the National Labor Relations Board trial examiner put it: "UE's highly successful strike ... motivated management to develop [a] new approach to employee and union relations, which approach was conceived in 1947 and developed by Lemuel R. Boulware."

Thus it was that the former accountant and marketing manager came to be transformed into the inventor, director, and promoter of a phenomenon which achieved wide recognition under the one-word epithet, "Boulwarism." Although Boulware, in his retirement, was to disown "good-humoredly" all rights to authorship of the name bestowed upon his baby, he nevertheless wrote a book about it called *The Truth About Boulwarism.* He did so, he explained, because of popular demand for definition of the term coming from corporation labor relations specialists, business school faculties, students, universities, the daily press, and "dictionary people." He went on to say that these elements desired "authentic reference material on the employee and community relations work with which I was associated from mid-1947 through 1960," at which point he—but not Boulwarism—retired from GE.

II   There was cause to assume in 1969, the year in which *The Truth About Boulwarism* came off the press, that this "ism" required both definition and the kind of "soul-searching study" which Boulware had said he gave to the 1946 situation, when UE, representing about 96 percent of GE workers, had shut down all the company's plants for the first time in history. But there is also reason to conclude, on the basis of the disparity between his book and the actual record of Boulwarism, that those who were demanding enlightenment from Boulware didn't get it. Nowhere in the book's 180 pages, for example, was the trained accountant as candid with figures as the National Labor Relations Board trial examiner, who reported that "as a result of the 1946 strike . . . the company was forced to raise its pre-strike offer of ten-cents-an-hour to 18½ cents." Nor did *The Truth About Boulwarism* clarify exactly why Wilson's 1946 under-the-sun-lamp-offer of the 10 cents to the UE officers, delivered as a take-it-or-leave-it proposition, could be rejected and subsequently converted by the union into a far better settlement.

In 1946 this General Electric approach produced something "little short of a debacle" for the company. In 1947 and 1948 the UE continued to improve the union's national contract. It was not until 1950 that Boulwarism really got going with a series of resounding triumphs which led corporation executives and lawyers, professors, management consultants, mediators and arbitrators, labor reporters, labor lawyers, and even some labor leaders to confess themselves dazzled by its ingenious conception and execution. Boulwarism was a hit. As the years went along, moreover, the show kept getting bigger and flashier.

A union negotiating committee would meet regularly with GE management representatives in collective bargaining sessions that came close to ritual. The union committee presented its demands for revisions in the contract. Management listened. Company functionaries scribbled copious notes. Once in a while a company spokesman might comment, in the manner of a supreme court justice, that such and such a union argument was unsound, unreasonable, and unthinkable. Or another might hand down the GE opinion that indeed everything in the contract disturbing to the union was perfectly all right just as it was. On the whole, however, the company people didn't say much. Nor make any counter proposals. They sat there, across the table, observing the form of collective bargaining as technically required by law. Thus weeks would pass.

At length, on a particular day, the show would open. Union

247

negotiators familiar with the routine of Boulwarism had learned to sense the signs. There was a kind of expectancy in the atmosphere. The company representatives seemed suddenly to have come alive. Then all at once the entire GE cast would put in an appearance with props. Curtain going up! Technicians, projection people, public relations specialists, various assistants, all were suddenly on the scene with documents, charts, graphs, slides, films, lights, screens, cameras. Everything but bells ringing, everything but a full-piece orchestra fanfare. In such fashion General Electric presented its package-style contract terms *à la Boulware.*

Simultaneously, across the country in every major GE plant, road show companies went through a miniature performance. Local company managements would gather workers together on company time as captive audiences. Supervisors distributed literature containing the company terms and the promotion therefor. Similar material would be found in full-page ads in community newspapers. Instead of one grand opening in Manhattan, there were a hundred or so, all timed, scheduled and run off like clockwork as if by pushbutton signal from GE headquarters on Lexington Avenue in New York. The gist of the sales pitch flowed from the formula which Boulware in his book described as the essence of Boulwarism: that the company terms reflected the "best balanced interests" of the General Electric family—stockholders, employees, and consumers of GE products.

In 1946, Wilson had presented his 10-cent-an-hour "take-it-or-leave-it" offer in terse, unadorned, even casual style. GE terms under Boulwarism were also conveyed as take-it-or-leave-it offerings. But very much dressed up in Madison Avenue promotion finery. After 1950, as the company succeeded in establishing its terms in the plants, almost everybody seemed to be ready to accept this as proof positive that GE's Boulware had without question managed to discover a scientific formula of "relations"—which, by sheer force of fact and dramatic presentation, was accomplishing its wonders among the workers. This was Boulware's and GE's own public estimate of their accomplishment—"trying to do right voluntarily," to quote the motto of the Boulware book—taken at face value by observers,

248

practitioners, and scholars of labor relations the nation over. Very few, if any, saw through the Madison Avenue wrappings.

III Between 1936 and 1946 the UE's long-range organizing plans had not only brought GE under national contract but had established the union as representative of all but a small fraction of the workers in the shops. It was the one big union in electrical manufacturing. At the time of the 1946 strike, moreover, the three largest mass production unions in the country—Auto Workers, Steel Workers, and UE—fought a united CIO battle to victory. In 1947 and 1948, with the cold war gathering momentum, and with the UE expressing differences within the CIO on the questions of organizing the unorganized, Taft-Hartley, and independent political action, the union still made advances in GE negotiations. Boulware had become vice-president in charge of "Relations Services" in 1947. Nevertheless, in that year, for the first time in mass production industry the UE won paid holidays from GE. In 1948 the union went on to secure an increase in wages which Phil Murray successfully used as a lever to reopen the Steel Workers contract on the wage issue, which to that point the steel industry had refused to do.

In the year 1949, however, drastic changes occurred within the CIO. Unity among the three large mass production unions had given way to civil war, with two of the unions, Auto Workers and Steel Workers, conducting raids upon UE shops. The UE, after repeated but unheeded requests to Murray to stop the raids, ceased paying CIO per capita tax, sent no delegates to the 1949 convention and thus severed its CIO connections. Murray between 1946 and 1949 had been surrendering more and more trade union ground under the pressures exerted by the cold war Truman administration. The result was to split CIO industrial unionism asunder. At the 1949 CIO convention, Murray's creation of a new union in electrical manufacturing, immediately followed by the CIO-corporation-government offensive against the UE, threw collective bargaining procedures into chaos. By the time the smoke cleared in 1950, the GE formula of Boulwarism made its appearance at the bargaining table.

This was the stage-setting for what the National Labor Relations Board trial examiner had called a new approach to employee and union relations. In its analysis of this new approach, the UE said:

> Take-it-or-leave-it bargaining is far from unique with GE. All corporations want to give as little as possible and all want to dictate their terms. To the extent that they can, they do. Charlie Wilson tried to dictate the terms in 1946 on a take-it-or-leave-it basis—but the union was strong enough to "leave it" and fight it out. What gave Boulwarism its power for collective bargaining was the splitting up of the solid ranks of GE workers—a joint enterprise of GE, the CIO and the Truman Administration.

IV   At the time of this UE analysis of Boulwarism, some years of union encounters with the formula had passed, during which period workers had been afforded opportunity to learn things not spelled out in *The Truth About Boulwarism*. In negotiations, for example, after union committees had been treated to the spectacle of the "best balanced interest" company terms, and the company sales promotion floodgates had been opened wide, GE standard operating procedure called for concentration upon the weakest links in the pattern of divided unionism which now prevailed throughout the GE chain of plants.

The UE and Murray's CIO union in electrical manufacturing represented between them about seventy percent of GE organized workers—and were the only unions with national contracts. From 1938 to 1949 the UE national contract had covered almost all of the workers in the GE chain. The CIO's creation of the IUE established a new pattern: a UE national contract for the plants it continued to represent, and an IUE national contract covering plants where this union had obtained representation rights. Other unions, which after 1949 came to represent approximately 30 percent of the organized GE workers, occupied isolated positions wherein they were obliged to negotiate individual local contracts for each shop. It was this new broken pattern which enabled the company to congratulate itself publicly on having done away with the "labor monopoly" in its domain—although, of course, GE maintained its own monopoly on companywide collective bargaining.

While the negotiating committees of the two unions holding national contracts would be meeting separately in New York with company representatives, local committees from the other isolated plant unions were going through the motions of bargaining individually with local plant managements. Everyone understood that this was no more than marking time, that they were waiting until GE handed terms to UE and IUE. This waiting period, however, both in the field and in New York, constituted an important element in the strategy of Boulwarism. It was intended to build up expectations and impatience among the workers, to make them hungry for whatever goodies the company, in its own calculated time, decided to unveil. A sort of "what will we find under the Christmas Tree?" situation.

GE practice, once the terms were out in the open, was to push for signing as many individual plant contracts with the isolated unions as rapidly as possible. At this stage of Operation Boulwarism, the company would proceed to make public, in all its plants and the communities where they were located, reports of the agreements that had been signed. It was similar to the "body count" method of the U.S. military in furnishing news of "progress" in the war against the Vietnamese. Similar, too, to the sales figures for a new product which a corporation releases in order to impress both stockholders and consumers with the idea that if so many are eating it up, it sure must be great.

Boulwarism, as a matter of fact, was not simply a "new approach to employee and union relations" but rather a product designed, engineered, manufactured, promoted, and sold by methods which industry has developed—and continues to refine—for its consumer items. "I was told," Boulware related in his book, "to come up with a program that would utilize in employee and community relations those principles and practices that had been found successful in dealing with people in other areas of the business." One such "principle," fundamental to the success of Boulwarism, was the prior creation of favorable marketing conditions for distribution of the product. When the UE analyzed Boulwarism, it pointed this out:

> Boulwarism in collective bargaining has learned from dealing with its employees powerfully united in one militant union—UE. GE now deals, as it brags, with a hundred unions. This is what gives GE power to enforce Boulwarism in labor relations—*and it is this alone.* To attribute, as many tend to do, GE's successful application of Boulwarism in labor relations to the flood of GE's propaganda is an insulting underestimation of the intelligence of GE workers. They are just as well able to see through the company's self-serving flood of hogwash as are the workers of any other company. It is not "employee communications" that powered Boulwarism. It is company-manufactured employee disunity.

V

Disunity made it possible for GE under Boulwarism to impose, at each round of negotiations, its economic terms upon the unions. When the company said "take-it-or-leave-it" in regard to such things as wages, pensions, vacations, holidays, and the like, both the UE and the CIO union had to take it. There was no escape. But nevertheless, the two unions were in different situations when it came to contract provisions covering job conditions. There, over a period of eleven years of previous contract negotiations, the UE had been able to build up—because of its overall organization of the company and the consolidation of the strength of the organized workers —a series of steady improvements.

Experienced managements are well aware that any effort to take away from a union already established contractual rights affecting conditions on the job is bound to provoke most bitter battles. For that reason the UE, its contract provisions achieved

252

by struggle since 1938, could resist successfully company schemes to tamper with these provisions. The new CIO union, on the other hand, was required to start from scratch to negotiate a new contract. By the time Boulwarism got done with the IUE–CIO in 1950, that union's first GE agreement had missing from it a number of important provisions on working conditions long-established in the UE national contract. Westinghouse, taking advantage of the Boulwarism lead, drove harder bargains still. Or tried to. Whatever GE compelled the unions to take, Westinghouse endeavored to force them to take in greater measure.

Thus it was that through the fifties the workers in the two major corporations of the electrical manufacturing industry began to fall economically behind their fellow industrial unionists in auto and steel, whereas, up until 1948, with their one big union, they had been marching forward in the same front lines. Waves of resentment rolled up from IUE membership, hard hit by Boulwarism. This placed James Carey, designated by Phil Murray to head the new CIO union in 1949, in an increasingly critical personal position.

Murray, Carey's protector and defender, had died in 1952, whereupon Dave McDonald took over at the top of the Steel Workers union and Walter Reuther, leader of the Auto Workers, succeeded Murray as CIO president. Reuther and McDonald had achieved public recognition as prominent labor leaders, while Carey, forever aspiring to be so regarded, had never felt that he was accepted in their league.

Boulwarism, also, had humiliated Carey. As each period of collective bargaining with GE approached, Carey fell into the habit of predicting the death of Boulwarism. But when the bargaining was over, and the contract signed, there was no mistake about Boulwarism's state of health. It was in tip-top condition. Every contract imposing take-it-or-leave-it economic terms on the workers provided concrete evidence of the renewal of Boulwarism vigor and vitality. At length, in 1960, Carey felt driven by all these factors toward a desperate fling at making the grade. He placed himself in the position of commander-in-chief of the IUE committee handling negotiations with GE.

VI   The manner in which his negotiations were transacted, and the results to which they led, can be conveyed in excerpts from a verbatim transcript of exchanges between Carey and GE representatives at 1960 bargaining meetings. The quotations are taken from a record compiled by the National Labor Relations Board, which held hearings upon complaint from the AFL–CIO union that the company was not bargaining in good faith:

Carey: Have you ever heard of Matthew Carey?

Northrop [a GE representative]:   Let's get back to farming out [subcontracting GE work] and get away from your favorite ancestors. . . .

Carey: He was chased out of Ireland, got a few dollars from Benjamin Franklin and went into the printing business. . . .

Northrop: You may be right.

Carey: Damn right. I'm seldom wrong. You know, that's where Boulware got his "balanced best interests" theories. . . . I would like to have the James B. Carey Testimonial Library, Rutgers University—some call it Memorial Library—I would like to have company minutes from 1955, '58 and '60 sent there so the students could look at them and study them. You see, I never expected to live this long. I thought the Commies would get me by this time. How I can live the life that *you* make for me, I don't know. You know, it is hard for me to hold my head up when I meet with Reuther and McDonald. Reuther has been able to get things that we haven't been able to get in our industry. He's looked at with envy. I was elected in 1933 to National Office and he wasn't until 1946. It hurts me deeply to see them get these things. When I met McDonald, he was typing agreements, not negotiating. [McDonald originally entered the Mine Workers Union as a secretary and stenographer for Murray.] It's embarrassing for me, Mr. Moore [a vice-president of GE]. . . . I am not interested in becoming a nervous wreck. When I write my book I want to say good things about you, Mr. Moore. . . . I'm

254

proud of Walter Reuther and I have respect for him. I have been working with him for years. If you'd listen to him, it wouldn't be as good as listening to me because I have been in the business longer. . . . I'd like to discuss your Marxism theories with you, too. . . . You know, in Oklahoma, in a small town that had a population of about 6,000 I was main speaker at an event at which 35,000 people attended. . . .

Hilbert [attorney for GE]: Mr. Carey, what does that have to do with what we are here for today?

Carey: It has to do with GE. Who is GE to shut me off? . . . You know Mrs. Roosevelt called me last night?

Hilbert: Was it a sympathy call?

Carey: She heard I was in town.

Willis [a GE representative]: She has probably been watching TV.

Carey: If you want to know the source of the proposals made by Walter Reuther, ask me. It was written by me and presented in a resolution in Cuba in 1939. I was the author of it. . . . You are talking to the dean of this meeting. Why talk to lesser people? I know most about it. I'm more effective. . . . It's a shame that you don't quote the two deans, Cordiner [GE president] and Carey . . ."

Toward the end of one of the final sessions, Carey introduced the prospect of a strike, saying: "You see, Mr. Moore, not one plant will operate. I doubt like hell if this building [GE New York headquarters] will even operate."

To which a company officer replied, "We're going to keep the plants open, Mr. Carey."

Very shortly there ensued what the labor editor of *The New York Times,* A. H. Raskin, described as "the worst setback any union has received . . . since World War II." It came about after Carey, without a vote of the membership, called a strike. Thousands of union members failed to respond. The company promptly launched a back-to-work movement which broke the abortive strike in short order.

Carey's four-year term as union president ran out in 1964.

In that year he was challenged for top office in the union by one of his previous supporters, Paul Jennings. The system of electing officers by mail ballot, instituted at the time Murray set up the IUE organization, permitted control of the election machinery by the incumbent administration of the union, whose trustees—all of them in Carey's camp—declared him reelected. Jennings contested the count in a protest laid before the Department of Labor, which found that the election had been stolen for Carey. After a year of court squabbles the issue was settled without another election, when Carey's resignation paved the way for a union executive board decision to install Jennings as president of the AFL–CIO International Union of Electrical, Radio and Machine Workers, the IUE.

VII   Even under the most exacting siege conditions, the UE over the years had consistently called for UE–IUE unity in contract negotiations with the two major companies. The demonstrated accomplishments of Boulwarism, exploiting for GE benefit the employer-manufactured separation of workers into a number of different unions, strengthened the UE argument for unity as time went by. Out in the field it began to make more and more sense to the workers in the shops. In 1966, however, the new IUE leadership was not disposed to cooperate with the UE. Each union in that year's negotiations continued independently to develop and pursue a bargaining strategy which, in both cases, could not help but be influenced by the restlessness of the rank-and-file.

For the first time since 1946 the UE conducted a strike vote by calling all its GE members out of the plants during working hours to cast their ballots. This tactic in itself, signifying a militant UE show of strength, exercised GE management. Even though Boulware himself had retired, the company took it for granted that his formula would endure, holding the divided workers in check. The results of the UE strike vote, which took place in October 1966 not long before the contract deadline, were even more disturbing to GE: overwhelmingly in favor of strike action if necessary. Soon the IUE also announced its readiness to strike unless a satisfactory agreement was reached.

At this point there occurred a high-level intervention. President Lyndon Johnson requested IUE leaders to postpone strike action, pending appointment of a special White House panel assigned to seek settlement between IUE and GE. The three panel members held presidential cabinet rank: Secretary of Defense Robert McNamara, Secretary of Labor Willard Wirtz, and Secretary of Commerce John Conners. Their settlement terms, after separate meetings with GE and IUE, prompted a statement from UE which began: "While UE was engaged in direct collective bargaining, the Administration used its power to force the AFL–CIO union to accept the GE formula."

The UE went on to say that the three-year contract terms provided for less than half of the wage losses sustained in the past by GE workers due to increases in the cost of living—and afforded less than 50 percent protection against future increases. This was a reference to the inflationary economic escalation at home following close upon President Johnson's 1965 escalation, by massive bombing, of the war being conducted against the Vietnamese people. The UE statement on the GE settlement imposed by the White House concluded: "GE's unyielding collective bargaining practice known as Boulwarism has again escaped unscathed as it has ever since 1949, when GE workers were split."

VIII   At its 1964 and 1965 conventions—and again in 1966—the UE had drawn attention to the horror, futility and economic consequences for the American people of the military adventure in Vietnam. Just as the UE was among the first unions in the country in 1946 to warn of dangers inherent in the Truman-Churchill cold war foreign policy, so it was among the first in 1964 to call for a negotiated end to the hot war in Indochina. "Efforts to apply military solutions to problems of international relationships are irrational in origin and ruinous in prospect. Only a foreign policy aimed at peace among all nations can serve the interests of people everywhere." So the UE had said since 1946. At the union's 1966 convention in Pittsburgh, a resolution headed *The Search for Peace* opened with this paragraph:

> The war in Vietnam has brought us face to face with the most serious crisis. Today, more than 300,000 of our men are fighting and many of them are dying in the jungles 9,000 miles away from home. Among them are our own young members who have been drafted out of the shops, and each day more are drafted to join those already there. The cost of living has been rising rapidly, taxes have been going up and the fight against poverty is being sacrificed, while corporations are wallowing in the greatest profits in history.

At the time that Johnson put White House weight and prestige to work in settling the 1966 IUE dispute with GE, the top leadership of the AFL–CIO, headed by George Meany, constituted strong institutional support for the Johnson war policies. This was a prime factor inhibiting in that year collective bargaining cooperation between the UE and IUE. But these same war policies were leading some former bitter enemies of UE to urge, in 1966, that the IUE and UE get together.

Among them was Monsignor Charles Owen Rice of Pittsburgh, who, back in the days when he had been Father Rice, a mentor of the Association of Catholic Trade Unionists, had few rivals in hostility toward the UE and few who could be said to have helped more to weaken and split the union. If Father Rice were to be awarded an honorary degree as masterplanner of the redbaiting war upon the UE in the late 1940s and through the fifties, it would be difficult to discover anyone knowledgeable of the period who might dispute his title.

By the mid-sixties, however, the Monsignor's public opposition to the U.S. military adventure in Indochina had helped to lead him toward a revised view of the UE's position in the labor movement. Writing in 1966 in the *Pittsburgh Catholic,* Monsignor Rice declared that the UE had been one of the victims of McCarthyism—and that AFL–CIO unions in GE, facing "the enemy as a unit," would be "even stronger if they were to accept the UE as an ally." Shortly after the Monsignor had so expressed himself, he put in a telephone call to the hotel in

Pittsburgh where UE president Fitzgerald had just arrived for the union's 1966 convention.

"Fitzie," he said, "you are surprised to hear from me. I read the news that your convention is in town and I'm calling to wish you well." When Fitzgerald replied that the good wishes were coming twenty years too late, Monsignor Rice said "Even twenty years is not too long for a man to change his mind." Telling the story at a later UE convention, Fitzgerald remarked to the delegates that Father Rice regretted "all the losses that you have taken for the last twenty years," adding, "I forgive him and I suppose you do, too."

IX   By 1966 the UE's low point of ninety thousand members a decade previous had been left well behind, as its resumption of extensive organizing work, and the return to the union of some shops lost during the McCarthy period, brought the organization to a stage where it represented about one hundred sixty-five thousand workers. It was the UE's survival, and increased strength, which provided the basis for continuing the struggle for unity of workers and their organizations confronting the two giant corporations in electrical manufacturing, GE and Westinghouse.

That struggle began to develop after the White House had imposed 1966 GE settlement terms upon the unions in the form of a three-year contract. The UE statement—that Boulwarism had once again "escaped unscathed" and that GE workers had received in wage adjustments nowhere near what the cost-of-living escalation justified—was a realistic analysis. Victory for Boulwarism in a period of war-induced rapidly rising living costs, combined with accelerated company speedup measures in the shops, began to crystalize rank-and-file sentiment for unity in the next negotiations. The imposed settlement of 1966 had furnished a lesson: Militant unity between the unions was imperative.

While possibilities for such unity were being studied and explored by the UE through 1967 and into 1968, tensions at the top of the AFL–CIO exploded. Walter Reuther and George

Meany had long been at odds. Finally Reuther listed a series of complaints against the AFL–CIO under president Meany's stewardship, charging failure to organize the unorganized, failure in satisfactory collective bargaining settlements, failure in legislative action. It sounded very much like a replay of the UE position in the CIO after the Second World War, at which time Reuther had been on the other side of the fence. Also, Reuther's condemnation of the Meany-dictated AFL–CIO policy on the U.S. war in Vietnam as being "unworthy of the labor movement" indicated, as in the case of Monsignor Rice, that the position of UE and some other unions against war and militarism in foreign policy was no longer a lonely one. People inside and outside the labor movement of the country were beginning to have second thoughts on the subject.

A decision by the Reuther-led union, the Auto Workers, to withhold per capita payments from the AFL–CIO, and to send no delegates to the AFL–CIO convention in Miami in the fall of 1968, resulted in a convention vote to expel the union. Another instance, in a house of labor, of the old "You can't quit, you're fired" procedure. Be that as it may, the departure of the Auto Workers from the AFL–CIO fold, occurring as it did at a critical stage of the UE's drive for unity in preparation for 1969's contract talks with GE and Westinghouse, posed several worrisome problems. Would the Auto Workers and the Teamsters—the two largest U.S. unions which as independent organizations had just formed the Alliance for Labor Action—agree to join hands and cooperate in a unity framework with AFL–CIO unions? Would Meany regard the Auto Workers–Teamsters alliance as "dual unionism" and, in effect, forbid AFL–CIO organizations to have anything to do with those unions?

The UE took the initiative in urging upon the IUE–AFL–CIO and the now independent Auto Workers the need for a unified approach to bargaining with GE and Westinghouse. Whatever differences might exist among the unions, the UE argued in preliminary exchanges and soundings with various leaders, they could not be permitted to intrude upon the primary job of confronting the corporations from a position of strength. In early January 1969, the UE and IUE leaderships agreed "to undertake steps to establish joint cooperation" in getting ready for that year's bargaining with GE and Westinghouse. Later, in a letter to UE president Fitzgerald, Reuther and executive vice-president Frank E. Fitzsimmons of the Teamsters Union, on behalf of the Alliance for Labor Action, committed their organizations to "the achievement of maximum cooperation and coordination . . . as they relate to the forthcoming GE negotiations." Thus, after twenty years, union leaders described by *The New York Times* as "long-estranged" embarked upon coordinated moves which, although they had not been among the objectives of Lemuel R. Boulware in 1947 when he began laboratory work on his GE formula, nonetheless were in truth produced by nothing but Boulwarism.

Many UE members, curious as the unusual get-togethers started, asked the union's international officers what was said when they met for the first time in twenty years with Reuther, Jennings and their associate officers. "No one on either side," the answer came, "said a single word about the past. All of us acted as if we had seen each other just a few days before." The UE, which had worked so long to bring these meetings about, opened up with, "Guys, we want to talk about how best we can pull ourselves together to handle the bastards this time around." That's all it took to get the discussions going.

17
The Great 1969-70 Strike

I   The first entry in a UE record of the united union effort to secure a 1969 settlement with GE ran like this:

Formal negotiations started with GE on July 28, 1969. Negotiations proceeded in the normal manner under the Boulware formula. The company just going along day by day listening to the union's proposals.

For almost six months, UE and IUE, as the two principal organizations, each holding GE national contracts, had been developing understandings on the presentation of economic and other issues. The most important understanding, however, was that on working as a team, allied in cooperation with the other unions. All agreed that come what may, they would stick together. For UE and IUE, once the meetings with GE began, this required a system of regular conferences on how things were going in their separate sessions with company representatives.

Under the Taft-Hartley Act the company could oppose meeting with a joint union committee. It preferred to continue, Boulware-style, the separate meetings which had been the custom for twenty years. During that period UE and IUE national negotiating committees met at the same time in the same building—the GE skyscraper headquarters on the corner of Lexington Avenue and Fifty-first Street in New York City—but on different floors and with different GE negotiating squads. During the long stretch of no contact between the unions, the company advantage, to say the least, was considerable. GE could exercise complete control until it came time for the Boulware spectacular. In 1969, however, the UE and IUE committees through August and September continued to keep one another informed.

Not that there was much to talk about at first. For two months we "tried to get some indication of company attitude on numerous contractual improvements in working conditions," the UE recorded in its notes. "Indication of attitude," a phrase used by the company in finally agreeing to place contractual issues, as distinct from economic issues, first on the agenda, turned out to mean very little in regard to union demands. Among the contractual matters were procedures for protecting workers against layoffs due to automation or plant closings, as GE followed its postwar practice of shifting some plants overseas or to low-wage areas in this country; and an end to the company policy of avoiding the equal-pay-for-equal-work standard by classifying certain jobs, mostly performed by women, at rates which might be lower than unskilled rates for cleanup or sweeper jobs.

Also, the UE raised several so-called "little issues"—meaning that they were confined to local plant situations or could be considered not to have the general import of the union's major economic demands. Nevertheless, these "little issues" were of extreme importance to workers affected by them— to second- and third-shift workers in plants where the company had refused to assign a doctor or nurse to infirmary duty, as was done for first-shift workers; to the women workers of a shop in Waynesboro, Virginia, whose need for replacement of "lint-free" dresses required on certain special jobs was not being met by GE. This "little issue," as it turned out, persisted in dispute until the last hours of settlement.

About mid-September, according to the UE record, the unions introduced economic issues: "wages, cost-of-living safeguards for the next three contract years, pensions, insurance, sick leave and others. Here the old pattern prevailed without the slightest change. The company would hear us out, hear all our arguments, then they would bring in their economists... and so it went on into early October." The UE record described John Shambo, chairman of the IUE–GE Conference Board, as nailing it right on the head when he remarked, "We were just shoveling smoke."

II   Although the company had given few "indications of attitude" on issues brought forward by the unions, the UE and IUE negotiators agreed that they had caught hints of GE intentions to include in this year's "Boulwarism gift package" some changes the company wanted to make in long-standing relationships between the two major unions and the company. These would be so extraordinary, and so patently unacceptable by the unions, that it was hard to believe the company could be serious about them. Unless, of course, it was counting upon shortlived union cooperation, anticipating that when the going got rough—and perhaps high government pressures once again applied—the unity among the unions could be broken down.

For more than thirty years, ever since the UE signed its first national GE contract with Gerard Swope in 1938, all agreements had been on this national basis. When the IUE appeared in the industry in 1946, it, too, established a national contract relationship with the company for the plants it represented. What GE now appeared to be contemplating was setting the clock back to before 1938, by opening options to negotiate individual local plant agreements and eliminating altogether the principle—accepted originally by Swope when proposed by the UE—that any time workers in a hitherto unorganized shop chose to be represented by the union, the national contract would apply to them. The changes at which GE negotiators seemed to be hinting amounted to little less than scrapping, piece by piece or wholesale, the traditional national contract.

Likewise with another tradition. From its inception the UE had insisted upon—and won at both GE and Westinghouse—the right of workers to conduct a stoppage because of a grievance unresolved after passing through all levels of the contract grievance machinery. Sometimes a very small number of workers in one department would be involved, as few as six, eight, or twenty. The rest of the plant might remain unaffected. "Indications of company attitude" on this matter pointed in the direction of a management prerogative to lock out perhaps thousands of workers—an entire plant—if a small group exercised its stoppage rights under the grievance provisions of the contract. The union negotiators frankly hoped that GE was touching upon these extremely sensitive issues only for

264

strategy purposes, that it would refrain from incorporating them in any formal proposal.

They hoped further, in fact, and so said to company representatives, that GE would hold off on any take-it-or-leave-it ultimatum and would, instead, engage in collective bargaining. However, with the contract deadline of October 26 about three weeks distant, there had been no sign of any company shift away from Boulwarism. At this point the UE leadership, in line with understandings over the years between union and company, suggested an informal meeting with the GE vice-president in charge of labor relations. This company officer, ever since Boulwarism replaced the Swope negotiating policies —wherein Swope's chief lieutenant met with the union committee—didn't appear at formal bargaining sessions. But he would, if requested, agree to an informal meeting.

International union UE officers Fitzgerald and Matles met on the evening of October 6 with GE's vice-president Philip Moore, who held the post Boulware had once filled. With Moore were the two company officials conducting bargaining with the unions—Everett Bickford, head of the GE team negotiating with the UE, and John R. Baldwin, manager under Moore of union relations, who headed the IUE negotiations. Fitzgerald and Matles tried to persuade the GE officials to hold off on the traditional Boulwarism spectacular and to negotiate all issues with the two unions. The company men listened but made no response. At the end of forty minutes or so there was nothing left to say. Bidding the others good night, the UE leaders departed. They carried with them the impression that GE was just about ready to spring the spectacular, perhaps on the next day.

Matles quickly contacted the IUE's John Shambo. Overnight, union committee members devised a plan. The next morning, October 7, the UE committee reached the meeting rooms before the company team arrived. After a while the doors opened. In came Bickford with his usual associates. Trailing behind them was the retinue of assistants, technicians, public relations specialists, and so forth—bearing equipment and piles of documents—which customarily heralded Boulwarism's big show. At once the UE committee, without permitting the meeting to open, requested time to hold a union cau-cus.

A few days before, GE representatives had been visibly taken aback by the appearance of an expanded UE committee, whose composition, under federal law, is left strictly up to a negotiating union, just as the law leaves composition of a company committee up to the company. Until the first week of October, the UE committee had consisted exclusively, as in the past, of representatives from UE local unions and the international union. During that week, however, sitting in as regular members of the UE committee were: James Ogden, administrative assistant to Auto Workers president Reuther; Frank Demerie, administrative assistant to then executive vice-president Fitzsimmons of the Teamsters; and Joe Mangino, leader of IUE Local 301 in Schenectady.

III   Joe Mangino, as soon as the caucus was called, left the third-floor scene of UE negotiations and went to the tenth-floor conference room, where the IUE meeting had not yet started. Once Shambo heard from Mangino what had happened down below, he also requested a caucus just as the IUE session was about to open. Both union committees then adjourned across the street to a hotel in which the IUE had rented office space for the negotiating period. It took a while for the company to discover that the committees had left the GE building, that the audiences on which they had learned to depend for the openings of Boulware-styled shows would not be on hand.

What to do? All across the country, GE wheels were in motion. Newspaper ads in the mill. News releases for press, radio, and TV all set to go. Unless, somehow, a "hold" button could be pushed—or another expedient dreamed up—the company would be vulnerable to an unfair labor practice complaint of publicizing its terms before they had been formally presented to the unions. Very soon, two GE representatives left headquarters under orders to find the union people and get the company's offer to them.

One representative headed for the hotel across the street,

where he delivered GE's offer to an IUE office secretary. The other GE official showed up at the UE building two blocks away. There he served the company papers, as if they were a summons, on the switchboard operator. In this fashion in 1969 the unions representing one hundred fifty thousand workers employed by the largest electrical manufacturing company in the world—its 1968 reported profit $357.1 million—received the GE contract terms.

These included the two propositions about which company negotiators had seemed to be hinting: destruction of the national contracts and establishment of "management rights" for plant lockouts. For the first time since 1946, GE was soon told that its take-it-or-leave-it offer was unacceptable and that the organized workers would, therefore, leave it. The 1969 response was delivered by the two unions which had received the offer—a far cry from 1946, when all GE workers were represented by one union, the UE. But the 1969 unity among the unions constituted, nevertheless, a big improvement over the past twenty years. Under the circumstances it was the best possible approach workers in GE could take toward Boulwarism.

It was ironic that as the unions on October 8, 1969, told GE they would "leave it"—the answer which Boulwarism had supposedly outlawed—Lemuel R. Boulware's book had been off the press only a few months, published by David Lawrence's Bureau of National Affairs. "The whole is offered," Boulware wrote in the foreword to *The Truth About Boulwarism,* "as a seemingly needed and desired addition to the educational material about . . . a program of such continuing current interest." He had written much more prophetically than he no doubt intended. Interest in Boulwarism possibly reached an alltime high in 1969, when the GE formula encountered its first challenge for restoration of genuine collective bargaining between company and workers. Boulwarism, in short, was meeting up with real life. Lemuel Boulware's book, in many respects, was outdated before it got into print.

IV   At eleven-thirty on Sunday morning, October 26, silence fell in the conference room where the UE committee for weeks had continued to meet with company representatives, running out the clock. As the zero hour drew near, a spokesman for the union committee said:

> We have spent three full months trying to work out an agreement with you and we have failed. For twenty years your labor policies have been based on a cult and on an ideology known as Boulwarism. So long as you continue to stick to it, no agreement is possible. . . . The last time we faced a national GE strike was twenty-three years ago, in 1946. Some of us who are here today have lived through that experience. We are under no illusions as to what we are going up against.

He went on to refer to full-page newspaper ads in which GE had "served notice on our people that if they strike, you will make every effort to break it." This was, he said, unlike the practice of U.S. Steel or General Motors, companies which "do not love unions" but had learned that "strikebreaking does not pay, that the scars created take years to heal." He added that the union, aware of the tremendous power of the General Electric Company, could not rule out the possibility that the company might prevail. The spokesman continued:

> The question you must however answer for yourself is how long it will take you to prevail and how high a price you will have to pay to break us. Should you decide to pay the price and at the end succeed in getting us down, we can promise you that eventually we will pick ourselves up and start all over again.

He went on to say that during the days ahead the company "would be hitting us with injunctions and back-to-work movements—and as our people take counter measures to protect their picket lines, things may get rough between us." With such expectations in store, he suggested that since unions and company would be immediately busy "putting our respective houses in disorder," the next meeting be scheduled for Wednesday the twenty-ninth, three days away. "If that is OK with you we suggest you call us so we can agree on the place and time." With that the union committee left the room, its departure later recorded in the UE's journal of events of that time:

268

There is something eerie about a skyscraper on a Sunday. The GE building was as dead as a morgue. A service elevator took us down to the lobby and we signed out. The guard opened the accordion steel gate and let us out on Lexington Avenue after which we walked west to the old Cornelius Vanderbilt townhouse that since 1943 has served the cause of trade unionism as UE headquarters. The old mansion was buzzing with activity this Sunday afternoon.

Within an hour the UE strike call had been transmitted by phone to about three dozen local union leaders standing by at stations over a three-thousand-mile front—from Ashland, Massachusetts, to Oakland, California. Citing GE's refusal to change so much as a comma of its terms of October 7, and "Nixon Administration . . . assurance that the company will have a free hand in the event of a strike," the call set the walkout time for midnight. At 1:00 P.M., as the call was released to New York newspapers, wire services, and TV and radio networks, IUE secretary-treasurer David Fitzmaurice, from a copy just delivered by the UE, read its contents to IUE–GE conference board members gathered at the Americana Hotel. The UE record of events noted: "It was well received. The IUE people must have felt relieved to hear that UE was already on the move. At 3:00 P.M. a radio bulletin announced that IUE and UE have shut down GE. Now it was UE's turn to feel relieved. Unity had met this test."

Next test would be midnight—and next after that the hour of Monday morning, October 27, when first shifts ordinarily started work. Reports flowing in to UE headquarters showed both of these tests also being met by UE and IUE local unions, as well as by some of the other AFL–CIO unions whose contracts expired on October 26. The great strike was on.

V Preparations for an action of this magnitude are not made overnight. From the inception of negotiations in July, the UE rank-and-file had been kept abreast of developments at the bargaining table by the *UE News*, by communications from their negotiating committee, and by appearances at local union membership meetings of representatives serving on the committee. On October 8, UE workers from every GE plant and service shop came off the job and approved the committee's rejection of company terms, voting by secret ballot in favor of strike. Between that date, and October 26, the union proceeded to put its strike machinery into gear nationwide. Conditions had changed since 1946. The 1969 machinery had to be adjusted to suit them.

One major new responsibility of the UE international representatives and field organizers assigned to every local union in the GE chain—just as in 1946—would be to maintain and strengthen the spirit of unity. This was still fragile because of the long conflict between unions in the electrical manufacturing industry. There were, furthermore, casualties of that warfare in the shape of unorganized plants, some but not all in southern states. And there were additional casualties among the white-collar salaried office workers, many of whom had once belonged to UE but had been pulled away during the period when the unions were split. They remained unorganized.

Another obstacle in the way of a successful shutdown of GE consisted of some salaried skilled technicians and specialists in the shops. These were a relatively new type of worker, created by the introduction of advanced mechanized and automated methods of production, who performed jobs on the shop floor side by side with the members of unions for which the salaried technicians, too, were eligible, although most had not joined. Disunity among the unions had left them adrift.

Also a product of disunity were dozens of shops where various AFL–CIO unions and others held individual local contracts—the weak links traditionally employed as initial points of company attack with a Boulwarism take-it-or-leave-it package. A number of these contracts extended beyond October 26, some of them running into January of 1970. It was expected—but not guaranteed—that the workers in these plants would join the strikers' ranks when their contracts expired. At the least, it would be essential to insure that none of them got Boulwarized into signing new local contracts until the national strike was settled satisfactorily.

270

Not at all the situation of 1946. Nevertheless it was obvious that if no cracks developed in the unity of UE and IUE, which between them represented about seventy percent of organized GE workers and were entrenched in the key and heavy-equipment plants, the chances for success would remain favorable. This became even more apparent as the strike was joined by members of the Auto Workers and the AFL–CIO Machinists in the only key location—a large jet engine plant in Evendale, Ohio —not represented by either UE or IUE. Everything depended, then, on their joint cooperation. And within each union, everything depended on keeping the strike solid in all plants and shops. The least exception could be exploited by the company in its strikebreaking campaign. For this reason the UE paid particular attention to Waynesboro, Virginia, and Rochester, New York.

VI At the recently organized Waynesboro GE plant—scene of the lint-free dresses "little issue"—only about half the work force of a thousand people, composed of almost equal numbers of men and women, were UE members. In Rochester the local union at a small service shop with two dozen workers, also recently organized, had not yet signed up all of them. These, then, were the potential trouble spots in a strike, all other plant locations being in strong organizational positions. Developments after October 26 at Waynesboro and Rochester provided sample stories of how a rank-and-file union goes about handling such problems, under conditions where their solution is critical to the effectiveness of a major union action.

When UE international representatives Liz Overby and Hugh Harley arrived in Waynesboro, they found, as they had anticipated, that about half the workers had heeded the strike call while half didn't. The work of the UE representatives was cut out for them, seasoned and skilled as they might be through years of experience in UE union jobs. Harley, later to become UE director of organization, decided to cast his lot with the labor movement a few years after he was graduated from Dartmouth College. New England–oriented, he was a natural—once he had served his appenticeship in organizing campaigns in several different states—for assignment to organize in Massachusetts and Vermont. In these states he devoted more than two decades of patient, active endeavor to the union's effort to organize plants building machine tools as well as cutting and hand tools—a task finally completed with the help of a Supreme Court decision in the Chief Justice Warren era. In the New England territory, too, Harley had opportunity to develop as a skillful strike leader.

Liz Overby, while in her early twenties, had taken a job on a shop assembly line, from where she was recruited for the UE and trained in her union jobs by Bill Sentner, UE leader in St. Louis and Iowa. Her life work became rank-and-file unionism in all its aspects, among which was much organizing duty. Not long before the strike, indeed, Liz had been in Waynesboro helping to organize the UE local there. In that sense, her return was a visit back home to people she had come to know well— an experience familiar to many union organizers. Once in Waynesboro on strike assignment, Liz had another familiar union experience: Along with other pickets she got arrested and hauled off to jail. Later another group of pickets, Harley among them, received the same treatment.

This came about partly as a result of the plant's location on a main four-lane highway. The space in front of its entrance gates at the time of the strike was declared off-limits to pickets by city and state police. When the union's challenge to this prohibition was met by arrests and jailings, the UE initiated a case in federal court, arguing that favorable decisions in similar constitutional cases of free speech and assembly—First Amendment rights—had been handed down by the Supreme Court, also during the days of Chief Justice Earl Warren. The court agreed with the UE. It also granted the union's request to order the city of Waynesboro to provide safe terrain wherefrom strikers could distribute leaflets without being hit by cars on the highway.

The court's order on this was specific. It directed the city to erect a wooden platform several inches high—in the form of a divider down the highway's center—for union leaflet distribution. Shortly after this was installed and in operation, a UE international officer, paying a midnight call on the Waynesboro picket line, had it pointed out to him by the picket captain on duty. "You see that thing in the middle of the highway? That wooden platform they had to build for us? I want to tell you it's the greatest single victory the workers of Waynesboro have ever scored."

Around-the-clock picketing and leaflet distribution were extremely important at Waynesboro, where the main job of the UE organizers was to help the local strike committee hold the ranks of those on strike solid while persuading other workers, even if one by one, to join the union and the strike. Things worked out in Waynesboro just about as planned—and in Rochester, too, where UE organizer Ed Bloch had been assigned.

Bloch, having completed university studies, took up work on an assembly line in a radio plant, where he became a local union shop steward. During the latter part of the Second World War he joined the Marine Corps, serving in the Pacific theatre, after which he enlisted on the staff of the UE. In Rochester for the 1969 strike he moved right in with the dozen strikers in the small service shop. Together they were able, before the strike ended: to keep the strike going; reduce the number scabbing by three; and set the stage, after the strike, for all but two holdout workers joining the union.

Nowhere in the country, in any of the forty-five UE strike locations, did the company succeed in breaking a line and inserting a back-to-work movement wedge, despite most intensive efforts to do so. These company efforts, launched even before the walkout started, had Thanksgiving in view as first target date for busting the strike. Whether or not GE under Boulwarism had calculated the difficulties any union would have in planning and conducting a strike during winter months, the record showed that one of the very first moves made to apply the Boulware formula—in 1950—included a change in the national contract expiration date from spring to late fall. Take it or leave it. In 1950 both UE and IUE had to take it.

VII

Shortly after Thanksgiving, in one of the strike reports which went out regularly from international union strike headquarters to local unions, there appeared among various accounts of events and developments in the field this brief item: "Local 563, Amalgamated Meatcutters and Butchers, donated twenty-five hundred turkeys to UE California strikers." Local 563's support was both typical of that forthcoming from all sectors of the labor movement and also significant in helping to explain why, at Thanksgiving time, with the strike going into its fifth week, GE's back-to-work maneuvers met no success. But the company's steady refusal to move in negotiations from its October 7 position, plus certain signs of impending strikebreaking activity out in the plants, made it more than likely that the next back-to-work target date would be in the vicinity of Christmas.

"Our estimate of the situation," ran a comment in the UE record of the 1969 struggle, "was that they would make another offer before Christmas—not an offer for the purpose of settling the strike but for the purpose of breaking it, to try and use the offer as part of the back-to-work movement." It seemed possible that GE was proceeding along an automatic course charted by Boulwarism without having given full study to the changed situation among the unions—which reflected a rank-and-file spirit whose depths the company might be misjudging. "The workers were determined to surrender no more. They were fighting back not only for dollars and cents but for dignity and respect. They were no longer going to permit GE to play one group of organized workers against another." So ran a passage in a UE statement issued after the strike was over, sizing up exactly what the company had failed to comprehend from beginning to end of the struggle.

Early in November a copy of GE's back-to-work battle plan "fell off the back of a company truck"—as UE members were accustomed to put it—into the hands of the union. The plan was an up-to-date model, refined and streamlined according to Boulwarism's Madison Avenue public relations methods, of the famous strike breaking Remington Rand Mohawk Valley Formula of 1936. To attain the plan's stated objective of motivating "hourly employees to return to work by December 22, 1969," foremen and managers were instructed to make "direct personal contact with employees," while at the same time a barrage of mailings, newspaper ads, and press releases would blanket the communities where GE plants were located.

The "Back to Work Plan"—headed as such by the company —laid out an almost day-by-day schedule beginning November 17, when "low-key" radio messages were to be broadcast, and extending to December 22, at which time foremen and managers would make "final phone calls." During the week of December 7 the plan called for transforming the radio messages from "low-key" to "hard-hitting," an escalation the reason for which became clear when, on December 7, as the UE record noted, "GE coordinated the back-to-work drive in the communities with an offer handed over to UE and IUE committees in New York." Continued the record:

> We were all ready for them. Just as soon as they came in with their offer, UE and IUE put our counterproposals on the table. Two things were now before the people: The company's second sweetened-up offer—and our counterproposals. They were obviously not prepared for that, having expected that only their offer would be in the works.

In the meanwhile the union, which had made the back-to-work plan public after confronting the company with it at the bargaining table, had been preparing its members for the pre-Christmas back-to-work push by GE. Although plant managers, foremen, supervisors, and public relations people followed the script to the letter, it worked no better than Boulwarism as a whole was working. "The strikebreaking scheme fizzled. The Boulwarism–Mohawk Valley back-to-work formula failed. Their December 22 deadline passed. The workers stood solid." So the UE's record of events noted.

VIII With negotiations in New York recessed for ten days over Christmas and the New Year period, Matles decided to spend Christmas week on the picket lines in Indiana and Ohio. Matles said some months later when a group of UE local union officers and shop stewards were analyzing the GE struggle:

We had been sitting with management for three months before the strike and for ten more weeks since the beginning of the strike. This had taken its toll. All of us were kind of down in the dumps. I went home for a few hours, packed a bag, then called the president of our GE local union in Decatur, Indiana, and asked him to pick me up the next morning in Fort Wayne.

When I checked into the Keenan Hotel, in Fort Wayne, my old standby, it looked as though I had it all to myself. It was 11 P.M. and the temperature was eight degrees and it was the night before Christmas. I walked for about a mile to the Broadway gate of the GE plant represented by IUE Local 901. The picket shack, tightly enclosed with yellow plastic, was brightly lit up. A roaring fire was going in the steel drum outside of the shack close to the gate and a couple of pickets were playing cards inside with a little stove keeping them warm and snug. I talked with them for a while and walked back to the hotel. Nothing that I had seen or heard would keep me from having a good night's sleep.

On Christmas morning the president of the Decatur local picked me up and together we visited the IUE Local 901 headquarters. We met with the local officers, visited with the men and women in the strike kitchen who were busy preparing Christmas dinner. We went out to the picket line to talk with the morning shift and then we took off for Decatur which is about twenty miles from Fort Wayne.

This started me off on a week of visits to our strikers in our strike trailers, strike kitchens, picket lines, relief headquarters and homes of strikers in Indiana and Ohio. This was a week of informal discussions with individuals and small groups of our rank and file strikers and their families, asking and answering questions, talking and listening. Listening was the most important part of the trip.

Flying home from Youngstown to New York, the day before the New Year, I felt pretty good. First, I had gotten my batteries recharged. Second, I had gotten my bearings and was much clearer in my mind as to what we would have to do when the real bargaining started. Third, I got a clear assessment of the strike, the shape it was in and what had to be done to maintain our lines solid during the crucial weeks ahead.

IX   For these weeks two possibilities appeared to be in the picture: either there would be serious bargaining as a result of company recognition of the meaning of the failure of its back-to-work-movement—or, just as in 1966, GE would go to the top, the White House, to compel a settlement in its favor. Just before negotiations recessed the day before Christmas, the UE learned that such company moves were being made. Presumably, while a UE leader was visiting the front lines in Indiana and Ohio, GE was in touch with supreme government headquarters in Washington. Now Republican Richard Nixon, not Democrat Lyndon Johnson, headed the federal administration. But such changes in party labels seldom mean much to corporations. Ever since the Civil War, they have almost always been able to gain influential access to high places of government, no matter which party is in power.

George Shultz, Nixon's Secretary of Labor, was the key official expected to arrange to have negotiations transferred to Washington, as in 1966. Some leaders of AFL–CIO unions favored this way out, taking the position: "We're not getting much of anywhere here in New York. What can we lose in Washington?" The UE, able to report high morale on the picket lines in the field, argued that GE power in Washington was far stronger than anything the unions could muster, that the basic power of the unions lay in the solidarity of the rank-and-file. These discussions occurred at the turn of the year, with negotiations due to resume on January 5, a Monday. It was impossible to predict just what course they would take.

In the early morning hours of Sunday, January 4, a snow and sleet storm drenched the northeast of the country. By 10:00 A.M. in New York, as the UE's CPA auditor struggled

277

through the slush on Fifty-first Street on his way to union headquarters to do a bit of work, the broad stone steps of the building were inches deep in wet snow. Fitting his key into the door he caught sight of a soggy Western Union envelope lying on the threshold. Once inside, he took a look at the contents, checking first the signature on the long telegram. It was from Senator Jacob Javits, Republican of New York, addressed to UE president Fitzgerald. The union auditor picked up the phone to pass on the news to top leadership of the UE.

Javits, whose state contained many striking workers, proposed in the wire that the "fact-finding" method be employed to help settle the dispute between GE and the unions. Specifically, he suggested a board of three members to make findings but not binding recommendations for settlement. Members of the board would be selected from lists submitted by unions and company—except that "if the parties are unable to agree upon the designation of any or all of the three fact-finders from those lists, then the parties shall accept the appointment of one or more such fact-finders by the American Arbitration Association." Two days later, after representatives of the unions had consulted and agreed, telegrams of acceptance went forward to Senator Javits. Said UE president Fitzgerald:

> While we firmly believe that the issues in dispute should be settled between the parties at the bargaining table, there comes a time when an objective review of the facts by a third party can be of help in bringing them into proper focus. We are confident that an objective examination of the facts must sustain the justice of the union position.

GE rejected the Javits proposal, "using the excuse," the UE said in its January 7 Strike Report, "that the Director of the Federal Mediation and Conciliation Service, J. Curtis Counts, has been assigned by Secretary of Labor Shultz to assist in negotiations." Commented Fitzgerald: "It is strange that this company which has spent millions of dollars on newspaper ads to get its position to the public is now dodging a public airing of the facts in this strike." The UE leader's reference to "millions" was later confirmed in a review of the strike by the magazine *Business Week,* which estimated that "at least 20 GE ads in a handful of major papers . . . not counting local ads and radio-TV spots" cost the company "$2.5 million to $3 million."

Perhaps, had it not been for the initiative of Republican Senator Javits, the Nixon Administration might have moved the negotiations to Washington. At any rate, there was no repeat of 1966. Negotiations did not move to Washington but stayed in New York in the hands of the broadly based, representative and cooperating union committees.

X   On January 7, the director of federal mediation J. Curtis Counts arrived in New York City to undertake efforts to bring about a settlement. For those union leaders and members who did not know him, his background appeared to offer cause for concern. He had entered government from a post as vice-president of labor relations for one of the large corporations in the aero-space industry, Douglas Aircraft. Further, his transfer to government came about because of his long close friendship with President Nixon, at whose wedding Counts had been best man.

Nevertheless, as a mediator (not an arbitrator), he was acceptable to UE, whose leaders were aware of his reputation as a "practical, no-nonsense negotiator" with the Auto Workers union, which represented the workers in Douglas Aircraft. This estimate of Counts on the part of UE leaders had to be explained to the rank-and-file of the membership. Some of them figured Counts spelled trouble. Often there are good grounds for such a feeling about a person coming from a career of labor relations responsibility on the company side. But not inevitably so. You can't always go by the book on matters of that sort. It happens often that a mediator with a union background will give a labor organization a shafting, just because he is trying to prove to the company that he is not biased in the union's favor.

Counts turned out to be an extremely able mediator, doing a workmanlike job of mediation in a very difficult situation. He let the parties do their work with his encouragement. On January

30, UE *Strike Report Number 67* (on the ninety-seventh day of the strike) contained a statement to the membership from Fitzgerald and Matles, announcing that the UE–GE national negotiating committee had reached an agreement for settlement with the company. The statement said:

> This is the first negotiated agreement with GE in twenty years. Six previous agreements were imposed on the union and not negotiated. It took fourteen weeks on the picket lines for the organized GE workers to convince the General Electric Company to respect the union at the bargaining table.

Strike Report Number 68, dated February 2, advised the membership that the UE–GE Conference Board, "with every local represented," had discussed and approved the settlement and recommended its acceptance to the membership. On February 4, *Strike Report Number 69* contained the text of a wire sent by Joseph Turkowski, head of the UE conference board, to all UE–GE local unions, informing them that the membership had ratified the agreement and that the "national strike against GE is terminated." At that point—and not until then—the picket lines came down for the first time in one hundred one days, while local union officers proceeded to notify local managements that members were ready to return to the job under the negotiated terms of the new agreement.

This, like most such agreements, did not represent everything the workers in justice had coming to them. When Matles was later discussing his Christmas visit to the picket lines in Indiana and Ohio with a class of local union officers and shop stewards, he remarked that it had "afforded the opportunity to convey informally to the grass roots the idea that the whole loaf was not going to be there." The agreement, nevertheless, set Boulwarism back, not only in terms of the negotiating process but in results. An eight-page summary of the settlement, made available by the international union to local union memberships for study before ratification votes were taken, began by reporting that the "solidarity of our strike" had brought about the withdrawal of the two demands that "threatened the existence of the union."

280

These were GE's propositions for scrapping the national contract and interfering with the right of workers to conduct a stoppage after exhausting the grievance procedure. Moreover, the new contract, covering a forty-month period, would expire in the month of May—meaning that the October termination time imposed under Boulwarism in 1950 had been successfully resisted and reversed. Wage increases amounted to 50 cents an hour across the board for the span of the contract, which also included a cost-of-living formula with four increases during the life of the contract. Also special adjustments in the rates of "low-paying jobs employing mostly women workers" and in the rates of skilled workers.

Improvements in pensions, sick pay, vacations, hospitalization, weekly sickness and accident benefits, life insurance, and nonhospital medical expenses—such as cost of eye exercises, hearing aids, tooth extraction, and root canal work—were listed among the general economic gains in the summary upon which the workers based their decision to approve the settlement. Listed, too, were most of "twenty-six contract improvements in working conditions, some of these extremely important, such as winning automatic progression to the job rate." All in all, the "first negotiated settlement in twenty years," although not the whole loaf, had quite a bit of bread in it.

XI The vote for ratification in Waynesboro, Virginia, had a particularly sweet flavor. There is where "Little Issue No. 1: The Lint-Free Dress," had hung on the negotiating line until the very end. In one of a number of news releases sent out during the strike, the union sketched the issue in these words:

> The Company gives each woman on this job two dresses. When these wear out, the women have to buy their own out of their already inadequate wages.
>
> During the three months of formal negotiations which began July 28 and ended at midnight October 26 when the strike began, the Union repeatedly demanded that as long as these women are required to wear special cloth-

ing the Company must continue to provide them after the first two wear out.

GE refused. This mighty corporation claimed that women sometimes wear these dresses outside of the plant and even to church on Sunday. So let them buy their own after the first two wear out, GE declared.

Every few days the Union raised the issue of dresses at the bargaining table. Every few days GE said it was studying the matter and might find contractual language to "ameliorate" the problem.

The day before negotiations came to a halt the Union again asked if the Company had a proposal to solve the dress problem. As a compromise, the Union suggested that the Company could put the GE emblem on the dress. We said we seriously doubted that the women would want to sport a GE emblem on their Sunday dresses, but if they would, it would be a free ad for GE. The Company repeated, however, that the problem was much too complex for so simple a solution and they wanted more time to study the matter.

This and other news releases during the strike were prepared by Charles Kerns, in charge of publicity and publications of the international union. The regular strike reports— sixty-nine in all—were also his work. As editor of the reports, in constant touch with every one of the forty-five units on strike, Kerns kept an ear tuned for significant displays of spirit among the strikers—and for the generous gestures of support coming from other workers, students, teachers, public officials, and community people. His "Final Report" to the members, dated February 6, 1970, contained a message and a last few words of "little issue" news:

We wish to thank everyone who kept us informed of the events in your locals across the country. We hope that this exchange of information in these regular *Strike Reports* played some small part in helping to maintain the solidarity and high morale that characterized this strike for 101 days and shaped the victory.

We are glad to inform you that this publication is now defunct.

PS: You remember the lint-free dresses for the women of Local 124, Waynesboro, Virginia? Well, the company has agreed to replace the lint-free dresses every 12 months. The lint-free dress is free. It's OK if the ladies wear them to church and there will be no GE emblem!

XII Never since 1946 had the national press felt obliged to give such studied coverage to a militant rank-and-file struggle by organized workers. Most of this press, indeed, for many years had helped to promote the conditions under which Boulwarism flourished by publicizing attacks made on such unions as UE. In February of 1970, however, events prompted reporters, commentators, and editors to pay attention to a fighting labor movement whose strength came from the bottom up.

Said *Time* magazine:

> In the minds of the strikers, the primary issue was not even economic. Their aim was to force GE to abandon its bargaining strategy of "Boulwarism." . . . Union loyalists have long regarded this strategy as an attempt to fix wages unilaterally, but the many unions representing GE workers were too divided to challenge the tactic effectively.

The New York Times, in a report and analysis of the strike written by A. H. Raskin, the *Times* editorial page assistant editor and the newspaper's specialist in the field of labor since the thirties, said:

> The chief goal of the 14-union coalition was to slay "Boulwarism," the papa-knows-best bargaining philosophy on which GE relied to dominate contract negotiations for two decades.

Although the *Times* referred in 1970 to the slaying of "Boulwarism," the UE leadership took a longer view, saying in a statement to union members after the strike was settled:

> This is the first negotiated agreement with GE in 20 years. Six previous agreements were imposed on the unions and not negotiated. Whether the company has

decided to permanently forego the old ways which led to the strike will be determined in the next 40 months of this agreement and during the negotiations of the next agreement.

Business Week, which had covered the 1969–1970 strike extensively, explained at its conclusion:

GE negotiators tried to use basically the same strategy that had succeeded in the past, but they were out-maneuvered. . . . GE made mistakes in the 1969 negotiations. . . . In the first long, hard months there was no real bargaining in the normal sense of the term. Confrontations, yes. Interminable talk, yes. But bargaining, no. At one point a union negotiator said, "We'd do better playing gin. At least something would be on the table." A company man wryly agreed. . . . At the end of November, GE began to prepare a second offer. UE's Matles urged the company: "Don't put anything on paper. Don't publicize what you have on your mind. Let's be informal: let's talk before you act."

But on December 7 the company made its offer on paper and it was given publicity. Key company people now concede this was a serious mistake. The offer was quickly rejected, and the parties were solidly frozen into new positions. . . . Just before Christmas, the ice began to melt, though no more than a handful on both sides knew it then.

XIII
This was the story at the top level of negotiations. On December 22 the UE *Strike Report* related what was happening at the bottom "just before Christmas" among the workers on the picket lines:

Today was the day the company's carefully scheduled back-to-work scheme was to culminate in masses of strikers streaming over, under and around the decimated picket lines. It didn't work out that way. Reports from all UE locations bear this out. There is deep resentment against company efforts to use the pressures of the Christmas season to try to force workers back to the job on company terms. Plans are going ahead to make this Christmas as bright as possible. Christmas parties for the children of strikers, and other social events, will be held. Donations of food and toys are coming in from community organizations and individuals all over the country.

If the ice in the frozen negotiations was beginning to melt around Christmas, the heat coming from the rank-and-file—supported by the whole labor movement and many others—produced the thaw. Unity welded on the picket line, as a UE officer later commented, did the job. UE and IUE locals joined one another's lines. Some set up strike headquarters together. In Beverly, Massachusetts, members of a UE local in United Shoe Machinery—not a GE plant—stopped work for the first time in twenty-eight years in protest against subcontracted material being shipped from their plant to General Electric plants in Schenectady and Burlington, Vermont, where IUE locals represented the General Electric workers.

Support for the strike, meanwhile, poured in from UE local union members outside the GE chain who were working and receiving income. Also from members of AFL–CIO and independent unions. Also from the highest levels of the labor movement. At the head of the AFL–CIO, George Meany raised more than $2 million which was distributed among all the unions of the coalition on the basis of the number of strikers represented by each organization. The Auto Workers, at the initiative of Walter Reuther, contributed $1 million to the UE and IUE—the two unions with most members on strike, with the smallest treasuries and the greatest need. That old friend of the UE, the Longshoremen's and Warehousemen's Union, with Harry Bridges at the helm, sent many thousands of dollars to UE strikers for which ILWU members assessed themselves.

Contributions were made on a straight trade union solidarity basis, with the UE—the only union which did not operate a weekly strike-benefit system—receiving its fair share. The fact that weekly strike-benefit payments were being made to members of all other unions on strike didn't adversely effect the solidarity of the UE strikers. The UE, as always, distributed relief according to need, members presenting their case for help to local union committees. Not once during the one hundred one days did any UE local union express a complaint about relief help, finances, or the manner in which support was balanced between what they could raise themselves and what came from the international union.

To those UE members who remembered 1946, old times were back again. Community people donated funds. Merchants gave food and extended credit. Mayors from eighty-five cities, at the call of Mayor James H. Tate of Philadelphia, met in New York City to discuss what could be done to "help bring about a settlement of the dispute." A group of more than thirty nationally known writers, scientists, editors, religious leaders, lawyers, and public officials requested "contributions to feed and support the GE strikers." Students moved into the picket lines. Professors helped collect funds. Student publications editorially endorsed the striking workers. Said the Columbia University *Spectator,* "Underlying grievances are directly linked to the Vietnam War. Why must workers be asked to assume the burden of inflation accelerated by a war which profits the largest military contractor in the nation?"

It was all this which melted the ice, induced the thaw, got negotiations going and brought about the first negotiated settlement in twenty years between organized workers and the General Electric Company. On December 24, Christmas Eve 1969, a bit of verse in the UE *Strike Report* of that date forecast the outcome of union unity, worker solidarity and support from the people:

'Tis the night before Christmas
And all through GE
Not a wheel will be turning
Until the Unions agree!

On the next day, Christmas, when UE's Matles was visiting the front lines of the strike in Decatur, Indiana, everything was summed up for him by a young leader of UE Local 924, who said:

They've been trying to tell us there are three separate

groups in GE: the company, the employees, and the union. That's what they've based themselves on. We have to show them they're wrong. The UE represents the workers. The workers are the union. We have to show them there are not three groups but just two: the company and the union. Them and us.

18
Seeds of Rank-and-File Rebellion

I   In the summer of 1966 two young welders were at work side by side in a large shop. All at once they took off their big welder mitts, set down their helmets, and shut off the machines. Picking up some quarter-inch welding rod, each of the young fellows carefully shaped a bend in the rod's tip. Then, with the rods slung on their shoulders, they strolled to the center aisle of the shop, which ran a distance of a couple of city blocks.

Out of their pockets they took a few Ping-Pong balls. Right there in broad daylight, during regular working hours, they squared off and began belting the balls down the aisle with their welding-rod golf clubs.

The foreman couldn't believe his eyes. Was it really happening? Never in his memory of many years had there been a sight like this in the shop. Such an infraction of every rule he could think of. Such a breach of basic shop discipline. Had they gone crazy? He demanded to know what in the hell they thought they were doing.

"Playing golf," one of them said as he took another swing. The foreman blew his stack. He threw the book at them. "Get your personal gear together," he said, "and get out."

The next move was up to the shop steward, an old-timer long active in the union. It was obvious that job pressure had gotten to the two young fellows. That in itself was nothing unusual. Pressures were bringing on protests from workers time and again, often in the form of spontaneous stoppages. But a golf-playing stoppage?

No stoppage at all, the young fellows explained. They weren't on working time. They were piece-workers and they were on their own time. They got paid according to the number of pieces they welded and delivered to the boss. So if they knocked off from the steady grind of the job nobody was paying them for that time off. They needed a break and they took it.

Company speedup, production pressure, the bosses constantly on the backs of the workers—these were grievances the shop steward was fighting every day in the shop. So even though he had never come up against a golf-playing grievance before, he had no trouble taking hold of the basic issue and going to bat with it. Management could not be permitted to impose any such penalty. No way. It was out of the question, considering the deep dissatisfactions and frustrations of shop workers from which the novel protest sprang.

The incident had been unique. But fundamentally it reflected a most serious stage of affairs starting to develop for all workers in shops in the mid-sixties. Management pressures for more and more production per worker, combined with the mounting economic pressures of life, were creating a mood of resentment and rebellion steadily on the rise.

II   Each woman on the final assembly line had an operation to perform that took only hundredths of a minute. Three-hundredths, four-hundredths, five- or six-hundredths. Their hands were in constant motion, their fingers flying. The same pattern of movement repeated over and over again by seventy-five women on the line, one of several final assembly lines in the shop.

Piece by piece, eight hundred thirty electric irons got assembled every sixty minutes on this particular line. The women were doing a mechanical job which became second nature to their fingers and hands. Performing their split-minute tasks, they found some relief from boredom by engaging in constant conversation. They kidded around. Or got on to such subjects as children, husbands, boyfriends, TV shows, plans for the weekend, for vacation. If the foreman bugged them, they bugged him back. They discussed job grievances and how to

289

fight them. They also arranged among themselves to switch jobs several times during the eight-hour shift to break up the routine.

Came the day the company had a new speedup idea: the module assembly system, as it was called. A pilot program got underway in one department, designed to replace the existing method of assembly altogether. Under the new system, one worker would assemble half of the iron, a second worker the other half—with each worker now performing not just one monotonous operation but a number of them. Instead of seventy-five workers the new system cut the number of workers down to sixty-four, to turn out the same eight hundred thirty irons every sixty minutes.

Eleven less workers. Several monotonous and boring operations instead of one. The increased speedup, together with the additional operations required from each woman, now demanded steady mental concentration as well as harder physical work. Little chance, any more, for kidding around, for chitchat, for grievance discussion, for helping each other and for switching jobs on the line. Faced with a choice between two evils—the old continuous assembly line or the new module system—the workers determined to stick with the lesser evil. The old line was bad enough but the new one was intolerable.

Many sociologists and industrial psychologists of the period were devoting themselves to study of "the nature of work" in modern production, especially its monotony and boredom. They went out on research expeditions into the shops. They brought their findings together at symposiums, institutes, and seminars. They wrote papers and books on the subject of "the changing work ethic" and so forth, focusing for the most part on the problems of job monotony and boredom and offering suggestions which they thought might help to "humanize" boring, monotonous work.

Boredom and monotony are indeed painful components of almost every modern job situation, blue collar and white collar. Workers subjected to such situations, when they see no chance of escape by upgrading to better jobs, are driven to distraction. But other miseries are even worse on them. Speedup and more speedup constitute the greatest of all job evils—they grind physical and nervous systems to shreds. Often, too, a job is backbreaking because of the constant heavy lifts and hauls required.

The continual noise in a shop can be so intense that it brings on deafness, even at early age. Smoke, soot, dust, gases, fumes, vapors, chemicals, and other poisons in the atmosphere of a shop damage the eyes, the breathing passages, the throats, the lungs of the workers. Conditions and hazards which management takes for granted can be hellish beyond belief, resulting in deaths, injuries, and disease assumed by all too many companies to be simply unfortunate byproducts of their natural need to speed up production and increase profits.

In the year 1970, according to the Bureau of National Affairs, there were fourteen thousand two hundred workers killed as a result of industrial accidents. The bureau also reported that in the same year more than 2 million workers were disabled by accidents on the job. If nondisabling but nonetheless serious accidents were included in the figures, "the yearly total would be twenty-five million injuries," said the bureau in its volume, *Job Safety and Health Act of 1970.*

"In a 1967 study," the bureau reported, "the U.S. Surgeon General"—top medical man in the U.S. government—"estimated that sixty-five percent of the workers in seventeen hundred industrial plants potentially were exposed to harmful physical agents, yet only twenty-five percent of these workers were protected adequately. . . . It was estimated that three hundred and ninety thousand new cases of occupational disease occurred each year." Known hazards, said the bureau, such as lead and mercury poisoning, went unchecked. "New dangers posed equally complex problems. The Public Health Service estimated that a new, potentially toxic chemical was introduced into industry every twenty minutes."

At the UE's September 1972 convention in New York, a leading scientist went to the heart of the matter of job-related deaths, accidents, disease, boredom, monotony, and all the dangers and ills to which working people are exposed on the job. Said Professor Barry Commoner, head of the Department of Biology of Natural Systems, at Washington University, St. Louis:

The system we are living under was created by management. They invented the whole thing. They did not take into account the impact on the environment or the impact on the worker. They have run up a debt to nature and to the worker and they can't pay the debt because every effort to improve the situation reduces productivity. . . . I don't see any escape from the fact that if we are going to improve the environment and improve working conditions, it is going to cut into productivity and cut into industrial profits.

Many of Professor Commoner's social science colleagues studying "the nature of work" had examined only the job picture alone, whereas he had included in his field of vision the whole profit system which governs jobs and the conditions under which they must be performed. In this perspective, it became clear that every least bit of protection and relief for workers had to be extracted from a company whose primary concern was cost.

One of the union's "little issues" in the 1969–1970 strike against GE had been the demand for a doctor or nurse to be on duty in the infirmary on second and third shifts, as was the case for first shift workers. The UE supported its demand with instances of demonstrated need for available medical personnel on second and third shifts. One such instance involved an experience in a plant where a third-shift guard had been assigned to handle any emergency that came up. It happened that a worker was badly hurt. The guard summoned to the scene took one look at the worker's blood and fainted dead away.

This and other evidence presented by the union could not move the company to agree to place a nurse on duty during the night shifts. Unlike the "little issue" of the lint-free dresses in the GE strike—when the company, in the final stages of bargaining, conceded that it would replace worn-out dresses of the type required by management for certain jobs performed by women in a Waynesboro, Virginia, shop—the night-shift nurses' "little issue" didn't get settled. It remained on the agenda for future struggle by the union. GE took and held the position all through the long strike and negotiations that second and third shifts had fewer workers than on the first shift and therefore didn't justify the cost of a nurse.

Cost is the issue involved in all such union efforts to protect and refresh in some small way the lives of workers on the job. Management measures "idle time" of a worker in hundredths of a minute. For the purpose of establishing production standards on assembly or machine operations, one minute is divided into one hundred parts. With each hundredth of one minute regarded by management as precious production time, it is not hard to find the reason why a union demand that workers on a continuous assembly line be given a five-minute break from the line each hour would be rejected out of hand by a company. Five minutes relief time per hour adds up to 500 one-hundredths of a minute every hour—4,000 one-hundredths of a minute for each eight-hour shift—an "astronomical" prospect of cost to the company.

III   There arrived in a UE heavy equipment electrical shop one day a gigantic new numerically controlled machine tool, embodying the latest in automation technology. It had taken several months to pour the foundation and to install this tape machine tool. Several more months would be required for three skilled machinists in the shop to "debug" it.

Soon twelve similar machine tools were due to be installed in the shop where the first one had arrived. Each one of them had the capacity to produce what had formerly been produced by four conventional machines, employing a total of twelve skilled machinists on three shifts. The new machine tool, operated around the clock, required a total of three workers, one for each shift. The result: nine workers displaced.

Corporations have claimed that automation creates jobs. The record of GE, the fourth largest corporation in the United States, does not support this corporate claim. General Electric —which is not only a user but also a builder of numerical controls for the machine tool industry—was among the first companies to start installing the most advanced technological equipment in its production facilities. In 1972 GE had sales of $10.5 billion—up 17 percent from 1970. Net profits in 1972:

$530 million—61 percent higher than in 1970. But in 1972 these impressive increases in productivity and profits had been achieved with twenty-eight thousand less workers than two years before.

The loss of twenty-eight thousand jobs in one corporation within a two-year period symbolized the effect of expanding automation upon jobs in industry as a whole. Unemployment was one important problem for workers in the new technology. A second important problem concerned the value to be placed on the jobs of those workers who would remain in the shop to operate these machines of the new technology. The value would be fixed by way of classifying the new jobs according to what was determined to be the degree of skill, physical effort, and aptitude required from workers doing them. There were no precedents by which proper classification of the new jobs, and the rates of pay they would carry, could be measured.

Negotiating the classifications for the jobs of the three skilled machinists who had debugged that first machine tool in the shop, and classifying the jobs of the machinists who would debug and operate all twelve of them, was therefore a major matter. The company proposed the same job classification, and the rate of pay, which had prevailed on the old conventional machines. By rights, however, said the company, the classification should be downgraded, and the rate it carried consequently reduced, because there would be less skill and physical effort involved, less pressure on the worker. Not so fast, replied the union. Said one of the skilled machinists who had worked on debugging:

> The pressure is greater. It is tremendous. With these new machines the mechanical is combined with the clerical. You are now more than a machinist. You are also a production clerk, a programmer, an inspector, a combination of everything. I work physically harder on that numerically-controlled machine. Before, I was physically tired enough. But now I'm more physically worn out and mentally exhausted as well.

The union fought for a higher classification. The battle between union and company negotiating committees went on for a long while. Meanwhile, in the shop, the twelve tape machine tools stood silent, as the machinists awaited the outcome of the battle the union was waging for proper classification. Management kept referring to them as monuments.

Monuments they possibly were, in a monumental effort by the company to deprive skilled workers involved in operating these machine tools—and others like them—from having the new jobs properly classified, while management reaped the full fruits of increased productivity. After months of struggle management agreed to a slightly higher classification, carrying a job rate of 20 cents an hour more. Balance sheet: Nine machinists displaced from their jobs; three remaining machinists on new jobs classified to carry a 20-cent-an-hour higher rate; production increased 300 percent while labor costs were reduced 75 percent.

Precedent-setting classifications for jobs in the new technology would affect not only the first workers to operate the revolutionary machine tools but also other workers hired for these jobs as time went by—among them white collar workers, largely unorganized, who under the new technology were occupying such jobs in increasing numbers. Throughout American industry, tens of thousands of the new jobs were in process of being downgraded, underclassified and underpaid, thus deciding the fate of contemporary workers as well as of their children—and perhaps their children's children—if they in turn were destined to handle jobs in the new technology. Incalculable billions of extra profits were the corporations' stake in this procedure of underclassification.

The appearance and spread of automation and the new technology in industry faced the labor movement with a question as revolutionary as the technology itself: How would the benefits of greatly increased productivity, only on the threshold of development, be distributed among the employed, the unemployed, the consumer, and the owners of industry? The battle was yet to be joined and would clearly have to be fought by the labor movement on both the economic and political fronts—a most enormous challenge.

IV   Five days a week, early in the morning, the young family of four drove in the one car they could afford thirty miles to the shop. Mother, father, two small children. It was the only way the young mother could get to her job on the first shift, which started at 8:00 A.M. At the shop gate she said goodbye to her husband and children, who then drove back home.

There, throughout the day, he took care of the kids. In mid-afternoon father and children once again drove to the shop, leaving home to allow just enough time for the young family man to make his second-shift job that started at 4:00 P.M.

That was also the hour the first shift ended. The young woman could not leave the assembly line until four o'clock and punch out her time card to leave the shop. The young man had to punch in a few minutes early so as to be on his job at four. Problem: What to do with the kids while she was punching out and he was punching in.

Sometimes it was solved by parking the car in the company lot, telling the children that mother would be along in a few minutes, and locking the car doors, so the kids wouldn't wander out into the lot where cars were coming and going. Sometimes the young father would leave them at the guard shack near the gate. There the guard could keep an eye on the children until their mother picked them up.

It was then the young woman's turn to drive thirty miles home and look after the children, prepare their supper, and put them to bed. Some time after midnight her husband, riding with a fellow worker, got back from the shop. Next morning the work rat-race began all over again. As for the necessary household, shopping, and other chores that family life requires, the parents shared these between them.

Such was the pattern of the lives of this young working-class family of the period. It followed a course familiar in the experience of many others.

V   A UE international officer said, in November 1968, to a group of shop stewards and local union officers:

For the past two years, as you know, we have been having widespread discussion in our union on the general feeling of rebellion, cynicism and disgust among young workers. Let's examine, now, why these young workers coming into the shops today feel and act as they do.

When a young worker goes to the employment office of a large corporation, the personnel man sits him down and launches into a big song and dance. The young man is told that he is about to embark on a new experience and career with one of the best companies in America.

In addition, he is given a whole kit of company pamphlets, leaflets and literature which tells him that he will be receiving the best wages, best vacations, paid holidays, hospitalization and insurance—and many other benefits that the company has waiting for him. He is led to believe that all these goodies are given to him by a compassionate company out of the goodness of its heart. Nowhere is there even the slightest hint that the union had anything to do with squeezing a little compassion out of them, although for thirty years they had to be dragged along—kicking, screaming and scratching all the time.

When this young guy starts getting his weekly pay check it looks pretty good, but not for long. Soon he buys a house with a thirty-year mortgage. He puts some furniture in the house. He buys a car, a refrigerator, washer and dryer. A TV—most likely a color TV. On top of all that, his young wife is pregnant again.

As the monthly bills start piling up, his pay envelope looks ridiculous. He sees no reason at all why America, the richest country in the world, can't give him a job that will provide him with all of the necessities and some of the luxuries of life—and what's wrong with that? He is frustrated, he is mad, he is ready to fight the Establishment that fails to give him what he needs.

VI   These several accounts from UE experience of the period of the middle and late sixties, and the early seventies, uncover the roots of the growing resentment and rebellion so evident in the mood of working people at that time. Speedup, inadequate wages, rising prices, repeated tax increases, unemployment for some, and the fear of losing a job for others, these were the returns for working people which a quarter-century of cold and hot war had helped to produce.

By 1972 the average wage of more than 50 million organized and unorganized production workers employed in private industry was $7,254. Before taxes. This fell about $4,000 below the U.S. Department of Labor moderate budget for a family of four. Not even the average annual income of those workers who were assumed to be raking in up to twenty or more thousand a year—the 2¾ million organized construction workers—reached the level of the government-established moderate budget.

In 1970, the latest year for which figures were available, the average annual earnings of organized all-year-round-employed construction workers—foremen and supervisors included—was $9,055. If the earnings of other organized construction workers not employed all-year-round were taken into account, the 1970 average dropped to $7,953. It would without question be lower still, provided government figures were recorded on the earnings of the seven hundred fifty thousand unorganized construction workers.

In this industry, also, annual rates of unemployment were twice as high as for industry generally. In 1972 the total unemployment rate in the country, according to official government sources, amounted to 6 percent: 5½ million people out of work. Many economists believed this to be a serious understatement of the true number of unemployed. Government sources reported further that 26½ million Americans were receiving incomes of less than $4,100 a year, which classified them, said the government, as living in poverty. Other millions, not far above the poverty line, were called "economically deprived."

But the most illuminating statistic on the condition of working people throughout twenty-five cold and hot war years could be found in what economists termed "distribution of national income." In 1947, at the start of the cold war, the income of the lowest fifth of all families in the U.S. was 5½ percent of total national income. Whereas that of the highest fifth of families, in 1947, was 41½ percent. In 1972 the breakdown remained exactly the same. No change.

VII   A review of corporate profits for more than three decades of hot and cold war shows the following: Before the Second World War, in 1939–40, profits of U.S. corporations averaged $6.4 billion. In 1943–44, Second World War years, the average was $11.2 billion. With the beginning of the cold war in the late 1940s, they started a steady climb toward heights unprecedented in the career of any corporate profit system.

By 1972, when the U.S. government was compelled to withdraw from the longest and most unpopular war in which the country had ever been engaged—that in Vietnam—U.S. corporations reported a net income of $52.6 billion, an all-time high. Corporations do not advertise gross income before taxes in the way they advertise the gross annual wages of their workers. Whereas the $7,254 annual average income for workers in 1972 represented income before taxes—the $52.6 billion corporate profit in 1972 was income after all taxes had been deducted.

Nevertheless, corporations were complaining about a crisis faced by U.S. capitalism. One of the reasons for the "crisis," they stressed, was foreign competition, principally from the corporate systems of Japan and Western Europe, where West Germany led the field. There was no doubt that the capitalist systems of West Germany and Japan had become robust rivals of U.S. capitalism. While U.S. corporations for twenty-five years had concentrated much research on military technology, and much production on war material—both financed by government out of taxpayers' money—these other foreign systems, also with major assistance from U.S. government grants provided by American taxpayers, had been developing civilian-goods industries. Their products began substantial penetration of markets all over the earth, including the United States.

The competing capitalist systems of that era were in a different position from those which had the whole earth as their oyster fifty years previous. The field for unbridled exploitation of people, raw materials, and markets of other countries had shrunken as a consequence of the two world wars of the twentieth century. After the First World War the Soviet Union dropped out of the territory available for that kind of exploitation, while Eastern Europe and China dropped out in the aftermath of World War II. If capitalism wished to continue doing business with the new non-capitalist nations, embracing one-third of the world's people, it could do so—but not on the old basis of uncontrolled exploitation.

Also after the Second World War, strong nationalist movements emerged in many previous colonial and semicolonial countries of Asia, Africa, and Latin America, asserting their right to independence and self-government, as well as to ownership of their natural resources. Thus more territory formerly open without restriction to U.S. capitalism and others continued to shrink. Such shrinkage, combined with increased pressure from the capitalist systems of Germany and Japan for sales in world markets, confronted the highly privileged and once dominant U.S. corporate profit system with what it called a crisis.

Examination of this crisis showed that the profit appetite of U.S. capitalism was insatiable. The 1971 net income of the largest electrical manufacturing corporation on earth, General Electric, was $472 million after taxes. Its chief foreign competitors in the industry had profit appetites of more modest dimensions. *Fortune* magazine of August 1972 reported the net incomes of the three leading electric manufacturing corporations outside the United States: Siemen's of Germany, Hitachi of Japan, Philips of the Netherlands.

Their combined net income for the year 1971 came to $278 million, compared with GE's $472 million. The three foreign companies employed a total of 836,063 workers in 1971, while General Electric employment was 363,000. This profit and employment comparison shows that GE could well afford to pass on a greater share of the high productivity of its workers to the workers themselves, as well as to consumers in the form of lower prices. Such benefits for workers and consumers, obviously, would still permit GE to maintain a profit advantage over its foreign competitors. The American corporate profit system as a whole, in its drive for higher and higher income at a time when the world was no longer its oyster for exploitation, turned the heat on its own workers. Speedup pressures in the shops, economic pressures on workers and families, escalating prices, an increasing tax load carried by working people, automated unemployment, other jobs transferred overseas to U.S. protectorates in such areas as South Korea, Taiwan and certain Latin American countries . . . all of this and all of these were the means by which corporations kept squeezing out increased profits for themselves. They chose to tighten the screws on the American working people.

VIII   In the spring of 1972 old-timer Wobbly and UE Local 107 leader, John Schaefer, now retired after forty-two years on the job as a skilled pipefitter in the Westinghouse turbine works of South Philadelphia, sat with a few old UE friends in the living room of his home, where many a group had gathered for discussion over these years. The union friends were discussing the impact upon the labor movement of the changing composition of workers in the shops, among whom were many young workers of different backgrounds and temperaments.

In 1971 the members of traditionally militant UE Local 107 had concluded the third strike for a new contract in thirty-seven years of the local union's existence. It lasted five and a half months, reminiscent of the historic 1955–56 ten-month struggle. "Johnny," one of the group observed, "the young fellows shaped up pretty good in that strike last year."

Pretty good on the whole, said Schaefer. Pretty solid. His wife, Maggie, thought that was an understatement. "Now Schaefer," she said, "they were as militant as the people in 1955. Not a single scab in five and a half months." Schaefer agreed that was true. "They've got the militancy, the young fellows," he said. "No question about it. The militancy is there. But have they got the working class consciousness?" Schaefer continued:

> Some teaching and learning has to be going on in working class principles, some study of past struggles. Reading about them, discussing them, picking up from there the principles for conducting present struggles. And

I'm not sure the rank-and-file, militant as it is, is getting that kind of education nowadays. I may be wrong. But from where I sit, I don't see much of it.

Not long before this conversation in Johnny and Maggie Schaefer's living room in 1972, UE workers in a bitter cold Vermont winter had been conducting a bitter strike. Two feet of snow lay on the ground early one morning as state troopers launched an assault on the picket line, to open a path to the plant for foremen scabbing on the production workers' jobs. One militant young fellow, a year or so over twenty years of age, was among those trying to hold the line as the troopers advanced. By his side was Matles, who, at the time, was in Vermont helping out in the strike.

In the crush of the action, as the picket line was being forced back by the pressure of the troopers, Matles said to the youth at his side: "Well, I guess this is what they call in the books the class struggle." The young striker came back with, "Class struggle bullshit, Jim. Just a bunch of lousy cops bought out by this bastard company to beat our brains in."

The history of the labor movement shows that over and over again American workers have conducted struggles on the industrial front as fierce and determined as those in which workers anywhere on earth have engaged. Nevertheless, as Johnny Schaefer observed—and as the young Vermont striker's remark revealed—class consciousness had been slow in its growth. One measure of its low level could be found in the fact that even after one hundred years of working people's struggles in the United States, it remained the only industrialized country where no labor party had been organized. The most politically powerful and class-conscious corporate class in the world had managed to keep the working class tied to the long-established political system dominated by two major parties.

IX   Eugene V. Debs once observed:
Ten thousand times has the labor movement stumbled and fallen and bruised itself and risen again; been seized by the throat and choked into insensibility; enjoined by

the courts, assaulted by thugs, charged by the militia, shot down by regulars, frowned upon by public opinion, deceived by politicians, threatened by priests, repudiated by renegades, preyed upon by grafters, infested by spies, deserted by cowards, betrayed by traitors, bled by leeches, and sold out by leaders. But notwithstanding all this, and all these, it is today the most vital and potential power this planet has ever known.

In the first half of the twentieth century more than thirty years of labor movement struggle took place, with advances and setbacks, before conditions prepared the ground for the rise of industrial unionism which Debs, among others, had foreseen as natural evolution. During those years a great world war, an all-out corporate assault on the American labor movement, and a vast economic depression in the United States—throwing millions out of work and shaking the corporate system to its depths—created conditions for a rebellion by working people. This rebellion assumed the form of a movement to organize the unorganized in mass production industry. CIO industrial unionism was born.

The leadership for such unionism emerged from the rank-and-file in the auto industry, steel, electric manufacturing, the machine industry, the rubber, glass, oil and chemical industries; from among the metal miners, longshoremen, the seamen, the transport workers; and from shops and plants all over the country. Most of them were young leaders. The movement had impact on the established leaders of the AFL. The old guard dug in to resist industrial unionism. Other AFL leaders, while not changing long-established policies and methods of running their own unions, recognized and accepted the challenge for the organization of the mass production industries.

They threw the energies, the resources, the manpower of their unions into the fight. They provided the indispensable element of their own experienced trade union leadership to the new movement, giving the young industrial union leaders not only guidance but full rein to get on with organizing the unorganized. Thus was the American labor movement realigned, strengthened and its membership increased by millions.

The CIO objective of the 1930s—to implant industrial union-ism in the shops of mass production—had been achieved. But the drive toward long-range objectives—organizing the millions of workers still unorganized, developing a strong independent political movement, redistributing the national wealth and income—was derailed by the corporate anti-labor offensive conducted during a quarter-century of cold and hot war. In the seventies, then, these objectives still remain to be won.

The ground for historic changes in the American labor movement which make possible the realization of important objectives has always been prepared by the pressures which the corporate class exerts upon working people. This powerful class, striving relentlessly for increased productivity and higher profits, brings into being the objective conditions which produce change in the labor movement. Intolerable burdens are imposed upon workers in the shops. Severe economic strain is inflicted upon working-class families.

Labor leadership, new or established, does not create movements. It is the other way around. Seeds for change in the labor movement are sown among rank-and-file workers by the conditions forced upon them. It is from this ground, from among these seeds, that new leadership springs to lead the struggle for change.

Index

305